P9-EJP-915

HOME TO THE WILDERNESS

"The popular nature writer, author of *One Day on Beetle Rock* and many other fine books, tells the extraordinary story of her life from her repressed and unloved childhood to her discovery of the joys of living with and communicating with wildlife."
—*Publishers Weekly*

"From poverty to attempted suicide to psychoanalysis to the point of becoming an extraordinarily perceptive if not mystical writer of the world of nature—this author writes from the deepest level and withholds nothing. 'One's own truth' is what Sally Carrighar's book offers the reader. Accept it with humility."—*Best Sellers*

HOME
TO THE
WILDERNESS

A Personal Journey

Sally Carrighar

PENGUIN BOOKS INC
Baltimore · Maryland

Penguin Books Inc
7110 Ambassador Road
Baltimore, Maryland 21207, U.S.A.

First published by Houghton Mifflin Company, Boston, 1973
Published by Penguin Books Inc, 1974

To Jack, my brother,
with gratitude for the light touch
he brought to some of our
darker days

FOREWORD

SIX YEARS AGO an English critic, reviewing an autobiography that described "the people I've known and the places I've seen," found it interesting, as those autobiographies nearly always are; but at the end the critic said, "We still await a life story written from the deepest level and withholding nothing."

Editors who have known that I have had some extraordinary companions — bears, wolves, lions — and have seen some intriguing places, from the arctic to Malaya, have suggested that I too should write an autobiography. Usually I have said that I would rather report these events objectively, in essays and narratives, but the thought of writing "from the deepest level and withholding nothing" was a challenge. I made a start to see how it would go. And since the way forward was a descent, it was easier to keep on than turn back.

To write "withholding nothing" requires an attempt to reach absolute honesty and that effort itself pushes one's consciousness down to a lower level. In trying to share perceptions that are not superficial, it becomes necessary to explore depths that may become uncomfortably obscure — but not too dark to see that a precipice is there, and to realize that one only jumps over it at one's peril.

Is that what the critic was asking for — a message from the very deep level of the subsconscious? It can be reached, but whether one will survive the drop is not certain. I did reach it and the terror is here recorded. Now I ask whether that expedition is wise. Perhaps there are experiences which remain hidden from casual thought because (*pace* Freud) they *should* be hidden. I truly don't know, though my experience suggests that my own dive was necessary. And it has had a reward not anticipated: loss of a degree of loneliness, a sense of coming back to a world where other people are now more accessible.

The 1971 Reith Lecturer on the BBC, Professor Richard Hoggart, said: "It becomes part of the purpose of writing to . . . feel more securely — past simple assertions or crying down the wind — that we are not alone. We hope that this effort, this sort of exploring, will help us reach more convincing ways of speaking to each other. It is therefore true in the end to say that part of the purpose of writing is to reach others: not to sell them anything or persuade them, but to be quite simply in touch. It follows that we best speak to others when we . . . concentrate on trying to be straight towards our experience, in the hope that honestly seen experience becomes exchangeable."

It works that way for the writer. Only a reader can know whether he too has felt an exchange.

○

The customary thanks given in an introduction to those who have contributed to the making of a book are in my case expressed on nearly every page. For this record of the earlier part of my life includes almost countless examples of others' kindness. Most of the people I knew in the years of my youth were presenting a picture of *humane* beings that contradicts the impression given in current headlines. They were generous and helpful beyond the bounds of decency and humanity. When I was older, a capricious fate threw me into the company of a different sort: those who wish to exploit each other. But later still two, Dr. Carl Renz and Dr. Susanna Isaacs, inspired trust that our species is basically benign, and that belief is one thing that I wish to exchange with readers. Another is the personal experience I have had in the wilderness, of a nature that also is benign, and law-abiding and consistently moral — and therefore reassuring and if one respects those laws, safe.

I owe a great debt of gratitude to the zoologists, named further on, who interrupted their own work to encourage mine; and to the writer, Katharine Scherman, who read this book in its various stages and allowed me to filter its intimacies through her sensitive judgment.

Among those people who themselves have experienced nature's healing art, more than a few are in bookstores, and they have recommended my narratives for what they are intended to be: guides to the wilderness. I am sure there are many such booksellers that I do not know about, but of those I do, I wish particularly to send grateful greetings to the staffs of the Sather Gate Book Shop in Berkeley, California, the Dartmouth Bookstore in Hanover, New Hampshire, and the Princeton University Store in Princeton, New Jersey; and to the one perhaps longest and most faithfully pointing out this route to the wilderness, Miss Constance Spencer, bookseller of San Francisco.

1973   SALLY CARRIGHAR

CONTENTS

ILLUSTRATIONS

following page 176

i

THE BLAST FURNACE

WE WERE a father and his first-born, a four-year-old girl, setting out every Sunday afternoon to see the industrial marvels of Cleveland, Ohio. The young man had grown up in a smaller Canadian town and he was delighted with Cleveland, which hummed and clanged with the vast new developments steel had made possible. In temperament he was anything but an engineer; here however he was excited to feel that he had jumped into the very heart of the torrent of progress.

Most often we walked on the banks of the Cuyahoga River to see the drawbridge come apart and rise up, like giant black jaws taking a bite of the sky, so that boats could go through: the long freighters that brought iron ore from Lake Superior, other large and small freighters, fishing boats, passenger steamers. My father's eyes never tired of watching them make their smooth way up and down the river. His father, born in Amsterdam of a seagoing family, had been a skipper on the Great Lakes. Perhaps my father too should have been a sailor, but he was something nearly as satisfying — he worked for a railroad.

And so we went to the roundhouse where the steam engines stood when they were not pulling trains. They had all entered through the same door but inside their tracks spread apart, as gracefully as the ribs of a lady's fan. My father knew a great deal about engines, he knew the names of some of these and he walked among them with pride.

On our way to the roundhouse we passed through the freight yards where long trains of boxcars lay on their sidings. My father said that the cars belonged to different railroads and came from various parts of the country, being coupled together here because all those in one train were bound for the same destination. This was getting too complicated but there was nothing complicated about my father's emotion when he said, "Working for a railroad is like living everywhere in the country at once!" A characteristic enchantment came into his eyes and voice, a contagious exhilaration which meant that anything it attached to was good. Living everywhere was something that even a child could grasp vaguely and pleasantly.

My father and I made other trips and best were the ones to the blast furnaces. He explained how the iron ore from the boats was mixed with coal and carried in little cars to the top of the chimney above the furnace. It was dumped in, and as it fell down "a special kind of very hot air" was blown into it. The coal and iron ore caught fire, and below they fell into great tubs as melting metal, a pinkish gold liquid, incandescent as the sun is when it is starting to set. The man and child were allowed to go rather near the vats, to feel the scorching heat and to drown their gaze in the glowing boil. All the rest of the building was dark; the silhouettes of the men who worked at the vats were black shadows. Wearing long leather aprons, they moved about the vats ladling off the slag. That was very skilled work, my father said; the men had to know just how much of the worthless slag to remove. For years afterwards, when we could no longer spend Sunday afternoons on these expeditions, we used to go out of our house at night to see the pink reflections from the blast furnaces on the clouds over Cleveland. We could remember that we had watched the vatfuls of heavily moving gold, and those events from the past were an unspoken bond between us.

Someone once said, "Your father must have been trying to turn you into a boy. He'd probably wanted his first child to be a son." Perhaps; but it was not strange to him to show a girl the achievements of men. He thought of women as human beings and assumed that they, even one very young, would be interested in anything that was interesting to him. He had absorbed that attitude from the women he'd grown up with, his mother and her four sisters, all of whom led adventurous lives. His favorite Aunt Chris had married a clipper captain and sailed with him all her life. When they retired, having seen the entire world, they chose to settle in Burma. Another aunt married one of the Morgan family, who established the famous breed of Morgan horses, and took up a homestead in Manitoba. Aunt Mary, a physician's wife, went with him out to San Francisco during the Gold Rush and stayed there. The fourth aunt had married the inspector of ships' chronometers at Quebec; and my father's mother, of course, had married her skipper from Holland. In the winter when he was not on his ship he ran a factory for making barrel staves that he had established in western Kentucky — all this and the fathering of five children by the time he was twenty-eight, when he lost his life in a notorious Lake Erie storm. His wife, a musician, brought up her five without complaint, just as her mother, also an early widow, had reared her five gallant girls. With his memories of women like these it was not surprising that my father would wish, even somewhat prematurely, to show his daughter the things that were thrilling to him. I did not comprehend all his family history at four but I did absorb the impression that girls and women reached out for life eagerly and that it was natural for them to be interested in absolutely everything.

Our house would be dark when we got off the streetcar and walked the short distance from Euclid Avenue along Windermere Street. As we came up the steps my mother would turn on the lights in the living room, a grate fire might be burning, it seemed warm and inviting and my father could never seem to resist saying something like, "I hope you had a nice afternoon."

"Oh, very gay. I read the paper and darned your socks."

"We would have been more gay if you'd come along with us." Then she would say something like not being satisfied with such pleasures as looking at ships and blast furnaces. She did have other pleasures. Almost always on Saturday night they went to the theatre or to parties or gave them, but my father never let the argument go so far as to point this out. He never let their talk become a sparring match, for one reason because my mother's answers weren't logical. When she was arguing she just played with words. And there was no need for my father to try to compete with her kind of wit — he never could win nor could anyone else. But if he did not try to win, neither did he lose. He retired from these games with always the same kind of laugh, one meaning, *We're not going to fight over this.* All the same, it was a sad little laugh.

She was in fact generous in putting up with being deserted each Sunday afternoon for that was often the only day when she and my father could be together. He, being a sub-assistant to the president of the New York Central, frequently traveled with him during the week. Soon she would no longer endure this routine. Our Sunday trips started when I was four and ended when I was five and at the same time my father gave up his work for the railroad. Now — lovely prospect! — he would be at home all the time, but in asserting her wishes my mother had made it known that the close tie between her nusband and child must be loosened.

My own joy was in eclipse already, because I had learned I never must talk.

"Today we saw nine boats go under the bridge! One was big, people ride on it, they eat and sleep —— " But mother had left the room.

"Daddy took me up inside one of the engines. It was dark but when I sat —— " To show that she was not interested mother had picked up the paper and pretended to read.

"Oh, Mamma, I wish you could see that beautiful fire. It is flat like water, but it's pink and gold and so bright! I wanted to put my hands —— " What was outside the window that mother must see? A horse's hoofs were approaching on the brick paving, not running away. She had not even allowed me to tell her about the time when I was visiting my grandparents in Painesville, Ohio, and the four horses pulling the fire engine had run away, down Grandpa's short lane, at the end of which they had piled up, a tumult of hoofs pawing the sky, broken harnesses flying. The horses crashed through the fence at the house of Mr. Beanau, Grandpa's helper, they were trampling over the garden, men were shouting, Cora Beanau screamed from the doorway . . . My mother may have learned all this in a letter from Grandma but she would not let me tell her about it.

As long as my mother lived she would not let me share with her anything that was in my mind. She would shut me up by telephoning, making a grocery list, beginning to read, or by talking, herself, which was increasingly the way in her later years. If I drew in a breath to speak, her words darted into the silence and continued without a pause until she saw that I'd given up.

After I understood that she did not want to listen I would tell my father about my childish adventures but ways were invented to interrupt those conversations too. My mother would dash about the room in pursuit of a fly or moth, real or imaginary. She would plump up the sofa pillows or rearrange flowers. Once she handed my father a wrench with the complaint, "I can't stand that dripping faucet one more minute!" When he said reproachfully, "I want to hear what the child is saying," her great green eyes widened and she shrugged. "Oh! Sorry I interrupted." The front door was closed rather more firmly than necessary, and through the window we saw her walk down the street, so spirited and so stylish. As my father watched her his eyes were sad. He said gently, "You might save up things to tell me before I read to you when you go to bed." I tried to do that but it was not the same. Gradually a silence came down between me and my father, although we always knew that we loved each other. The silence lasted forever.

When I could not tell anyone about something exciting, wild horses raged through my mind until the event faded. Though one does not see runaway fire-horses every day, every day something worth telling happens and for most children, I imagine, the need to talk is adequately discharged. It was not for me, but energy thus unspent can build into a kind of power — in a child as well as a grownup. Stored away, it can become a sort of personality capital, giving an inner sense of having accumulated significance as an individual. One has had this experience, and this, and their memory has not been dissipated by describing them. The storing is not a comfortable process, but it may not be entirely unfortunate.

Yet no child would choose this verbal isolation, and in wondering how it came to be, I used to think of what I knew about my parents' relationship before I was born. Each of us has been formed by the sort of marriage our parents have had as well as the combination of the two individuals' genes. I know that my father and mother had been in the same young crowd in Cleveland and when he won her she was considered a real trophy. She was graceful and rather tall, and with her large green eyes and dark hair, in which a white streak rose from one side of her forehead up over her pompadour, she was always conspicuous. She dramatized her personal color scheme by often dressing in black or white. I remember her later in a white evening gown covered with rows of fine white, black-edged lace as she sat at the piano, rings flashing over the keys while she played "Sounds from the Ringing Rocks," the only piece she knew and she could play it without ever practicing it, a curiously permanent, showy part of her dazzle.

But conversation was her great gift. It became irrelevant when she was piqued and shooting off verbal fireworks, but she kept well-informed and at other times she could talk compellingly and with wit. This almost daunting fluency may have been one of her chief attractions for my father, for he was not very articulate. That is, he never launched forth on the plight of the street-railway system, or the price of steel, or the next election as some of the men in their crowd would do, holding the attention and winning the admiration of everyone. My father, who often was called a jolly man, did his talking in humorous little asides. He could see through pompousness and deflate it amusingly with a word or two but that was not playing the game of intellectual dominance that my mother admired. My mother would feed flattering questions to the men who talked analytically; sometimes she could pull together their arguments better than they could — but in always a graceful way. My father would shine with pride whenever my mother talked thus brightly in any group.

He was a man who, as the English have been known to say, "had the misfortune to be born poor and gentle and unselfish," and he wanted little more than to make his wife happy, to give her her own way most of the time and provide as much as possible of whatever she wanted. But what she really wanted, I think, was not such devotion as much as a partner who challenged her. Very competitive, she thrived on opposition that she could try to break down. And how compete with a husband who greets your darts with only disarming smiles?

My parents never came to the neutral state reached by some couples with unlike temperaments, but to avoid it they paid with grief. Was the disillusionment already setting in when my father took me away on those Sunday trips? Were they a means of sidestepping, for a few hours, the ready weapons my mother had on her tongue? As time went on he sidestepped further and further.

When I was five and a half we moved from Windermere Street to Fernwood, and I can date situations by which house was the background. We were still on Windermere when I realized that I must not only keep silent but must never approach my mother if I could help it. If I walked to her she would move away with a rejecting throw of her hand. Recognizing these signs I tried to keep a little distance apart from her, but when she was sitting relaxed and looking beautiful sometimes I wished so much to be near her that I would come up to her knee. With a shudder, as if she had been touched by a snake or lizard, she would start up from her chair, and if in passing along a corridor we happened to brush each other, she would involuntarily shiver. Fixing my hair was an ordeal for her; often she suddenly threw down the comb and went quickly out of the room. She would not make my dresses, although she sewed well, because she would have to touch me in fitting them. This repugnance became even stronger as she grew older. When she was ninety and we were walking together in Berkeley, California, where she lived, I thoughtlessly put my hand under her elbow as she was stepping down from a curb. With a spasm of loathing she went rigid from head to foot and could only begin to walk again when I moved away from her side.

An aversion so strong can become uncontrollable, as it did a few times with my mother. I hoped that after a long time and lengthy separations it would lessen, and eventually we even drew fairly close to each other in letters. I know that she too wished for a better-relationship. She usually seemed glad when I proposed visiting Berkeley — but at the first sight of my face at the airport, she froze. I try to imagine the suffering it must have been to have such an odious child and look forward to years of daily association. I wonder that she could stand the prospect. My poor distraught mother!

But also poor daughter.

2

To my father I never mentioned my mother's antagonism, nor to anyone else, with a single exception, until I was well into adult years. Several grown-up friends gave me openings, for they observed what was happening, but I remained silent. Why? I don't know. Children have these reticences and besides, I thought it disgraceful not to be loved. My mother's hatred was such a denial of normal maternal feeling that I thought of it as one would of a congenital deformity in myself. I did wonder how it all began. Probably when I was born, I decided — and in that was exactly right, although I could not have known why for at that time no one could have explained the reason. Only the patient recent studies of child psychologists have made it clear why some babies are not accepted.

Mine was a dreadful birth, to my mother a terrifying, traumatic experience. High forceps were used and her coccyx, the bone at the end of her spine, was broken. It is said that even the most severe birth pains quickly fade from a woman's memory but that was not true of my mother. The experience remained in her mind so vividly that again and again, from an early age, I heard all the details. Even after ten years, when I was in the hospital following a ruptured-appendix operation, she took me down to the entrance hall in a wheel chair to show me a pair of high forceps in an exhibit of surgical instruments. They are much more skillfully designed now but then they looked as big and brutal as meat cleavers and similarly shaped. They sharpened my anguish over what she had undergone.

The birth had wounded me too. Part of my face was smashed in and the flesh had been bruised and cut. Even without the use of instruments, babies' faces are sometimes put out of shape during birth, but if the injury isn't too great it usually corrects itself in the first few months. My disfigurement lasted longer. Slow, steady improvement was made but the deeper damage was not eliminated until a dozen years later when dental artistry reconstructed my upper jaw.

While my mother was still recovering from the birth, what a shock to have such an abhorrent baby brought to her breast! The surface bruises and cuts soon healed but she still was not left with a handsome child and she must have hoped for one, especially because she had feared that having a baby would make herself less attractive. In our house was a framed photograph of her taken two months before I was born. It was said that her friends had urged her to have it made because after bearing a child she "would never again be so beautiful." Her friends must surely have been mistaken, for most people think that a woman is most beautiful when she has reached the fulfillment of motherhood. But the warning had stayed in my mother's mind. Being much admired, she must have been very conscious of feminine beauty and she probably had anticipated the reward, at least, of having a lovely child. Her antagonism was reinforced when it developed that I was also impossibly difficult. After the frightful birth and the sight of a baby so marred, it undoubtedly was a great strain to find that the child would require more than the normal amount of patience and love. It was too much to ask.

I was difficult not because of wilfulness but because I was too excitable. I know both my parents recognized this unfortunate trait (but not its cause) and tried to temper their baby's excessive reactions. That must have been hard to do since such children are irritating, but any show of annoyance only increases the sensitivity.

As far back as memory goes, I know that I had to be shielded from stimulation. Conversations were obviously censored and the reading of stories was often stopped because I became hysterical if they were sad. I had to have longer naps than most children and go to bed earlier at night because I had worn myself out by responding to every stimulus too intensely.

Some of my pleasantest early memories are of impressions that probably should have been more mild; these, almost painfully sharp, alternated with moments of panic. I had a whole repertoire of terrors, among them the rumbling of horses' hoofs on the bridge at my grandfather's mill, the swift flow of the river, the cow in the pasture, the sight of the dark watery depths of a toilet tank, and larger fears such as those of fire engines, thunder and lightning, burglars as soon as I knew about them — and my mother. I can remember a Sunday breakfast when I was still small enough to be sitting in a highchair with a ham bone teething ring on a string around my neck, and how I seemed to sense danger from my mother, who sat on my left, but I was exquisitely happy because this was a morning when my father, on my right, would not be going away and I would be safe all day. Already I had a feeling of something amiss in the emotional atmosphere of our house. My father spoke sometimes of an anxious look on my face. It distressed him and when he put me to bed at night, as he always did when he was at home, his last words, in a concerned voice were, "Wake up happy."

Emotional swamps are intolerable. One must get out of them somehow and the way is to hunt for the causes. Does a difficult birth, of even a high-strung and disfigured child, cause a mother to feel revulsion against the child for all of her lifetime? Eventually I had to know and many years later was given the answer by two who have worldwide fame as psychiatrists specializing in mother-child relationships: Dr. John Bowlby and Dr. Susanna Isaacs of London.* The information was very enlightening.

They agree that an abnormally painful birth may cause a mother to feel some resentment against her baby — some mothers, not very many. But those difficult births can also result in the baby's having a type of neurological damage that may give an uninformed mother a reason to feel a deeper antagonism.

When a birth problem has been anticipated it is often avoided by removing the baby without injury by Caesarean section. But such a need cannot always be foreseen and when the birth is unusually prolonged (the birth itself, not the labor), and especially if instruments have to be used, the umbilical cord can become compressed and thus cut off the baby's supply of oxygen. With his mother's blood he has obtained oxygen all along while he was in the womb and ordinarily he will continue to receive it through the cord until he is out and can breathe for himself. But if things go wrong on the way and the cord is squeezed or injured, sometimes the mother's blood can no longer pass through it. Before he is ever born, then, the baby will have suffered oxygen starvation, however prompt he may be in drawing in his first breath.

It is familiar knowledge that asphyxia, oxygen starvation, can cause the death of brain cells in people of any age very quickly — in

* Dr. John Bowlby holds an appointment at London's Tavistock Institute of Human Relations under the joint auspices of the National Health Service and the Medical Research Council. He has been advisor to the World Health Organization on the mental health of homeless children and is the author of a two-volume work, *Attachment and Loss*. Dr. Susanna Isaacs has been Physician-in-Charge, Department of Child Psychiatry at St. Mary's Hospital, London. More recently she has been at the Paddington Green Children's Hospital. Her articles on parents who injure their children have appeared in various scientific journals.

less than five minutes. Doctors have long been aware that this sort of brain damage can occur during births. If complications arise they work as rapidly as they can, but they are not always able to get out the child fast enough so that its supply of oxygen is not interrupted. If, then, the injury is done to the cells in the baby's cortex, some of the reasoning processes may become crippled.

What has been recognized now more recently is the fact that cells can be destroyed too in that area of the central nervous system which regulates automatic reactions. A child with that kind of birth injury will be able to think and reason logically, but the involuntary part of his nervous system may have been flawed. That is the part which maintains nervous balance and prevents our reacting too feverishly to small events. It does prepare us for emergencies, for flight or fight in the case of real danger, by releasing adrenalin and withdrawing blood from our skins and sending it to the larger muscles so we can run away fast or grapple with an opponent. It prepares us for stress, but when the nerve pathways have been damaged in a delayed birth, even the mildest disturbance may be interpreted as stress and the whole stress-mechanism be set in motion. A child with that handicap is apt to respond to a slight harmless noise as another child might to a nearby explosion. He over-reacts to everything, is excitable, panics easily, and in living with such an inner sense of emergency probably cries a great deal. By those who don't understand his problem he will be called high-strung, to such an extreme degree that taking care of him is exhausting. Sometimes the mother of such a baby, at her wit's end and despairing of ever straightening out her child, will withdraw her affection. The baby, then, sensing that he lacks the normal support from his mother, may have still more exaggerated reactions.

Dr. Isaacs emphasized that these nerve-damaged babies are not the ones now so famously "battered." In the so-called battered-baby

syndrome the baby is normal, not unusually annoying; and most of
the parents have no deep-seated animosity towards the child. They
are just people who are quick to lash out when irritated, in some
cases because they were hit and beaten in their own childhoods.
Many are troubled about their short tempers and can be helped
rather easily; and when the parents become more relaxed the battered youngsters are apt to be reassured and their emotional wounds
become healed.

In the case of birth injuries on the other hand, it is the children
who innocently are the cause of the friction. Their mothers are
usually conscientious but the tension accumulates — although Dr.
Isaacs said that a very equable woman can withstand these assaults
on her tolerance. And actually this kind of nerve-damaged child
will improve. The *tendency* to over-react may be permanent but he
will cope with it by himself when he is older. The more one of
these youngsters can experience calmness, the sooner he may achieve
it. A mother can do much by saying gently, "It's not that important,
is it?" Or, "We don't really mind that very much, do we. Let's forget about it."

I have explained this type of birth injury in some detail because it
is fairly common and an understanding of it can do much to lessen a
mother's stress. It seems that I almost certainly did have that early
handicap — but in my case the difficulty could not have been recognized by my mother, or accepted by her, for a rather startling reason
that Dr. Isaacs finally explained.

When she, after Dr. Bowlby, had diagnosed my nerve damage as
having made me irritable and demanding, Dr. Isaacs became curious
as to what happened next: how did my childhood progress? She
asked many questions, in a series of interviews, and I told her some
of the happenings described in this book. She listened until a picture of my youthful years and some later years lay before her and
then she asked, very tactfully, almost casually:

"Did you understand that your mother was psychotic?"

"Psychotic!"

"It seems unmistakable that she had a paranoid psychosis."

"If you mean insane, I don't think that's possible. She was one of the most intelligent people I've ever known."

Dr. Isaacs said, "Her type of psychosis is often no more than a narrow gap in an otherwise perfectly rational mind. It is not inborn. Usually it is the result of some highly traumatic experience."

"My birth?"

"Probably — the stress of the difficult birth itself, for which a beautiful baby would have been compensation. But she may have expected that the disfiguring of your face would be permanent."

"My aunt said that she took one look at the baby and turned away."

"Such an emotional shock, coming right after the dreadful birth itself, could have caused a wound in her psyche too deep to heal. It would have been made still worse when she found that her child was high-strung and almost unmanageable."

"But I improved," I protested. "My face did, and I became less excitable."

"She would hardly have been aware of that improvement," said Dr. Isaacs, "because she was not able to see you the way you were in reality. She had developed delusions, like other paranoiacs, and you were only a character in her fantasies. Your birth nearly had cost her her life and after that you were always seen as a threat."

"A threat!"

"A threat of one kind or another — different kinds at various times in your childhood. The delusion of being menaced is typical of a paranoid psychosis."

I told Dr. Isaacs I thought my father realized that my mother found me disturbing: "and so he was very tender." Dr. Isaacs' comment was that it would have been a paranoid reaction "if she saw you then, even a tiny child, as a danger. She may have had the delusion that you were replacing her in your father's affections."

I said it was still hard to realize that she was not sane. "She managed everything, money, the household, the committee work at her church, so well. She made such good friends and kept them for life." Again Dr. Isaacs emphasized that wide areas of her mind were entirely normal. "But you know," she said, "that at times you were close to losing your life."

How well I knew. I recognized through most of my childhood that I was not safe, that anything I might do, believing it harmless, could be considered so wicked that I might have to die for it. I lived with that dread every day; yet one can learn to tolerate quite distressing things. Even the threat of death could be almost ignored except after narrow escapes. But I did develop an unchildlike carefulness.

Dr. Isaacs continued her explanation: "Paranoiacs sometimes believe themselves at such risk that they feel they simply have to eliminate the danger. They are responsible for some tragic crimes that seem incredible because they are committed by people who have been known as intelligent and dependable." And then she said:

"You were fortunate that you lived to grow up."

Since Dr. Isaacs defined paranoia I have been reading other authorities on the subject. They confirm what she had described. Dr. Norman Alexander Cameron, until a few years ago Professor of Psychiatry at Yale University, says of paranoid disorders that they are "delusional reactions in patients who show neither serious disorganization nor deterioration. They develop . . . under conditions of unusual anxiety, emotional arousal, strong personal need." But I like best the definition by Dr. Harvey Cleckley, psychology professor and author of the book, *The Mask of Sanity:* "The ego structure * of the

* The ego structure is the knowing, willing center of consciousness (Dr. C. G. Jung).

paranoiac . . . may be thought of as having sustained a tear or a lo-
calized break which is patched or concealed rather effectively by
forces within the patient."

A "tear in the psyche": could there be a better excuse for paranoid actions? Behavior which originates in such a scarred mind will
be blameless, and I only wish that I could have understood the true
situation much earlier. Dr. Isaacs said finally, "Your salvation has
been that you were able to face most of what happened, and so you
could cope with it realistically." I would say only fairly realistically.
More of the time I have felt bewildered by the many fearful events,
but now that I know their cause they are no longer so damaging and
seem even interesting.

They are like incidents in a fairy tale, a Grimm fairy tale, for
much of what happened was simply my mother's way of treating her
fantasy child — who was the only daughter she ever knew. For example, she thought that my high-strung reactions, due to the nerve
damage, were a personality defect, that when I was frightened by
thunder or runaway horses, that was an ominous sign of flightiness,
probably leading later to dissipation. This delusion was alarming to
her because there had been some emotional instability in her ancestors, but she insisted that I could "master my character weakness" if
I tried hard enough. Feeling therefore disgraced when I was
frightened, I learned to hide that distress and finally to be less af-
fected by it. Being afraid didn't seem wicked to me however, and so
I lived in a limbo where things were not what they seemed and my
mother's face could suddenly be the face of an unreal sort of person,
abnormally terrifying. As a child I thought of it as her "terrible
face," for what it expressed was an impulse to do the ultimate violence. It of course was the face of her madness, and it is likely that
no one else ever saw it, that it was only shown to the menacing fantasy child.

3

The ancestors who gave my mother the raw material for her delusions had not been lawless or even raffish. They were just what she thought of as weak reeds who bent in a wind if it was very strong or if it carried a whiff of alcohol. One was my father's sister, but the complications she caused did not appear until later. Two on my mother's side gave her the mental pain of an obsession.

One was a Presbyterian minister and a cool view of him cannot but fill one with pity. He felt so strongly about the evils of slavery that he used his farm as a station on the Underground Railway, that bold venture for passing on escaped slaves to Canada, yet the church officials forbade him to preach on this issue and thus shattered any chance that he might have had a satisfactory preaching career. He drifted away from the church and into a long series of other work including journalism, teaching, shoemaking, storekeeping, the manufacture of carriages, the cooperage trade and finally, and disastrously, wholesale dealing in whiskey. Invalided out of the Northern Army, he died at home in 1865. The family history describes him as a scholar and a tormented soul, and his wives (he had a succession of three) and his children as always insecure and leading almost a nomad life. It appears that whiskey and the ambivalent attitude of his church have to share responsibility for his failure.

When she was eighteen one of the daughters had a chance to escape from this luckless environment. Her mother's sister Amanda had married a prosperous widower with eleven sons, and she wrote to young Sara, "Come and visit me and I'll give you one of my boys." Sara's daguerreotype shows an engaging little girl (she never grew to be five feet tall) with a face full of spunk and ambition. She arrived in the household of John Harden of Mt. Gilead, Ohio, with all the advantages of a girl from away and a managing type of aunt to make the best possible match for her. So Sara looked over the available sons and made her choice: Calvert, the black sheep, the only ne'er-do-well among all the eleven, an alcoholic.

He, who became my grandfather, had joined the Union Army at seventeen in that proud branch of the service, the Sharpshooters. His regiment, like many others during the Civil War, was short of food, the men were kept going largely on rations of whiskey, and he came out of the war with a permanent thirst. He fought his addiction; several times he went into one of those institutes that promised "the cure," and for a while it would be effective but never for long. He bought a mill in Brecksville, Ohio, and then a larger one in Painesville, where his life beside the Grand River, flowing through sunny meadows, appears to have satisfied him. The weeks I spent there in the summers were for me an emotional oasis. I never saw my grandfather when he was not sober, at least when I knew he was not. We had a happy relationship. According to my cousin Donovan I followed him around like a puppy.

There had been a period after his two children, my mother and her brother, were born when he disappeared and his young family lived in his father's household. It was an educational experience for the young wife after that floundering youth, for the Hardens had arrived fairly late in the United States and they came from a titled family of Ulstermen, bringing into this western wilderness the values of a European culture as well as some of its practical benefits. With his manorial background John Harden felt a certain responsibility for less fortunate neighbors; he was known for his generosity to them, and with his own books he established the first free public library in Ohio.

John Harden managed things well. He bought and sold land in

Ohio and Indiana, he harvested good crops of walnut trees from his tract of timber, he held local government posts. Most influential on the daughter-in-law were the ease and artistry of his household. There she learned to appreciate the best quality in dress and home furnishings and the fine points of social etiquette. In her father-in-law she encountered a wider point of view than her own father's, for the Hardens were not churchgoing people and yet John Harden always provided the hospitality for the circuit riders because, he said, he liked to cross swords with an educated mind. He was not tolerant of his son Calvert. In his will he made some provision for Sara but he specified with acid bitterness that her husband was not to receive a penny.

Finally Calvert came back for his family and Sara began a lifelong effort to create a household like the Hardens' but with a Harden husband who was "a drinking man."

As a child's companion my grandfather was delightful, although not always entirely responsible. He once took me to the Painesville theatre to see a movie which turned out to be of a naked man being tarred and feathered and ridden out of town on a rail. I was not in the least disturbed by it but it must have had some effect because I remember so vividly that fantastic garb of feathers and my wonder that the man could keep his balance on the rail. I can remember too how extremely interested my grandfather was — like a boy. He probably forgot I was there.

He would not allow me to go into his mill, among the open shafts and the whirring belts, but I could go in his office where, in his high desk, he kept a quantity of cheap costume jewelry and when I had especially pleased him he would give me a piece of it. He was tall, with a bearing which had given him the universal nickname of The Colonel (not his Army rank), but under this commanding manner he had such a nonsensical turn of mind that I would rather hear him talk than have someone read me a story. Once when he'd decked me out with his brass and glass he said, "Now you look like the Queen of Sheba." Who was she? "A pretty lady. But if you're going to be the Queen of Sheba you have to act pretty too." To act pretty: that piece of advice, tossed off so lightly, stayed in my mind more effectively than much repetitious talk about firm self-control.

My mother frequently told me about her father's drunkenness when she was a child, how when he didn't appear for dinner she and her mother would go to the mill and find him insensible on the floor, how they would rouse him and give him support as they led him home. I don't know why her brother, older than she, did not do this but perhaps he did and she only described the incidents because she was so anxious to impress upon me the shame that can come from "giving in to a weakness." She always emphasized the moral but it was really not very effective because my grandfather as I knew him was a gentle and lovable man.

Sara treated him coldly and with the silence which seems by then to have become a family weapon; her daughter, my mother, immensely proud and mortified by his drunkenness during her girlhood, felt for her father, and showed it, an icy contempt. His protests were nonverbal. I think one reason he gave me the trashy jewelry was that it horrified my grandmother and mother (it always disappeared during the following night); and he provoked them in other ways. For one, he chewed tobacco, a habit the women considered revolting. When my grandfather went out after lunch, usually to tilt back a chair on the sunny porch of his mill while he waited for farmers to bring in their grain, he never left without saying he was leaving to "have a chaw tobaccy," using even a phrase that offended them.

And yet I believe that he loved his child-sized wife, for when she died he quite went to pieces and never again really pulled himself together. At lunchtime when I was visiting them she would say, speaking into thin air, "I want the horse at three," and he would amble off in his relaxed way with no reply but at three the horse would always be ready, freshly groomed and the buggy and harness dusted.

And we would take a drive. Sometimes we went to the shore of Lake Erie to watch the fishermen bring in their catch and to buy some sturgeon, plentiful in the lake at that time — unforgettably delicious! Or we would call on one of my grandmother's friends, or most often we went to the nurseries, for Painesville was in a flower-growing area, and we would sit in the midst of acres of sweet peas, carnations, or roses, almost faint with the fragrance, and eat cupcakes and apples.

On another favorite drive, we would go to the cemetery, as beautiful as a park, where we often stopped beside a vault on which a marble child played with a marble dog — there for my interest but I guessed quite early that my grandmother saw herself in that cemetery, as she probably did, for her down-going was the long slow hill of pernicious anaemia, then incurable. We drove home past a large white house where the daughter, a girl of my age, had a duplicate playhouse built on the spacious lawn — a vision of what wealth could mean and that was an ache not accepted easily.

For those afternoon drives it was always necessary for me to have on a crisp clean dress, my grandmother with the white bun of her hair very smooth and wearing a black alpaca skirt with a white shirtwaist. To be expected if visiting friends, but also for the workers in the nursery lanes and the old man raking leaves in the cemetery? Rather for me, I think, to instill the habit of doing the decorous thing. Because she was so tiny and not strong, it seemed touching to me even then that she always *tried* so hard. From the bone china and sterling silverware to the stuffed canary under the bell glass in the parlor, there was everywhere evidence of her effort to create the amenities of a civilized life. Her house, mostly by her own efforts, was spotless, but she always found time and strength to make my long visits a pleasure.

I was instructed but also welcomed. Did she know the feeling I aroused in my own home? She probably sensed the animosity, not its real cause, and wished to give me the experience of warmth. She did not preach about giving in to a weakness but she did sometimes speak about having a strong will; even a child could be "like a mustard seed, which is small but powerful," and she would give me one so I could chew it and taste its strength. She also gave mustard seeds to my young cousin Donovan, and I doubt that she attributed my excitable reactions to a personality defect — for one reason that she was patient and kind, so that I was more calm when I was with her. Dr. Bowlby has pointed out that an infant's ability to stand stress is greatly dependent on the amount of physical contact he has with his mother, on the way she holds him, on the effectiveness of her soothing techniques. I believe that my mother tried conscientiously to give what I needed, though perhaps never much cuddling or holding, and when even her best efforts failed to make me a placid baby, gave up all except the most perfunctory and mechanical care-taking. Yet I did receive tenderness from my father and grandparents and a touching protectiveness from small Donovan, and Dr. Isaacs pointed out that I was lucky in that, for out of their reassurance I was able "to build up the bits and pieces of comfort which made it possible to live."

My grandmother lived until I was ten and although she never said anything to make us aware of it, we knew she was losing ground. She was still courageous. Alone she made a farewell visit to relatives in Toledo, and when they were on the railroad station platform waiting for the train to bring her home, some ruffians snatched her handbag and to cover their escape threw her down on the track in front of the oncoming engine. At the precisely necessary instant she jumped onto the cowcatcher, and her only comment about this escape was that she was glad the thieves had not got her gold watch, on its long gold chain, which was tucked into her waistband.

When I went alone to the Cleveland rest home where she was being nursed in her diminishing strength, I believe we both realized that this would be the last time we would see each other, and I was hurt to find that she was up and dressed as meticulously as for one of our country drives. So much formality, in her manner too, when I only longed to have us put our arms around each other and cry because we would soon be separated — when could formality be abandoned if not at a time like this? Yet now I am moved to realize that she wanted me to remember her as presentable as she had been when she was well.

After my grandmother died at our house in East Cleveland, my mother and her sister-in-law made the trip to Painesville to distribute between them my grandparents' furniture and other worthwhile possessions. On the interurban car they discussed what was there and agreed on what each should have. Warning of a shocking dénouement came as they walked down my grandfather's lane. He was standing in the door of the house, leaning against the casement, for he needed support. Even then they could see that the curtains were down, and their first glimpse of the interior told them the rest. He had sold everything, all the carved walnut furniture, the silverware, the embroidered linens, the carpets, the stuffed canary. The house was stripped to its bare boards. At the sight of my mother's face he laughed — he had had a final chance to repay her for her lack of tolerance, for her frozen scorn. He laughed, and then turned inside to his silent and empty life.

The origin of my mother's dislike for her father, almost her loathing, may have gone all the way back to the early years Calvert's family spent in the John Harden household. John Harden's will showed an attitude towards his wayward son that was unforgiving, and so Calvert probably was referred to with disdain. I have gone through the farmhouse and town house John Harden built, obviously the homes of a man with taste, and his will proves that he was a man with a strong sense of public responsibility, of leadership, of the belief that no virtue is more important than helping to set the social tone by personifying the most worthy values. It is *noblesse oblige,* not only an obligation to dispense charity but as much an obligation of honorable behavior, an upper-middle-class habit of mind and it was my mother's. To be a "substantial citizen," her frequent phrase, was an intention always dominant in her mind.

And she certainly succeeded. Friends spoke of her often as "such a lady," although she had a slight handicap, curiously, in her compelling charm. Being aware that the family's position of authority had slipped in the last generation, she was eager to re-establish it and to do that she relied a little too much perhaps on her captivating manner. Those whose social position has never been threatened don't make quite so much effort. But she did very well, especially considering that her husband, although entirely respectable, never thought of himself as setting an example to anyone. His family knew the right and wrong way of doing things, but they didn't feel any urge to demonstrate their preference to others. They wished to live fully and they had a talent for that, but none of them, including my father, ever tried to be a community bellwether.

It is typical of those steadfast, dependable people like the Hardens that they put loyalty to one's class ideals ahead of loyalty to a member of one's own family. An example is John Harden's disowning of his son when he failed to live up to the Harden standards. Defection like Calvert's can undermine the whole assumption that a family embodies impeccable virtue, and how then can they function as models? Such families have always found it hard to acknowledge unconventional offspring. In England they were often paid to stay out of the country — the "remittance men," and if the Hardens had remained in Ulster young Calvert probably would have been sent to America. I don't know what they would have done with a daughter who seemed unstable from early babyhood. Drowned her perhaps?

4

Three years after I was born my parents decided to establish themselves in East Cleveland where, due to an unexpected opportunity, they almost immediately became prominent. The families on and near Windermere Street were ruled, almost literally, by a Mrs. Reid (I'll call her), a woman so sweetly but firmly authoritative that few would question her status or guidance. There was no question either about the status of anyone sponsored by Mrs. Reid, and she took a fancy to my mother, who became the court favorite. It must have seemed a great stroke of fortune, for it lifted my mother, the newcomer, at once into second place in the social hierarchy.

Mrs. Reid certainly was intelligent, she probably had a college degree in even those early days, and she was willing to share her expertise in many things, especially the rearing of children. There was a Mothers' Club, organized by Mrs. Reid, of which she was the president and my mother the secretary. Through it all of us, the young, were being taught and discplined by regulations laid down by Mrs. Reid, and my memory of her is colored by the fact that she thought it was good for children to have to take bad-tasting medicine. Castor oil and various unpleasant dark-brown nostrums became the accepted therapy up and down Windermere Street.

Mrs. Reid had a special advantage in her chronic frailty, which had been diagnosed as diabetes. This was before the discovery of insulin, and so Mrs. Reid was going to die and that doom gave her words a kind of holy meaning, as if coming from an oracle on the other side of the curtain. The Reids could afford the best medical care and she did in fact live for years after she had prepared her children and all the community for the impending event.

The pervading melancholy in the Reid household made me reluctant to play with one of their daughters, a girl my own age, but there were other reasons as well. "Elizabeth" had an air of superiority much like her mother's and also her mother's habit of giving advice: "You should have stepped back till my mother went through the door first." "You forgot to say thank you for the junket."

At the time I was intensely concerned about becoming a trapeze performer and with a little neighbor, Walter Bailey, was practicing on a broomstick my father had put up in our apple tree. To leave this sunny activity for the Reid's house was like entering a tomb, but I was under a good deal of pressure to play with Elizabeth, for her mother and mine had decided that we should be special friends. They'd even had made identical dresses for us which we were supposed to wear on the same day, to me an embarrassing obligation. Nevertheless I was made aware that my avoidance of Elizabeth was a handicap to my mother; it could even have an unfortunate effect on her precious relationship with Elizabeth's mother, and frequently therefore I had to give up learning to hang by my knees while I gave Walter a push in the swing, and went to play with Elizabeth — except that she didn't really know how to play. She just wanted to show me the things in her curio cabinet and instruct me in whatever information her mother was currently giving her.

"This is a rock from the wall of the church where a famous artist is buried. First his wife died, and then his son died, and the artist didn't want to live any longer, so he died. And he is buried in the church."

Trust me to say the tactless thing: "If people keep taking stones out of the wall the church will fall down."

"I didn't say it was *taken* out of the wall. It had *fallen* out. It was lying on the ground. My mother picked it up when she went abroad with her parents. And this is a piece of the Rock of Gibraltar. My uncle knows I collect rocks and he sent it to me. The Rock of Gibraltar is one of the Pillars of Hercules. That's just a myth, but I guess you don't know about myths."

I had seen trapeze performers at the county fair in Painesville — frosty white bodies in the night sky, standing on glittering silver bars as high as the treetops, and then swinging on silver swings, higher and higher, until suddenly they dived through the air, just trusting that they would be caught by another performer, hanging by his knees. Would that be so hard to learn? Oh, and while you waited for the dive, the drums, beating so softly and fast you could hardly breathe . . .

"In the olden days they never sailed through the Pillars of Hercules. This stone was lying there even then, when they weren't sailing through."

I never said much during Elizabeth's six-year-old lectures. At any time I could not think of much to say to her, and anyway the whole question of permissible talk had become very confusing. I did know that I was supposed to talk to the Reids, if they talked to me, but of course not to *tell* them anything — telling was the kind of talk that was forbidden, to me but not to Elizabeth, who was always telling things, most of which you would be willing not to hear about.

Since the Reids were indirectly, innocently, responsible for a disastrous episode in my life, a word about Mr. Reid also is needed. As Mrs. Reid seemed to my mother an ideal wife, so Mr. Reid

seemed the ideal husband — very successful and handsome in a dy-
namic way. He must in fact have been brilliant, for already, in his
thirties, he was an influence in Cleveland and in the state of Ohio
and was slated for a consulting appointment in Washington. I remember Mr. Reid well: tall, rather heavily built, with a don't-inter-
rupt-me voice and a manner which always seemed to imply that he
could not waste much more of his time in this company. My father,
unfortunately, had too little of that kind of presence. My mother
had heard that Mr. Reid could do three things at once: converse
with a man on the other side of his desk, talk on the telephone, and
write a letter. She admired that quality (more I imagine than Mr.
Reid's callers did) and referred to it often, probably as a way of
trying to stimulate my father, who was one to put all his mind on
what he was doing, whether mowing a lawn, reading a newspaper,
or listening to someone who was talking to him, which was very
nice for the talker. There must have been many meetings between
my father and Mr. Reid and I wish I could recall them, but in any
case Mr. Reid would have sensed that my father was unimpressed,
and my father would just not have been interested. That Mr. Reid
could have thrown opportunities in his way was a thought that
would have had no effect on my father, although I imagine the
point was made. In our family's contacts with the Reids my father
and I were both failing my mother.

5

She was always quick to see and grasp any social advantage such as
one which occurred in May of my sixth year. My parents and I had
often spent weekends with a family of friends who lived in a wooded
suburb west of Cleveland, on the shore of Lake Erie. This time the
Brownells were going away themselves and they asked if we would

like to come and spend a few days while they were gone. We would give companionship to an elderly relative and meanwhile could have suppers on the beach and walks through the woods, then alight with new leaves and spring wildflowers. Gladly accepting, my mother thought of inviting Elizabeth to come with us. Elizabeth and I could sleep in the bunkbeds of the Brownell boys — all in all a fine chance to deepen that special friendship both mothers tried to promote. Pleased as she was at this prospect, my mother may have been slightly surprised that the Reids were willing to let Elizabeth go, for their children were being reared with a vigilance almost as close as if they were royalty. Nevertheless Mrs. Reid agreed and in the middle of a rainy week we set out. All day Friday and Saturday the downpour continued, growing ever more murky, and with all the water everywhere suppers on the beach and walks amid flowers were not even a hope.

Elizabeth became difficult. The boys had plenty of games but she didn't like to play games. She was very frank about being bored. "Don't they even have a curio cabinet?" I didn't know what to do with her and kept starting to play by myself, when my mother would take me aside and hiss (the only possible word), "She's your *guest.*" My mother never understood children, as I realized when I saw her with grandchildren, and she probably could not have realized that a girl of six might be lacking in the techniques of being a hostess. She tried to entertain Elizabeth herself, for I am sure she was thinking about the report of this weekend that would be made in detail to the Reids, but by the end of Saturday even my mother's social gifts seemed to be running out.

It was still raining on Sunday. Plans were taking shape for us all to go to church when the Brownells' nanny goat got away. The goat was there to supply milk for the elderly lady, and a neighbor's boy was taking care of it but since milking it on Saturday he had not come back. On Sunday morning the goat broke its tether and went leaping off through the woods. My father, not waiting for even a raincoat, took after it. For some time they were out of sight; when they reappeared my father was holding the frayed end of the rope with the goat pulling him on at an awkward and stumbling pace. Near the house my father's foot slipped on the wet leaves and he fell face-down in mud. He continued his hold on the tether and when he had the goat tied up again, he came into the house, dripping mud from his hairline to his shoes, and laughing. He evidently expected that we all would have seen the humor of his mishap, but my mother was livid. What would Mr. Reid have done in the same situation? Let the goat go, of course. No doubt phoned the police or waited for the boy who would come eventually and then could find it and bring it back. In any case he would not have considered splashing off through a soppy wood and finally he would not have fallen down in the mud. With what ridicule this event would be greeted in the Reid household! My mother wept and my father went to take off his suit and clean himself up. He wore a housecoat of Mr. Brownell's to dinner, and his scrubbed face looked embarrassed but gently defiant.

I touched his hand: "Oh, Daddy, you make so many jokes for us!"

He, brightening: "Goats are always good for a laugh."

My mother: "Goats and some people." She and Elizabeth shared their scorn with a glance.

I would have no more to do with that girl. After dinner I went up to the boys' room and lay on the floor, looking at picture books. Perhaps an hour went by. The room was chilly, rain dripped through the swaying trees and wind ruffled the ivy outside on a wall. I had seen all the books now, but I stood at a window wondering what to do, feeling helpless about Elizabeth.

The very click of my mother's heels approaching along the hall sounded angry. As she strode into the room and towards me her face was frightening, it was her most terrible face and all of her pent-up humiliation had taken over without control. She was striking me on my head, my body, anywhere, and soon, with one arm binding my shoulders, her fingers had tightened upon my throat with a strangling grip. I tried to tear myself loose but fury had given her an iron strength; I tried to cry out but my throat was closed. All I could see, with my head bent back, were two high casement windows, oblongs of light which swiftly darkened until they were black. (They would be a significant memory later.) Yet I was still faintly conscious and struggling when the old lady's cane came tapping up to the open door. As she saw her my mother flung me aside and, passing the elderly relative, she disappeared down the hall.

I fell onto one of the bunks but had to be sick and was able to get to the basin in a corner of the room. The old lady was still there and she held my head and helped me back to the bunk. She went away but returned with a cool damp cloth and sponged my face. She stayed with me for a while, all this without a word but with unmistakable sympathy, and finally she left. Feeling very ill and from time to time nauseated I lay on the bed until dark, when my mother came up for me. We were going home now. There was no question of whether I would be able to go — I had to and therefore somehow I did.

After that episode I was ill all summer and not well enough to start school in September. I had developed such a severe tic that for a while it was believed to be St. Vitus Dance (chorea) but the later decision was that it may have been due to some kind of shock. It began to subside in August but I was still in too distraught a condition to enter school. At a moment's notice people, any people, could throw me into a panic and my relationship with my mother was almost hysterical. Waking and sleeping I lived with two nightmares: the memory of my mother's face as she came into that room, and the pressure of her hand on my neck. And the very sight of her hands, if I ever became conscious of them, smothered my breath.

On that fateful Sunday there must have been bruises on my throat. In my hearing nothing was said about them, but I was treated by a neurologist and from the questions he asked and from the fact that he had private talks with my mother, I believe he may have suspected what happened. It was not he but our own doctor who discovered a damaged heart valve. It did not seem to be very serious. Playing tennis or other strenuous games or gymnastic exercises must be avoided, but those might be the only handicaps, a surmise, it turned out, that was too optimistic. (If the tic was in fact chorea, that would explain the heart problem, for chorea is a form of rheumatic fever.)

All my life, it seemed, had been a pilgrimage to the great moment when I could start to school. My father's schooling had seemed a wonderful opportunity to him, cut short too early, and therefore he had a contagious enthusiasm when he often said, "You'll learn that as soon as you go to school." Going to school, besides, was what the older boys and girls did, passing so enviably with their books while I sat on the front steps and watched them disappear. Going to school was the objective for which I had fairly pushed myself towards being six — and now I was six and I couldn't go. It seemed my own fault that I could not, because I wasn't brave enough to walk along Euclid Avenue with the other children. It was such a mix-up of fear and disappointment, guilt and self-doubt, that it may be surprising I ever came out of it.

One thing that finally made the venture possible was the friendship of a little boy, Jamie. Although the tic did not disappear for some time, by late autumn I started, soon with some confidence because Jamie, who sat next to me in the first grade, called for me at our house and took me home every time. On our walks he talked fascinatingly about railroads. His father worked for a railroad, as mine had, and Jamie said that his father was going to build a child's size railroad to connect their house and mine and the school so that Jamie and I could ride. The track would go along on the grassy strip between the sidewalk and curb. There were trees there and I was skeptical but, said Jamie, the tracks would turn onto the sidewalk to pass around them. Then wouldn't we run into people? He'd be careful. He would run the engine, I'd sit in the car behind. It was just for the two of us. The engine was going to be red, also my car would be red and the coal car too (he liked red). When the plans seemed complete I told my mother about them. "You little fool!" she flung at me. "Are you always going to believe what men tell you?" The remark probably meant that at some time she had mistakenly believed what some man had told her, but it also showed that she didn't understand how much fun it is, at six, to make believe, to blur the borderline between fantasy and reality. Anyway she spoiled my faith in Jamie. He became somebody else that I couldn't trust, because he told lies, and my fragile courage nearly broke down again.

But meanwhile I had found out how much I loved school. Geography: like my father's sense that he lived everywhere in the country, I soon felt that I was living everywhere in the world. And reading — oh, reading! That was living not only in every place but at all times. Elizabeth's mother and mine tried to instill a rivalry between us: which would get the better grades? Even most of the neighbors became involved. On the day the report cards came out, that year and later, adults would stop me to ask, "And which of you is ahead this time?" This annoyed me extremely, for what did it *matter* who was ahead? I just loved to learn, to learn almost anything, as I always had since the days when I learned about boats and blast furnaces. Besides, soon after I entered school something so wonderful happened that it was nearly overwhelming, and most of the recent tumult went out of my mind. It was no longer even important that I might not talk, for I had found a much better way to communicate — I had discovered music!

ii

CLIMB A STEEP LADDER

IN THESE DAYS when music is present always and everywhere, it must have been heard by most children from the day they are born. Perhaps nowhere in the world, unless in remote wild areas, could a child live as I did to the age of six without knowing that sounds can be arranged harmoniously in the patterns called music. In this today's children may be deprived, since before the time its marvel could sweep with meaning into one's consciousness, it is music of trivial kinds that usually has become familiar.

I have a dim memory of being rocked on my grandmother's lap while she sang a lullaby, but of no other music (we did not have a piano or phonograph then) until I experienced music suddenly and in one of its richest forms.

There can be few human revelations with a more profound impact.

It was on a Sunday afternoon in December when my parents took me to a Vesper Concert in the chapel of the Western Reserve University. There we would hear Sol Marcosson, one of the country's outstanding violinists. It was a beautiful setting for my great event: lofty space, pews and panelling of dark polished wood, the shine of organ pipes, all in subdued, magical light. My mother went first into the pew, my father was on the aisle and I between. But when

Marcosson began to play I seemed to receive this magnificent sound not through my ears alone but through the skin all over my body, and I slipped out past my father to stand in the aisle so that I could sense more of it. This was not necessarily an illusion. People totally deaf can hear sounds through their skin if the vibrations are sufficiently magnified and when one thinks of it, is this not true of us all? The sound at close range of an engine backfiring or tire exploding, or a nearby jet plane taking off seems to me to be felt through tactile nerve endings as well as ears and sometimes that may be true of sounds with less volume. But perhaps the experience at the Vesper Concert would have been as moving heard only through ears, and perhaps that is the only way I did hear it and it seemed to touch all my skin simply because the effect was so powerful.

When I turned back to the pew my father whispered, "You look as if you have seen the angels."

I remember well how it seemed that the music was another kind of talk, especially so since the soloist's violin was held against his throat. Anybody could talk like that! I could! And surely nobody would object, for this was not *telling*, this was just saying how happy, comfortable and safe — or else sad, lonely, fearful — everything is, but if sad, nevertheless beautiful and therefore with its own kind of joy. I did not clearly say all of this to myself, but I did experience a new hope, for of course I would learn to play like that. That would be my kind of talk. It was so absolutely necessary for this to happen that it certainly would. When I went out with my parents into the rainy night, where the street lights were giving a kind of Christmas spell to the wet boughs of trees and the pavement, I had an almost overwhelming assurance that my doom of silence was simply going to be lifted away.

I don't remember pleading for music lessons — it was just understood that I would have them. Perhaps my parents recognized even then, what turned out to be true, that I had inherited the musical talent which ran through my father's family. And perhaps they realized that such a delight would help me to become well again, for my terrors were still, at times, unmanageable. If that was their thought, they were right. A piano was moved into our house almost immediately and I learned, at six, one of the greatest sources of confidence that can come to one of any age: that there is always present an escape from personal disaster in impersonal joys and satisfactions. I was already learning that in school. That my mother's beautiful face could become terrible without warning was less fearful if one knew that the people of Egypt "live on dates and honey" — so at least the geography textbook said. One could imagine being a child among such Egyptian delights and thus partly escape being a child in a troubled East Cleveland home. But music seemed a quicker, more widely opened door. To slip onto the piano bench and touch the piano keys was almost as good as having Aladdin's lamp.

Sometimes we forget why music can be so fundamentally reassuring. Among all the innumerable, conglomerate sights and sounds of everyone's daily life, in a single musical note there can be perfect order — no longer the mixture of vibrations which is ordinary sound but vibrations in an arrangement so completely regular, so the opposite of random, as to seem hardly natural. Yet a pure tone is natural in the grandest sense. Occasionally an absolutely pure tone is heard in the voice of a bird, and that tone is true and orderly in as elemental a way as the movements of earth and stars in their orbits. Intuitively, at least, Sir Thomas Browne in the seventeenth century must have meant something like this when he wrote, "For there is music wherever there is harmony, order or proportion; and thus far we may maintain the music of the spheres."

Something as tremendously moving as this I felt when I touched the keys on our new piano. It was disappointing that it could not have been a violin. My mother had said, "I'll be wanting you to play for our parties and with a violin you would have to have an accompanist" — an unsatisfactory reason, I thought, for the meaning of my music was not going to be a social accomplishment; but later I was glad it had been a piano. For my own pleasure, too, it was better not to need an accompanist, and anyway one could talk with fingers almost as well as a throat. Talk I soon did, through my own compositions, but what I had not anticipated was the talk of the great composers to me.

My teacher was a widow named Mrs. Grace Bunce who had studied with Dr. Calvin Cady, head of the Music Department at Columbia University. I never have known anyone else who was taught by his system or even anyone who has heard of it; yet it seems so brilliantly right that I want to make a brief record of what has been lost.

The system was based on the assumption that beautiful sound is produced primarily by the imagination — by hearing in one's mind, before ever touching a key, the tone or tones to come and hearing them as ideal, as perfect as one is capable of conceiving. In my music lessons I started by learning to play only single keys: by learning to hear the tone that I wanted before a key was struck, hearing the tone as sharp, quick and bright, or perhaps round, resonant, whole. If one "hears" a tone very clearly in imagination, hand and arm marvelously do reproduce the tone in one's mind, no doubt due to the working of autosuggestion, which in many other ways will reproduce thoughts in actions. The imagining requires practice and it is a skill which improves. That, first of all, was what Mrs. Bunce taught: to create a beautiful sound in one's mind. Later one learns to hear in the mind what will be coming next even while the previous phrase is being produced; one hears it, that is, ahead of the fingers. In its more advanced stages it is a skill which simply occurs without effort. Incidentally, I suspect that most fine musicians use this technique in their playing whether they have been taught to do it consciously or not.

And so I began by playing single notes. It was an exciting day when I could first "hear" and then play do, re, mi in the key of C.

I had three lessons a week: one in performing, in the way explained here, one in musical theory, and (actually the most thrilling) one in composition. Every other week I had an assignment to make up a little poem, then the following week to express the words of the poem in appropriate musical sounds. The very writing of the poems was an enlargement of my world into new and brighter horizons.

I was fortunate in having the materials for poems immediately at hand (although one can write poems of course about almost any experience). Surrounding my life there was much that was beautiful. Our own yard backed up against the rose gardens of the John D. Rockefeller estate, and my walk to school followed other boundaries of the estate, along a high wrought-iron fence which enclosed vistas as lovely as landscape architects could create. There were both a brook and a small river, an artificial waterfall descending through rocks to a pond with waterlilies and lotus blossoms and a few white swans; and as a background to all this, groves and rolling green velvet lawns. Part way along to school was the entrance, with wide gates always open onto a straight tree-lined avenue with the pond at its end. I don't know how many of my little songs celebrated these inspiring scenes, but I should think many of them.

The final wonder: when my father became aware of how much I enjoyed the sight of the Rockefeller gardens, he secured permission from the manager of the estate for me to go in, to play in the grounds as much as I liked, and from then on that's where I was, a solitary but delighted child, in all my spare time. The gardens came to seem so much like my own that I have accused the Rockefellers of giving me a slight permanent sense of disappointment because I had felt during those youthful years that such elegant beauty was my rightful environment. With amusement I used to remember that vision when I owned my first house, in Nome, Alaska, where not a tree existed within a hundred miles and not even weeds would grow in my yard, which was paved with the crushed-rock tailings from gold-mining dredges. Wanting at least a few twigs of green in the summer, I took an Eskimo out on the tundra and we dug up some spindly little willows to transplant around the base of the house. Within a week the town's Husky dogs had eaten them.

There were two Rockefeller incidents about which I did not make up poems. One concerned the appearance of the four Rockefeller grandsons on the other side of the drive while I was feeding the swans. They just stood there and watched in a row, all in white shirts and short tight pants, looking as if they wondered at the audacity of anyone's so intruding. When I mentioned them at home my mother said brightly, "What did you talk about?"

"Oh, we didn't talk. You said that a girl should never speak first and they didn't speak to me."

"Well, for goodness sake, you could have started a conversation some other way." How?

"Oh!" Exasperated at such stupidity, "For one thing you could have fallen in the pond."

She was right, I could have.

The other episode was even more humiliating. I knew vaguely that things were not going very well for us financially, and I thought that Mr. Rockefeller might make us a gift — I had decided that ten thousand dollars would be a nice round sum — if he knew that my brother, recently born, was named John D. I hoped Mr. Rockefeller would think he was named for him, although my father reminded me that this was not honest since Jack was named for a relative. Nevertheless I composed letters to Mr. Rockefeller, none of which was sent because they did not seem persuasive enough. One day I was in the estate, sitting at the edge of the pond with my grandmother and the baby in his push-cart when Mr. and Mrs. Rockefeller came along in a fawn-colored four-wheeled chaise, he driving the pair of matching horses. They stopped. Were they going to ask us to leave? No, Mrs. Rockefeller looked down and said, "That's a charming baby."

I, oh very gracious: "Would you like to hold him?"

"Indeed I would."

My grandmother handed up my brother and both the Rockefellers talked to him and won his shy dimpled smile. This was an exciting event to report at home. "And what did Mr. Rockefeller say when you told him Jack's name?"

I had forgotten to tell him.

2

After the incident at the Brownells' house a new kind of tension came into my mother's attitude. I believe now it was due to her dreading that I would tell someone about her attack. She had become even more aloof and made more attempts to keep me subdued. Her impression that a six-year-old child could endanger her friendship with Mrs. Reid had been a delusion, but there was some logic in the belief that I, with a shocking secret, could be a threat. Nothing could have dragged out of me a description of what had happened but my mother could not have known that. Then and at later times she was curiously on the defensive with me.

In fact the elderly Brownell aunt may have said something about what occurred. From about that year on we no longer went to visit their family, only once again seeing them when, six years later, we were moving away from Cleveland.

As for me, with music, the "poetry" and the gardens I had overcome pretty well the aftermath of the attack. But when I was in the second grade there was a sharp reminder that my happiness was precarious. Just before the afternoon session at school one day, when most of the children were on the playground, a cyclone struck Cleveland. I was late and had been gone from home only a few minutes when, with no warning except a great, swiftly rising roar, a wind threw me face down on the sidewalk. Most frightening, all the breath was sucked out of my lungs, perhaps by a vacuum in or near the center of the storm. Next a cloudburst, the water falling in sheets and swirling over the walk. To get my face out of it I put my arms under my head and this made a pocket of air with which I could breathe again. Trees were falling, debris sailing through the air and crashing, a tumult. Then almost as suddenly the disturbance was over. I picked myself up and with water cascading out of my hair and clothes, went on to school.

The other children were all indoors when I arrived, some of those in my grade were crying but soon mothers began to come. Many burst into tears when they found that their children were safe. Most mothers had brought dry clothes, and the boys and girls, unselfconscious in the emergency, were undressing and dressing together. Some of the mothers continued to weep, holding their children on their laps, kissing them, pushing the wet hair back off their foreheads, searching their faces with love and relief that they were alive.

My mother and those of two boys were not there. The boys said their mothers were out but they both had keys and so were sent home. The teacher told me to sit down in a chair by the window and wait till my mother came. When she hadn't by the time the class was to start work, the teacher said, "You'll have to go home. You can't sit here all afternoon soaking wet like that."

I was the only one in a large class whose mother, able to come, had not done so, but that fact impressed me less, as I walked along through the fallen branches, than the way the other mothers had taken their children in their arms and caressed them. I never had seen a mother do that and of course had not experienced such affection myself, and I wondered what made me so hateful. Even so I was unprepared for my reception at home: an outburst of rage. "What do you mean, coming home at this time of day! Why aren't you in school?"

"The teacher said I couldn't stay, so wet."

"Well, get yourself upstairs and into some dry things and hurry back."

She was fearfully angry and she didn't ask, then or later, where I had been when the cyclone struck, or what had happened, and I never brought up the subject. But walking to school again, slowly, the confusion that I had lived with for more than a year straightened out, spun itself into a clear and coherent thought: she was angry today because she'd been wishing that I had been killed. There, it was said now, what I had not dared to tell myself: my mother wished I was dead. That explained everything, the violent Sunday, the outbursts of anger, usually over nothing, today's fury. It all made sense except the reason why, and I didn't waste time trying to figure that out. The important thing was to absorb the discovery — an impulse not stated to myself articulately of course. The discovery itself was a kind of relief. It let in light.

Children can live with the truth about situations. The knowledge — and I am sure it was correct — was crippling but better than mystery and confusion, dread and uncertainty. The important thing now was how to cope with it, how to stay alive.

I thought a great deal about that in the next few days and came up with a plan that today seems amusing. I told myself I'd be my own mother and then maybe I would be safer. That was a game I played for the rest of my childhood. First I must stop doing dangerous things like jumping off the shed roof next door, walking along the joists of a new house above the basement, and coasting in winter down the curving hill with a busy street at the bottom. I'd thought that I had to do these things because the boys in the neighborhood did and it was not honorable to be afraid. My real mother knew and did not object but my new mother did.

At home I would be more polite and helpful and unobtrusive. I would learn to fix my own hair so I would not have to be touched. I would never talk to my father if my mother was there wanting all his attention. I would read and do homework in my own room or the den, not with the others. I would avoid even the smallest offence because that could mean the end, actually the end. And in the future I would avoid a kind of disappointment that had become all too familiar, by resolving not to hope that my mother's attitude ever would change (a resolution not very well kept). She was an unfriendly stranger: if I always remembered that I would be cooperative and inconspicuous and possibly safe. Such plans occupied my mind during the next days at school. The other children were learning the alphabet and I never did memorize it from E to K. I still have a blank in that space, which can be a great nuisance for one who lives with a dictionary. All the time wasted finding the page and place on the page of grith, jackaroo, hagride, fissile, imbrue!

The new self-control was not as complete as I should have liked. With my mother it was effective; I was so much on guard with her that I could check my over-reaction to her almost before there was any sign of its coming. In that way I avoided triggering her anger, which was so hard to ignore that soon we would have a rising emotional spiral. But I still over-reacted to other people and situations, to good things and bad, especially those for which I was not prepared. "Oh, *why* can't you have poise like Elizabeth's!" she would lament in tones of exasperation. Yes indeed, why couldn't I? I didn't know but resolved to be more calm *all* the time.

She never pretended that she was fond of me, whether others were present or not, and I respected her for that honesty. It would have been intolerable if she had called me Dear, or smiled in a tender, approving way just because somebody else was with us. I accepted her view that I was not loved because — I didn't know why — I didn't deserve to be. I would just have to carry on, feeling that I was somehow monstrous.

In my relationships with other children I carried over from home two impressions: of the way I thought my personality probably would repel people, and the prohibition against my talking. Neither was a particular disadvantage with little boys, who may have welcomed knowing a girl with no down-putting sense of superiority and one who apparently recognized that only boys were worth listening to. When we first moved to Fernwood I was taken into a gang of boys to act as their spy and learn from another gang such essential bits as Tommy's trading his collection of cigar bands for Lawrence's dragon kite. I functioned in this role until my new mother forbade my playing hazardous games.

I had no lasting friendships with girls except the dreary relationship with Elizabeth. To get along well with her own sex a girl (or woman) needs self-assurance; and in my silences I simply failed to communicate. There were a few on the fringe, such as a nice child whose home was so religious as to be depressing — the main staircase, for example, "the Sabbath stairs," could not be used on weekdays, and crawling up the narrow dark stairs from the kitchen seemed humiliating and didn't make me love Jesus. Then there were two or three girls so undemanding that I had confidence with them — a retarded child, and a daughter of Hungarian immigrants, whose house was warmly welcoming with all the red in its carpets and draperies and the delicious smell of strong spicy cooking. The girl I liked best was so dedicated to becoming a ballet dancer that she went to school only often enough to escape the truant officer. With those three I could feel relaxed but they showed so little promise of ever being substantial citizens that my mother treated them coldly whenever they came to my house to play and afterwards she would make fun of them. I would not submit them to this kind of treatment and soon stopped inviting them.

In this loneliness I did not feel deprived at the time. It was assumed now that I would be a musician when I grew up and I accepted gladly the hours of practicing and became like the child who trained for ballet — with almost no other interests. My music teacher had discovered that I had absolute pitch, the type of musical memory, if it is that, which enables one to recognize tones. "Sing F," and I could sing F. "Shut your eyes and tell me what key this is." "A flat," and A flat would be right. That was great fun and I went around hunting for "shadow keynotes" in ordinary sounds — our mantel clock chimed in G, a stick dragged along the picket fence sounded a lovely rich B, when the motorman on the streetcar stomped on his bell it clanged in E, the wind in the gables outside my bedroom moaned from A to D. The whole world seemed to sing.

My small brother was such a delight to us all that, for a while, the tension at home was eased. (I see him learning to walk, insisting on making his trails at the steep end of our graveled driveway, where he reeled up and down, falling at every third step and crying to himself softly but refusing, at age one, to practice walking on easier ground.) My father was at home, my mother less frustrated, they were leading a pleasant life in their dancing and whist clubs, amateur theatricals, play-going with groups of friends, vacations on Lake Chautauqua with the Windermere Yacht Club — I don't know of any young people today who have such continuous, varied and innocent fun.

For me there was fun too. I remember these years as happy, though not all the time. On my ninth birthday I was sitting on our front steps with my eight-year-old friend, Norman, when my mother opened the door and threw out a bowlful of venom. She did not accuse me of doing, or not doing, anything specific — it was just an outburst of anger, and when she had closed the door Norman said, "She's not your real mother, is she? Isn't she your aunt or something?"

"She's my real mother. But I'll make it all up to a little girl of my own some day." That was my new mother speaking, and the little girl was the nine-year-old. As soon as possible I would start trying to make it up. But I was on a steep ladder, and the question was, could I continue to climb?

3

In carrying such a heavy emotional load any child, indeed any adult, is liable to have physical breakdowns. The damaged heart, too, meant that my strength was limited and I frequently went beyond it. I wanted to stay at my place in the class at school, for Elizabeth and I were still supposed to compete — a curious kind of obligation which seemed somehow related to family honor. And I also practiced music each day, usually till the moment when I would be swept by exhaustion. It was all rather too much and I became so susceptible to infections that I was always having to catch up from time spent in bed. When I was ten years old then came the rup-

tured appendix. I remember it chiefly because of the part my father
played in it.

There had been an attack in the summer while we were away at
Chautauqua and my parents were only waiting until I was strong
enough to have the appendix removed. But one night in the autumn there was a pain so sudden and sharp that I screamed aloud.
Soon I was in a horse-drawn ambulance, moving jerkily along
midnight streets. The surgeon, gruff but very skilled, was waiting
at the hospital, though I don't remember that or anything else until
the next day. The appendix had grown to the wall of my bladder,
and besides that complication I had peritonitis at a time before there
were antibiotics. Not surprisingly Dr. Hammond warned my father
to be prepared for the worst. I did not hear him say it, I did not
need to. I knew I was close to dying. Even a child will know. I
have known the same thing again and I believe everyone in that situation does. It is one of the most convincing of intuitions.

My mother sat at the right side of the hospital bed, she just sat
there with no sign of concern or affection. But my father sat at the
other side, leaning forward and firmly holding my hand, and he
saved my life with his love.

That is not an illusion. There must have been acute pain but I
was not aware of it nor of anything that was done by the nurses, I
was aware of nothing except the enormous strength of my father's
love and how he was using it somehow to keep me alive. Was he
silently praying? Perhaps not consciously. He was a man with always a hopeful outlook, a belief, not related to any religion, that
things could be made to turn out well in the end but only if one
makes an effort to bring that about. I believe he wished me to live
so intensely that somehow he made it happen. I knew at the time
he was doing it. I knew there was nothing else that could keep me
from dying — but I was sure that he would.

He gave me my life on that day. His love gave it.

Those who do not have faith in the power of love can say that I'd had a discouraging lack of it and that my father's convincing evidence of his love strengthened my will to live.

o

That serious illness and the solitude of the long convalescence marked the end of my childhood, really. During that time I lost altogether my slight friendships with other children, and without being able to do any serious practicing for a few months there was nothing left in the empty days but to think, to become more aware, to grow in my own resources.

The conditions were somewhat unusual but I do believe that a child of ten is in most cases ready for such development. One of that age is still lacking in many kinds of experience but probably has all the inner capacities he or she ever will bring to life. Some of those children are still unawakened and probably few of the others are willing to talk about any new depth of feeling. But having gone through that period of quick enlargement myself, I sometimes see in the eyes of children around the age of ten years a look of swiftly expanding consciousness. Often it is the rather solitary, uncommunicative child in whom the new consciousness seems to occur, or a child already dedicated to developing a talent and therefore somewhat detached. For me both of these reasons were working, with the added impetus of the illness. I nearly had gone away and in turning back could see everything from a new point of view.

It was a spiritual awakening, not the questioning characteristic of adolescence but a different way of observing and feeling. There has been only one other time when I had perceptions anything like as profound. That was much later during years when I lived in the arctic. The strange Northern tundra and the white expanse of the frozen sea, broken by mountains of blue translucent ice, are a scene utterly primitive, lacking in any sign of civilized living. A world beyond this one, a nonhuman, nonmaterial world seemed very real while I was there, and it reminded me that I had had the same pervading awareness of something we cannot know with our usual senses when I was ten years old. In each case I was shocked out of the habitual way of looking at things, in the first instance by the illness and in the arctic because I was in an environment unlike anything I ever had known before. Both times the new vision was rather bleak by ordinary standards but immensely satisfying. The satisfaction lay, I believe, in a degree of truth no longer distorted by the demands of everyday living. One's mind has to be, in some way, emptied; then I found that it fills up in this unaccustomed and very rich way.

During that convalescence I was allowed to play the piano for my own pleasure though not strenuously nor for long at a time. Actually I did not lose through being unable to practice seriously. The songs I composed became more mature and some of the poems expressed things I had not been aware of thinking. That probably happens to all writers — words falling out of one's mind which are a total surprise — but that was the first time it had happened to me. I wrote one small poem about some trained dogs I had seen doing tricks in a circus. It ended:

> Sometimes we seem like the little dogs
> Jumping through hoops.
> We jump too. An unseen ringmaster
> Cracks his whip at us.

Who was the unseen ringmaster? God? Fate? I never had thought about such an idea consciously and wondered where it had come

from. There were others. Writing poems now seemed like recon-
noitering through a strange country, and the tunes too took unexpected, more original directions. By then I could hear music with
my mind's ear when sitting quietly reading the score and I did some
of that during the convalescence, going over the pieces that I had
played earlier and planning new interpretations for them, more full
of musical meaning. Thoughts like these were in my head during
the latter part of my idle months. But I was having the uneven development of all youngsters. In more ways than one I was still a
child. I still put twenty-two dolls to bed every night.

4

As my grandmother's death approached and she came to stay at our
house, I was sent for that interval to my uncle's family who had a
farm on the outskirts of a village thirty miles west of Cleveland. In
the family were three cousins and I might have gone to their school
but it was thought that I could benefit from a few more weeks of
idleness.

The days were very boring, especially so because the family had
no piano. They had an asthmatic organ, which I did not enjoy. So
my aunt took me to the house of her mother, a Mrs. Harper, who
did have a piano and invited me to come and play on it and I did
that every day.

The company there were an extended line of in-laws, including
Mrs. Harper's brother's sister-in-law and her daughter, who had become engaged while visiting the Harpers the previous year and for
sentimental reasons had wished to be married there. The last stages
of her trousseau were being put together by this Lois Biscomb, her
mother, Mrs. Harper, and a cousin, and when the wedding was still

nearly a week away, the bridgegroom arrived. He was a young attorney, twenty-eight, who had just accepted a position doing some new kind of work which would not start until shortly after his marriage. In the meantime he was idle and the Harpers had invited him to come too. His name was John Craig and he was due on a Monday.

That day I went up as usual to spend part of the afternoon playing the piano. Alone in the parlor I didn't hear any commotion but as I finished one piece I looked up and discovered this young man who had quietly let himself down in a chair. Our eyes met and for a tremendous moment my hands were motionless. I had never seen him before and yet I had an immediate impression of being understood and completely accepted. I played again, a few Chopin *Preludes,* poignant, actually ominous music; at least I was not tempted to show off with technical acrobatics. Soon afterwards I left. All the young man had said was, "Will you come walking with me tomorrow? Good — I'll call for you at your uncle's farm about ten o'clock."

Tuesday was cloudy. We started out on a road that crossed my uncle's farm and we walked a fair distance, John holding my mittened hand, before either of us spoke. I found that his eyes were brown and so dominated his face that I thought, His eyes are all that you see. Yet I did also notice that he was not exactly handsome but had a nice face, as people say, lean with a squarish chin and a thoughtful mouth. In the parlor he had looked hollow-chested, perhaps only due to the way he had sunk into the high-backed chair.

John spoke first. He said, in words that were unforgettable:

"I hope we can make a start towards becoming friends as we walk along. I imagine we'll have a lot to say to each other."

"I don't talk very well."

"I doubt that, and if you do feel like it you can say anything to me because I'll be interested and I'm safe. Or if you just want to be silent, of course that's all right but forgive me if I hope to find out what goes on in the mind of someone who plays the piano so eloquently."

This was a miracle. Apart in my solitude I had not learned any spontaneous way of getting a relationship going, but now someone had simply opened a door and come into my isolation and confidently was saying, Let us be friends.

Since I didn't know what to answer I just turned and smiled and found him already smiling with reassurance. It didn't seem like the encouragement of a thoughtful adult towards a child. With his tone and manner John somehow was bridging the gap in our ages, and he made it appear that he needed and reached for some quality he had found in my music and therefore hoped to find in me. For myself, I turned my face to him as one does to the sun, to a warm joining of spirit that was a new experience for one young and lonely, and yet, now, right and natural — even it seemed inevitable.

The countryside on that day was barren. A late-winter thaw had melted most of the snow but no new green life could yet be sensed in the drab brown fields. The pines were still black, and black on the sky were the crazily patterned branches of maples. The last of what snow remained, in ditches, hollows, and on the lee sides of barns, had sagged into griminess but at least the road was dry.

John said, "I'm glad this land looks so bleak. On a bleak countryside people can come together more honestly." I was puzzled and suppose I showed that I was. "On a moonlit lake or a sunny beach or any other attractive place you may be in a glow because of the surroundings — and you think that you feel a glow for the other person. There is no chance of that mistake here!" John said it lightly. "So there is more truth in what we feel for each other."

What I thought was that the bare fields and trees made me feel threatened, therefore want to be close to another person, but that was not a thing I should say.

Apparently truth and honesty were important to John, for next he said, "I find a stark kind of truth in your piano playing."

I asked him if he thought I could put more truth in my playing by special study or training. He believed it was just something you find for yourself although the more technique you have, the more you can express of course. But in the end the amount of musical truth you give to a piece depends on the degree of honesty that is in you.

All this would be a great deal to think about. I wondered whether I should speak of musical truth to Mrs. Bunce but I was afraid she would think of it as simply playing the notes accurately and I was sure that John meant something much more profound.

This walk was a mind-stretching experience. For even more than John's words his manner seemed to imply that we were two people on a perfectly equal footing. Did he really feel that I was grown-up? Or did he, for some reason, just want to say what was in his thoughts whether I would know what he meant or not? Was he all bottled up, as I was, without perhaps having the outlet of music? I asked him if he played any instrument or possibly sang. He said no, he just liked music very much and tried to understand it. So maybe he did have some special need to talk.

The road divided ahead of us, one branch swinging back along the upper edge of my uncle's farm and we took that way. Soon we came to a green stucco house above the road on the right. I knew whose it was, the people were legendary — a man who had retired early to come and spend his life here in the country with his Spanish wife, who was blind. The wife had a beautiful singing voice and on warm, even fairly warm days like this, she often sang outdoors in their patio, which was open on one side to the valley. It was said

that she liked the acoustic effect of the land falling away and rising
on the opposite side. She was singing now, and John and I sat on
my uncle's stone wall to listen.

The songs had the suggestion of quietly borne heartbreak that is
typical of Hispanic art — the art of a country as barren as ours on
that day, but in Spain (I had learned in geography lessons) spring-
time as lush as the spring in Ohio can come briefly after a rain. The
woman did not, however, seem to be singing of dry arroyos and
olive trees with small, dust-gray leaves. John didn't think so; he
asked if I knew the songs and when I shook my head he said:

"I don't either but I'd say they are love songs, with all that haunt-
ing sadness and intimacy. Love is sad everywhere but maybe especially in Spain."

What could I say? I hardly ever had thought of love, much less
love in Spain, which was only a pink peninsula on the map of Europe the teacher pulled down like a window shade in front of the
blackboard. From Spain olive oil and oranges were exported, also
sad songs, it seemed of love. I could think of nothing intelligent
as a comment, and yet I wished to come into this new adult world
John was offering, and I asked, "Why do you suppose love *is* sad in
Spain?

"It's just an impression I have. I probably mean that Spain is still
rather mediaeval and the Spaniards may not have developed the
emancipated kind of love we aspire to. Some of us — there are mediaeval people in every country. But I'm not being logical.
Emancipated love is sad too — maybe as sad as any other kind."

John was thinking out loud, saying that to me just because he
needed to say it to someone, I guessed. But — emancipated love?
A bewildering thought. I knew the word emancipated. My grandmother had often spoken of emancipated Negroes when she told me
about the Underground Railroad station her father had operated

when she was young. It had been a risky venture — they could have lost their farm and everything they owned if they had been discovered passing on slaves, and it was not very pleasant either, the house always full of the Negro strangers, as many as twenty sometimes. But my grandmother had felt it was all worthwhile because "we were helping to emancipate those poor people." But emancipated *love?* Would I ever know what John meant?

The husband of the singer waved to us from the front of the patio — a slight motion which seemed to say that he was glad we were enjoying his wife's music but he was not inviting us to come up, which of course we did not plan to do.

Mrs. Harper had put up some sandwiches for us. John took them out of his overcoat pocket and we ate them there. I had been afraid that our walk would end by this time but it seemed that it wouldn't. Radiant, unforgettable day! I tried not to think of how much I was enjoying it, which could be unlucky. We stayed a little while after the singer went indoors and then walked on farther and higher.

So far John had kept the conversation focussed largely on me, but he wanted me to know something about himself, suitably in the relationship that seemed to be growing between us, and up there on the hilltop he told me about the new kind of work he would be doing. He told it in terms I could understand and later I translated it into an adult vocabulary. He had been a partner in a law firm which handled criminal cases and from time to time he had had to defend as not guilty clients in whose innocence he did not believe. The crisis came when one of his clients went free but a woman who, John felt sure, had not committed the crime was sentenced to ten years' imprisonment. John's partners had thought he was unduly sensitive to be so disturbed by this case, but John had resigned over it.

Almost immediately he had been offered a position in the office of

Ohio's state prosecuting attorney. Now John said that he was going to be an accuser instead of a defender and he was not entirely happy about that, but at least he hoped that in the future he could be more instrumental in keeping the innocent out of jail. Since I knew exactly nothing about law and government, John's explanations were a swift enlightenment, but some of what he said I was still puzzled about. The missing pieces were supplied by conversations about John in my uncle's family, then and later.

At the end John said, "Lois is not very happy about our having to move to Columbus. She doesn't want to leave her friends but I'm sure she will make others." He was putting the integrity of his work ahead of Lois's choice and that seemed right. I was suddenly interested in the proper role of a wife.

The next day our explorations took us to the other side of the village and then to the cemetery, which seemed to me a grim place to eat our lunch but John was not bothered by all the evidence of tragedy around us, and he said he was a collector of epitaphs. Before we left he had read them all, had copied some down and had discovered a few situations that he considered especially interesting. In the 1830's one man had lost three wives in five years. John: "Weren't his neighbors suspicious?" I said maybe not. "One wife could have died in a fire, and one been killed by a runaway horse, and one struck by lightning." John laughed and said he would appoint me attorney for the defense.

We sat on the church steps to eat our lunch and afterwards we stayed there a little while. John told me that he had had a brother, Jordan, a year younger than himself who was so much like him that people were always asking if they were twins. That gave his brother the idea of saying they *were* twins and they did that so often, they almost thought of themselves as being identical. "We liked the same sports and the same girls," and, John said, "We thought so much alike that there may have been some kind of thought transference between us. I would open my mouth to say something like, 'Grandfather's failing,' and before I could get out the words, Jordan would say it." They both used "we" for "I" — "We don't like hot weather," "We think Dr. Arnold's in love with Miss Emmett."

Jordan died of pneumonia when he was sixteen years old. I said that it must have been wonderful to feel so close to someone and John said, "It's so good that you have a little difficulty in feeling close to anyone else. Other people all seem a bit like strangers. Ever since Jordan died I have been as solitary as if I didn't really belong anywhere. You have this room and this furniture, these books and these clothes, but you don't have any place of your own among people."

When I heard these words which had so much meaning for myself, I felt a great sob starting to rise in my chest, but I had my own way of preventing myself from crying: I always thought, *Stomp on it, STOMP on it,* and I could.

John continued, "Now it seems that almost no one understands what I say in just the way I mean it, but maybe I look for that because, being a lawyer, I know that the other side is always trying to twist your words to gain an advantage." John and his brother were being brought up by their grandparents. Their parents had been in the diplomatic service and were drowned in a flood in South America. "You can't expect grandparents to understand a boy very well, but for ten years I've always felt as if I were alone. During all these years without Jordan I've kept hoping I would meet a girl who would seem like a twin — be as understanding as a twin. Lois is not a twin but I am sure she'll make a good wife."

John took one of my hands between both of his and he said, "Now I am going to tell you something that will have to be just between the two of us. When I wake up in the morning, I've often been dreaming that I was talking to Jordan, telling him what's going on, how things are. In my dream today I was saying, "I've met the most extraordinary young girl. She's musical, and the moment I heard her playing the Harpers' piano I knew that she was a twin. Everything she has said so far has been just right for me — just the kind of thing you would say."

We walked down a little grade to the Harpers' house where it was understood I would play for John. When we went in Mrs. Harper said, "You're a very good little girl to take this young man off our hands every day." I played Bach. It was the only music that seemed capable of expressing what I felt for John and also the intensely other-world sense I was having again. The dark sky of those days, the bare brown earth and the land falling away from the hills we had climbed fitted exactly the vision I had had when I was recovering from the illness. And now it was stronger than ever because, of course, this young man had been stirring my deepest consciousness. Whenever I thought of him later, and that would be forever, he would be moving about in my spiritual landscape.

There were shreds of clouds in the sky on Thursday, and an uneasy small wind prowled about the farm. My uncle said that a storm was building up and he was glad, for no one could hope that a false spring in February would go right on into the real spring with no more winter weather. Buds were already swelling and unless checked, would be bitten later by hard frost and mean a bad year for the fruit trees.

By ten o'clock we were on the slope, starting for the stone wall below the singer's house. We waited there for almost an hour but she didn't appear and we went on up the hill.

John asked if I ever had made up songs.

"Mostly songs! A new one every two weeks. That's part of the musical method I'm learning."

He asked me to sing one. I had forgotten some of them and thinking of others, now, they all seemed too simple and childish. He insisted and I told him about the Rockefeller swans and sang a little fragment I had composed for them:

> *The sun shining up from*
> *The pink lotus blossom*
> *Puts a pink palm on*
> *The white throat of the swan.*
>
> *She will not let me touch*
> *Her white feathers, but I*
> *Tell her that the reflected pink flower*
> *On her throat is my loving hand.*

John asked what was my latest song and I told him I had started a poem last night when I was going to sleep. It probably would begin:

> *The sun is failing, and the*
> *Shadow of the hill*
> *Elbows its way across*
> *The dark brown furrows.*

What would be the rest of it, John asked. I told him I wanted to say, but without saying it outright, that shadows are always trying to conquer the light. If the light is strong and bright, like the sun at noon, the shadows are small and thin, but when the sun is going it is a weak light, so the shadows conquer it completely and we have night.

"Shadows and dark are a kind of enemy that is always there. You should watch out and protect yourself by being very thoughtful and bright and clear: that will be the meaning of the poem."

I guessed that John was a little disappointed because I had not started a song about us or about himself and Jordan perhaps, but I already knew that you never can make up a good song in order to please another person. I explained that I had begun four years ago by thinking of music as a way of saying something to one other person but lately I had come to understand that it is a way of saying something to everybody, something which already exists, waiting to be told.

At the end of all this it occurred to me how freely I was talking to John these days, and how the talking did not seem to be wrong because I felt, for the first time, that my life was like a song which already existed — I just had to live out something that was there in the same way as the music waiting to be written down. Talking to this new, inspiring friend was permissible because it was part of events that were waiting to be lived.

John said he would like to hear another song. Was it part of the unknown design that with my next words I started down a very steep track? I said, "I have one poem that I just cannot find music for. I really believe almost anything that happens can become a song, but I can't find the music for this one."

Without knowing what was coming John asked to hear the poem. He laughed and said, "Maybe I can help you spot what the trouble is."

> *Someone is dead.*
> *The curtains hang too quietly,*
> *The scarlet flowers are odorless,*
> *No warm heart makes a record of*
> *The passing hours.*
>
> *Who is dead?*
> *I do not think I care. What kind*
> *Of pleasure could my dull mouth take,*
> *What beauty could my dry eyes find*
> *When life has fled?*

Darkness falls
And no one comes to light a lamp.
No one speaks, for none can hear.
A wind blows through the emptiness
Of someone dead.

The poem astonished John. He walked off alone a little way and when he came back his eyelashes were wet and he said, "That's a very unusual poem for a child to have written. You are the one you are imagining dead, aren't you?"

I nodded.

"What made you think of that?"

I couldn't tell him, of course. To do that would be the wildest departure from the no-talking rule and would put a quick end to our friendship. So I said nothing. He was persuasive:

"You do know why you wrote it, don't you. Did one of your friends die? Or someone else you loved?"

I could not answer.

"I think this is something you should talk to me about. It probably wouldn't hurt so much after that."

It might not hurt so much — what a skilled questioner he was!

"No one really died."

"But someone almost did. You almost did?"

It came then, the flood held back for all of a short lifetime:

"I almost died once because my mother wanted me to die. She tried to choke me but an old lady came and stopped her. She never cares how much danger I'm in — she hopes I'll be killed."

"This is impossible! What do you mean?"

"She hates me so much — you can see that I am a hateful person. I don't know how, but I must be or a mother would love me and she can't — she really can't." I told him about the cyclone.

"Does she say she hates you?"

"We don't talk. She doesn't talk to me and she won't let me talk to her or my father. I don't talk to anybody so I don't have any friends. Oh ———" The tears, the sobs, the words came out in a deluge together, and I don't remember how coherent the story was, but for the first time ever I was showing someone my private diffi- culties. For the first time my emotions and my voice had made a connection, and the loneliness and the fear, the great anxieties of the years were pouring forth in this unfamiliar experience of sharing them. John had taken my hands and was holding them very firmly. He pulled me close to him, and when all the words were spent and nothing remained but the tears and the ache, he leaned over and put his cheek against my forehead. That was all — he just waited until his protective strength made me feel safe enough so that I could stop crying. When I was quiet he said, rather gruffly but I didn't mind that, "Where is your handkerchief?" and he mopped up the fallen tears.

I don't think we said anything after that. We walked around a little while longer and then went back to my uncle's house, slowly. At the door John said, "I'll be here tomorrow at ten o'clock and we'll go out again. In the meantime don't reproach yourself for talking to me. It probably was the best thing you ever did."

The next day it was snowing. I thought that John probably would not come but he did and we set out up the hill on a road that was starting to be rather wet. The snowflakes were the large ones that drop so slowly and gently. They were coming down in a thick fall and soon our shoulders were white. "We're getting to be snow- men," I said and we laughed about that, about whether to put a pipe in my mouth. Although we were gay with the usual enjoyment of being together, now there was an undercurrent of sadness because of what I had told John and I was feeling rather sorry that he knew those unpleasant things. But the usual tight band of fear was no longer around my chest. That morning I was simply not afraid of anything at all.

We didn't turn back up the road that ran past the Spanish house but continued on westward and before long came to a little bridge over a brook. That brook, which I had loved in the summer, was muddy now, with tassels of dead grass and leaves caught on all the streamside stones and brush, but its sound was musical — like one of the Japanese wind-bells made of glass. John and I leaned on the railing and watched the water.

After we had been silent a moment John put his hand over mine and said:

"It may be that it would be painful for you to talk any more about the poem you let me hear yesterday, and unless you want to I won't ask you to say any more about it. But now that I know those things I believe you might need my protection some time." He took a piece of paper out of his pocket and gave it to me. "This will be my address in Columbus. Keep it, and if you ever feel that you are in danger you must let me know. You can send a letter or telegram and I will come right away. My new work will give me the right to do that, and you must promise to let me help keep you safe."

This was such a tremendous relief that I started to cry again. But John said firmly, "This is not something to weep about. It's something — I hope — to be glad about."

Something to be glad about! It was overwhelming. It had been all right to talk to him after all. That was to be the only time in twenty-eight years that I told anyone about the disgrace of not being loved, but with John the telling had been permissible. It had been good.

John and Lois were married the following Saturday in the Harpers' sitting room. The way they had it fixed, the bride and groom faced the relatives and friends who sat in a few rows of chairs. I was there. During the ceremony John's brown eyes turned to my face. I would always remember their look of reassurance, yes and affection.

o

After they left on their honeymoon people kept talking to me about "my friend John." Didn't we get cold out in the wind all day? What did we talk about? They guessed that I told him about my operation, school, teachers. They supposed that he told me about his romance with Lois. An intolerable intrusion! They asked but they really believed that they knew. It was terrible the way grown-ups were always sure they understood about everything, fully. They thought they could walk into anyone's mind the way you walk into a room and look around and see everything, and they assumed that they had a perfect right to do that. I stopped going up to the Harpers' but my uncle and aunt were just as bad if not worse. So inquisitive.

Before long my grandmother died and was buried in the town where my uncle lived, my parents coming, of course, with her body. It was strange to see her, my dear grandmother lying so still in the coffin, but I was not shocked. She was dressed very nicely, in black silk, and I was glad for her. There was much discussion about the fact that her mouth had opened slightly. I was not allowed to go to the cemetery.

During the train ride home my mother said, "I hear you got on well with your friend John." She spoke sharply, probably because she suspected that I had confided in him. I did not respond.

A year after I'd known John, one afternoon of a cold spring rain I was standing in the window of my bedroom, holding the large doll I had bought with savings from my allowance. The doll was a symbol, although I did not realize that she was. She was just a great comfort and the recipient of my love for John.

My mother came to the door of the room, behind me. She did not come forward far enough to see my face and as soon as she had spoken she left. She said, "I have a letter from Auntie Bess. Your friend John Craig has died. He died last week of pneumonia."

.

iii

LEGACIES FROM ALICE

MY FATHER was one of those unassuming people whose influence can be underestimated while they are present. When they are no longer there it may be found that their even temper and their essential decency have been holding at bay looming and ruinous dangers.

He never talked very much. Sitting looking out of the window with his mind obviously seeing a private landscape, or reading a newspaper or magazine, he would seldom express an opinion, except at times for a short, sensible, often humorous comment thrown out without demanding that anybody agree with him. Or he would be listening to my music, with a contented smile although only occasionally giving me praise. He was just there among us with a sunny amiability that we all borrowed while hardly recognizing from where it came. But when a new kind of work took him away from home, the demons of emotional illness came creeping in closer around us.

For my father the different work was fulfillment of a kind that few, I imagine, can get from commercial business. After he left the railroad he had gone into two or three ventures of his own, but none except a furniture factory, later destroyed by fire, had seemed intrinsically worth doing. He was proving that when he sold something in which he believed for its own sake, like his fine furniture, he had a very persuasive way, but to sell merely to make money or to break down a customer's resistance did not call forth his effective effort. Understanding his temperament, an older friend offered him the chance to train the salesmen of a large paint manufacturing company, and paint proved to be the product that, for all time, would inspire my father's engaging enthusiasm — paint because it was such a bright agent, it brought cheer into dull lives, especially the light, clear colors recently introduced. He loved to sell them for schools, hospitals, prisons, city halls, all such depressing institutions, and he was phenomenally successful. Wherever he went, sunlit color began to replace dinginess, and this became his lifelong crusade.

In two years he had jumped to one of the company's top administrative posts — in charge of manufacturing and sales for all the Southwest, with present headquarters in Kansas City and a branch to be opened in Texas and a new territory to be developed from Louisiana to the Pacific Coast. For a man who loved to live everywhere these boundaries gave a sense of wide, free opportunity, and his success shot up like a rocket. We had moved to Kansas City, but he soon got the factory there and its crew of salesmen so well organized that he could spend much of his time in the South, and we saw him from then only rarely.

Starting when I was twelve we lived in that different part of the country, and Kansas City, after Cleveland, seemed to offer only an arid isolation. In Cleveland there had been a yeasty stir of comings and goings. People were always making trips up the Great Lakes, or to Canada, or the east or west coast, or Europe. Our New York relatives came to visit, we went there, and a family friend sent me dolls from Paris. We felt that we were a part of the world scene and adventure was always beckoning. In Kansas City no one seemed to go anywhere, nor did strangers come through bringing the stimulation of new perspectives. The town had a romantic history; it had been the outfitting post for covered-wagon trains to the West, but all that was in the past. The Missouri River, a fabled waterway, seemed to carry no traffic and at Kansas City it looked like a meandering slough of yellow mud. For a sense of adventure one could take a drive along the parkway that bordered the stockyards or out on the flat surrounding prairies.

If, as my brother says, it was known as one of the wickedest towns in the country, perhaps the explanation was boredom. Few of the women were chic, there was no first-class hotel — people used to give dinner parties at the railroad station. The only glimmer of high life seems to have been a businessmen's lunch where the customers were served by waitresses in topless uniforms. In those days before air conditioning, on stifling summer noons a blue-plate special could raffishly be combined with the sight of perspiring cleavages.

But Kansas City did have its sedate Establishment and due to my mother's social skills we got into it more or less, via membership in an upper-class church and ownership of an inviting house in a pleasant neighborhood. This environment could have been promising when the wind didn't blow from the stockyards, but our changed way of living — more affluent though it was — meant a kind of doom for my mother. Gallantly she set about making new friends for herself and her family, not easy with a husband who was not often there. Of course a certain amount of money is necessary to support the status of social leader, my mother's natural role. Now we had it but our new prosperity was tied to my father's absence. When he did come home my mother always arranged evenings of bridge and he was well liked. How frustrating then that he was soon gone for another long period. Social activities that involve only women are limiting. Since, however, those were all that my mother was finding available, she made herself brightly and gracefully helpful, and therefore welcome, in the church-women's daytime world. But her greatest talents, of charm and intellectual conversation, were always called forth by men and as things were, those qualities were not used. Emotionally, too, my mother needed the balance wheel of a husband's presence. She must have been very lonely there in that strange city, away from her lifelong friends, and the outlook for her ambitions must have seemed bleak. At home she became tense and irritable, but the circumstances excuse her.

At that difficult time her unloved daughter presented her with a crisis. What she had long predicted and dreaded seemed to come true. A five-minute talk might have cleared up the situation but talk was impossible. The lines of communication between us were almost completely down.

Near our house was a pretty small park, only a block wide and two blocks long but picturesque. At one end it was below street level with rock walls forming a kind of amphitheatre; at the other end the descending streets levelled out with it. Lush planting around the smooth grassy center made the park seem like a secret garden. I loved to go there, especially to watch games on the two tennis courts — a sport considered too strenuous for me, but I devoured the sight of the beautiful skills.

One Saturday afternoon I was watching the players when I became aware of a small pointed face peering around the edge of a tree trunk. The instant my eyes met his he was gone.

Almost at once the same little face appeared at the other side of the tree. His fur was striped brown and whitish — a chipmunk. I watched him while keeping my head half-turned aside, since it seemed that a stare was alarming. The ruse worked. The chipmunk risked a dash down the front of the tree, then jumped into a crack between the rocks. I wished I had had a cookie in my pocket. A piece of it tossed his way might have lured him closer.

He came back. Out from the rocks, a quick dash to a nearer tree, out of sight behind it — and then on the ground boldly, sniffing along the grass, fast, urgently, but soon in a bush, again hiding.

The next time he appeared he found something he liked — a seed? — and ate it sitting up, holding it in his forepaws, very alert, the tip of his furry tail held aloft, twitching excitedly. He still watched me intently, watched my eyes. Are eyes so revealing of purpose? I risked a full glance and he whisked away. I laughed and said in a quiet voice, "I think you're playing a game of hide and seek with me. Please come back. I won't catch you. I promise."

The chipmunk was gone for several minutes. I sat very still guessing that I was observed. And then he was on the ground, turning this way and that, on guard — but brave! Only a few feet from my shoes. It seemed a pretence that he had to search here, then with sudden fear flicking away out of sight, quickly back, each time closer. The belief was unavoidable that the chipmunk enjoyed this. He *wished* to come nearer! Incredible. Now and then I would murmur a little talk but while sitting so motionless I was hardly breathing. Would the friendly small animal ever come up on the bench? I didn't have any chance to find out. The couple who had been playing tennis had to give up their court. They came and sat on the grass near the bench and the chipmunk vanished for good.

Monday morning I left for school twenty minutes early and went to the park. With a nut-encrusted cookie I hoped I could make progress in winning the chipmunk's confidence. But he didn't appear until five minutes of nine, when I had to go. Hopefully I left the cookie on the bench.

The next day and following days he was there when I came. I fed him a cookie by throwing him bits of it at a time. He ate them only inches away from my shoes. It didn't occur to me that he was tame because other park visitors might have fed him. It would not have mattered anyway. He was my friend and the meeting with him each

morning, the evidence of his trust, was a lovely grace note to start
the day. Soon he did come up on the bench and finally would put
his forepaws on my fingers while he ate the cookie out of my hand.
The tiny paws vibrated so fast they seemed full of electricity — like
the electric current for treatment that I had been allowed to feel in
my grandmother's rest home. The chipmunk's fur too, and all his
motions, seemed electric. He was a spark of life.

Nothing was said at home about my new habit of leaving early.
No doubt my mother was glad, for usually it took a lot of scolding
to get me away on time. These days I dressed quickly, ate breakfast
without dawdling, and was off towards the school, which was on the
same street as our house, Warwick Boulevard. At the next corner I
turned left on Thirty-seventh Street and walked the short block to
the park. No one ever was in the park at that hour and of course I
did not tell anyone that I went there. To have found this small
friend was a piece of luck too sacred to speak about.

I was twelve years old at that time, at school in the seventh grade.
One afternoon a boy privileged to run the principal's errands came
to our room with a note. The teacher, Miss Prentice, read it without
expression and said I was wanted in the principal's office.
Bewildered but perhaps anticipating praise, I went down. My
mother was there, looking tense and angry. The principal, always a
grimy, unkempt man and that day needing a shave, motioned for me
to sit down. He said abruptly, "Who is the man?"

I hadn't the faintest idea what he meant and could only ask,
"What man?"

"The man you meet in the park every morning," my mother said.
"Don't try to lie out of it!"

"Probably some tramp you've made up to," said the principal.

I was too stunned to reply. But I wouldn't have done so anyway.
I had acquired the habit of simply turning away when I was falsely

accused of anything, and I certainly would not tell these two evil-minded people about the chipmunk. Nor would I deny their suspicion, so ludicrous and so ugly. And how had the principal dared to be so insulting? Only of course because my mother had shown no impulse to defend me.

I just sat there looking out of the window into the pale autumn sky while the two of them tried to break me down. When they realized that they couldn't, the principal told me to get my coat and since it was near dismissal time, go home with my mother. "After this," he said, "she will always watch when you leave your house to see that you don't turn off to the park. And in the afternoon she'll be waiting to make sure you get home by five minutes after four." Not glancing at either of them I left to get the coat and then walked home with my mother in mutual silence. But inside the door she murmured, "You little harlot." I didn't know the word but guessed from her tone that it meant something despicable.

I didn't practice that day, just played for my own consolation — Bach, the little dances that Sara Heinz arranged for the piano. Especially I played the *Gigue* from Bach's *First Partita,* which must be one of the sunniest melodies ever composed — healthy-minded music, seeming utterly kind, by a man who fathered twenty children and still had all this affection left over to send down the centuries to anyone who might need love. I played it again and again and told myself that I was Bach's twenty-first child.

Since I didn't have any young friends I have no way of knowing whether other girls of my age would have been as mystified by that event as I was. Were they equally innocent, or by the time they were twelve were they sharing confidences that revealed the facts about sex? At least they were not sharing any with me, and although I had been told by my mother in great detail about the process of bearing a child, there had been no hints about the essential preliminary. I did sense some cloudy disturbing unknown, and the accusations in the principal's office made me feel quite enveloped in it but without making anything sharper or clearer. But one thing did develop the next day: that my mother believed I had inherited weakness of will from my father's family as well as her own. The culprit on his side was his young sister Alice — not an alcoholic but something that was much worse apparently: she had lived with a man to whom she was not married.

2

There were many books in our household and sophisticated, even esoteric art objects including paintings that my parents had neither the wealth nor the background to have chosen themselves. While I was small they were simply taken for granted; later I learned that we had inherited them from my father's sister. The books, especially, were a haven to which I turned later — a legacy wholly beneficent. But from Alice there was another legacy — her example, which my mother now seized on as additional proof that I was born bad.

Alice, the youngest and dearest of the five in my father's family, died when I was two and so I do not remember her, but her photograph showed a delicate girl with a kind of communicating gentleness. She had made an unfortunate start by being married at seventeen to a compulsive gambler in Canada, and had had two children by the time she was twenty. Her husband neglected them; at times they were nearly destitute. But Alice had three devoted brothers who persuaded her to divorce the husband, come and live with her mother in Cleveland, and let them support her and the children.

Somehow, perhaps through a brother, Alice met English Jeremy. The attraction was instantaneous. Jeremy wrote to his family about the girl he was planning to marry, how they soon would meet her for he was bringing her and her children to Europe. Firmly they closed the door. He was a younger son, a trained architect though as yet without any income or his inheritance. It had been expected that he would spend a few years in various European capitals studying the world's great architecture *in situ;* for that his family were giving him a generous allowance and had agreed, first, to a tour of America. But they would cut his income to the last farthing, they said, if he married the American divorcée with children.

Perhaps it is to be expected that the English have never cared very much for their American ex-colonials. Prejudice may be understandable, but it must have been fed by such writers as Anthony Trollope, his mother, and Dickens. Anthony Trollope wrote of women in Western America (Ohio, Indiana, and Illinois): "They know, doubtless, all they ought to know, but then they know so much more than they ought to know." De Tocqueville had been more generous: "If I were asked to what the singular prosperity of the American people ought mainly to be attributed, I should reply; to the superiority of their women." De Tocqueville was the more intellectual observer, but of course he was French and therefore perhaps more lenient in his view of all women? Jeremy's parents, literate people, probably had read all those writers.

Finally they may have been influenced by Robert Louis Stevenson's Fanny, another divorcée, from Indiana, the state next to Ohio, who also had children. The impulsive Fanny, Stevenson's "Tiger-Lily," had been welcomed by his family but had offended his friends. Well, Jeremy's family would save him.

They couldn't. The ship that was to have taken Alice and Jeremy on their honeymoon still took them, including the babies, with Alice as Jeremy's mistress. Just as originally planned, they were bound for the European capitals where Jeremy would study architecture. They stayed for seven years.

Alice's children were at that time one and two years old and any woman can turn her imagination loose on the thought of life in foreign hotels with very small children: the problems of proper meals, laundry, lack of play space, accumulations of toys, go-carts and other babies' equipment, of preventing annoyance to other hotel guests. Frequent packing for a new journey is always confusing and the disruptions to the children's routine must have had their effect on their temperament. And what of the difficulty for Alice of keeping herself attractively dressed and receptive: how could she be a proper mistress? She was said to have had a delicious sense of humor and that would have been relaxing but not the same thing as rest. There is a saying in India: one who is loved should have nothing else to do.

The fact that the children were always with Alice and Jeremy, requiring their time and attention, helps to define the lovers' relationship. It seems apparent that they were engaged in more than a light superficial affair. It must actually have been a very rich time, for they were living among the intellectuals of *La Belle Epoque,* that great creative release from Victorian suffocation. Jeremy was gathering the books and other fine things he would want for their eventual home.

Finally the children were eight and nine. They should be put in school. Jeremy and Alice returned to America and established a household in New York City. Jeremy hoped to join a firm of architects there and start to earn his own living so that he and Alice could marry. First, though, while his income from England could still be depended upon, they would have to wait, for he had contracted tuberculosis.

Sometimes he seemed to be getting better, but the sad truth had to be faced that the disease was progressing. Alice nursed him to the end and contracted his infection and died of it two years later. Her mother died immediately after her, brokenhearted at the loss of her favorite child. Alice's sister took the daughter; the son lived with us, off and on. He was always running away. He was imaginative and full of pranks; during church services he used to swing on the bell rope, out from the belfry stairs and across the church vestibule to deposit himself on the walk outside; he would drop a hook from his little wagon into the slot for the cable cars and go sailing down Euclid Avenue. Undoubtedly he was difficult but my parents were tolerant. They let him dig up our back yard to make a cave large enough to hold several pieces of furniture.

Jeremy had left all his possessions to Alice and it was her wish that on her death they should go to her sister and brothers. Details about her affair were told to me by that sister, my other aunt — perhaps with some idealizing and that was one reason I had never been impressed by the strong disapproval my mother always expressed when she spoke of Alice. But anyway Alice and Jeremy had loved noble things, therefore they must have been noble people. Wasn't that obvious? Since our house was filled with their treasures it was almost as if Alice and Jeremy lived there, a comforting thought, for I visualized them as safe to be with, humane and large-minded in the way of the few sophisticated people that I had met. I had simply shut out my mother's censuring of them. Very startling it was then when my mother accused me of a disgraceful inheritance of Alice's temperament.

The day after the incident in the principal's office I was looking at one of Jeremy's paintings, a transparency hung in one of our living-room windows, when my mother came up behind me. The transparency, which belongs to me now, glows outside at night from the lights in the house and during the daytime glows indoors from the sunshine. It is a picture of a peasant girl smiling with earthy amiability, the girl with her parted lips almost seeming alive. On that afternoon as I turned from admiring it, my mother drew in a breath and in a voice husky and trembling said, "You are another Alice."

The implication was not clear at first.

With her voice rising: "You are another Alice and when you grow up you will follow her footsteps and everyone will despise you."

"If you mean the way Aunt Alice lived with Jeremy, I am not going to do that."

"Oh, yes, you will! You will! It is in your blood! I know you better than you do yourself and there is no help for it. You are another Alice!"

She was wearing her terrible face. And her voice was now shrill. "Everyone will *despise* you! And no man will ever be willing to marry you."

Nobody has to listen to that kind of talk, not while she has two feet to carry her away. I left and went upstairs to my bedroom and closed the door. I was shocked and confused and shaking, but my mind was clear. I said to myself, I never will be an Alice. And I never will risk being trapped in a family again, so I never will marry anybody. Never, *never!*

o

In the years of my youth it would have been greatly disturbing for any mother to hear that her twelve-year-old daughter was having a secret daily rendezvous with some unknown man — disturbing for any normal mother. For mine, with her hypersensitive scarred emotions, the enormity of the distress is hard to imagine. It was an age when prudish gossip seized upon any hint of questionable behavior and condemned it ferociously. That would have been the reaction to a girl suspected of being wayward at twelve. My pseudodisgrace does not seem to have spread beyond the school, but anticipating that it would, my mother must have wondered if humiliations like those of her girlhood, due to her father's intemperance, were going to pursue her through all her life. She must have felt almost, if not quite, hysterical on the day she was called to the principal's office.

Could I have straightened out the whole misunderstanding by telling about the chipmunk? Since I had adopted the practice long before of never defending myself — most accusations being illogical and this one most groundless of all — I did not even consider explaining. I was still the abhorrent fantasy child and my mother would simply not have believed any tale that did not fit into her tortured illusions.

My view of her was not much more realistic. I did understand that most mothers are loving and mine was not, but I had no clue as to why I was misunderstood — nor, at my age in that time, why one would be proved as born bad by meeting a friend in a park, a friend like John Craig as I thought of it. And so the episode in the principal's office and the later scathing remarks at home created a tumult in which I too was almost hysterical.

My first conscious thought on the following day was the wish that I never would wake up again. It was Saturday, when I was supposed to be up early to do my part in keeping the household going, to dust all the low places, baseboards and rungs of chairs, hose down the porch floor, water the flower boxes and other tasks. On this day however it was impossible to get out of bed because I was absolutely paralyzed by the thought of seeing my mother. How to get out of bed and dress on this bright sunny morning and act as if everything was as before, when I was to understand that I was predestined to lead an evil life and was certain to be despised forever by everyone?

Mercifully I was not called and lay quivering between the sheets trying to straighten out what had gone wrong. By noon I had come to a few conclusions. The one who had seen me go into the park was no doubt my teacher, Miss Prentice who, I remembered now, lived in a house with other teachers on Thirty-Seventh Street, from where I could have been observed entering the park's bush-bordered path. She never had liked me, perhaps because I didn't like her. She had a large thin nose through which she sniffed ineffectually and continuously, a small nervous habit that bothered me to an irrational degree. My usual attitude towards teachers had approached adoration but I had felt no warmth for Miss Prentice and assumed that she had reported my trips to the park in a vengeful spirit. The attitude of the principal I just dismissed as what one could expect of a man who failed to shave on some days and wore wrinkled suits.

But what to do, how to face the future? I wished passionately that I could run away. If John Craig had still been alive, somehow I would have gone to him. If Alice and Jeremy hadn't died I would plead that they let me live with them. If my father did not spend most of his time traveling, I would have found him in Texas. All impossible; and what was left but to sleep under hedges, cold and dirty and without a piano? Every escape route was blocked. Maybe one just had to stand things like this. And so at noon, being driven out of my bed by hunger, I went downstairs. My mother was not there, having gone shopping, it might be. I went off on my bicycle and stayed away all the rest of the day, an escape of a sort. And on the succeeding days, for many weeks, I set out on the bicycle after school and didn't come home until dark. By then my mother and brother would have had their dinner, but my place would still be set at the table and my food hot in the oven. I ate it alone. She never asked me where I had been. She probably thought I was meeting the man, whoever he was, but she didn't seem to care. Maybe she wished I would go away with him, out of her life for good. Anyway she didn't mind my being gone from the house every afternoon. She was probably glad. It must have been as hard to have a hated daughter there as, for me, a hated mother.

Music was no help for me at that time. I would slide onto the piano bench as usual and look at the keys, but I couldn't touch them and after a minute or two I would leave. Nor could I study. I would just lie on my bed and look at the ceiling but without seeing it. School was unendurable. It *was* Miss Prentice who had told the principal that I went to the park. She spoke to me now in the same insulting tone that the principal and my mother used. All that year was an ordeal, and the next year, when I was in the eighth grade, that teacher too was insulting. But fortunately my reputation did not precede me into high school. Several teachers there became my friends, they *wished* to become my friends, and they were people with whom I could feel at ease. But for that year when I "became an Alice" there was no comfort with anyone, anywhere. I was so desperate that I wrote a letter to the Kansas City *Star,* telling what it is like not to have a single friend in the world. The *Star,* amazingly, published it (without my name, of course), and someone answered and they published the reply too. I still have the clipping. It reads: "Your picture was so vivid that I felt when reading it, 'Here is someone who could interpret for us what Christ wrote in the sand while he was waiting for the guiltless to hurl the first stone.'"

The beautiful words sang in my mind that night when I went to bed, on a pillow drenched with solacing tears.

3

Into that unnatural solitude came another animal briefly, a small white dog. He joined me one day as I walked home from school, from what direction I hadn't noticed, all at once he was there at my side, his feet twinkling fast to keep up. I talked to him most of the way but going up the steps I said, "You'd better go home now.

Somebody will be missing you." He followed me onto the porch however, waiting expectantly at the door. I wouldn't have risked allowing him to come in and I thought he would leave but he still was there when I came out to start on the afternoon ride. When he saw what was going to happen he jumped around like a little white symbol of joy and then ran beside the bicycle. I pedalled slowly enough to keep him with me since it would have been wrong to lose him too far from wherever he lived, in our neighborhood it seemed probable, though I never had seen him before. He went all the way and back and was still on the porch when I finished dinner, leaving enough so that he had some dinner too. I told him again that he should go home but I tipped two of the porch chairs onto their sides for a shelter and hoped that he would still be there the next day, as he was.

Since he did not have a collar I convinced myself that his owners had turned him out and that I was justified in continuing to take care of him. He was not permitted to come in the house but no objections were made to his being fed scraps and given a bed on the porch. He walked to school with me, was always there at recess to play with, and was waiting to walk home and then go on our bicycle expeditions. These became shorter because the happy experience of having this friend cleared my way back to music. Now I practiced again, though I'd stop two or three times to play with my dog on the porch.

He had erect brown ears, the tips turning over, and looked very much like a white fox terrier that my grandfather had had, a dog named Dandy. My pet too became Dandy. He was an eager little dog. The moment that I appeared he would bounce around with a sweet barking, and I discovered an unsuspected ability to frolic with him, and more surprising, that it was easy to talk to him. I talked to him all the time and the huskiness of my voice began to improve.

Through lack of use my voice had lost so much of its tension, its timbre, that sometimes it cracked like the voice of a very old woman. Our doctor had mentioned it, urging me to "Speak up! Talk strongly!" and I had tried but there had been no improvement until I was recovering use of it in the talk with Dandy.

He had adopted our house as his home and it was both amusing and touching to see him sit at the top of the steps, a proud little figure who seemed to declare that he was accepted here, that here he belonged. Sometimes other dogs would come to the foot of the steps. Dandy, down on all feet then, would bark boastfully, a barking I loved and interpreted as meaning, "You can't touch me. I belong to the girl who lives here and she will protect me." I would go out on the porch and pick him up in my arms, from where he barked even more boldly, but I don't think he needed that intervention. In the dog hierarchy of a neighborhood it may be that the self-confidence which comes from being well loved helps a dog to maintain his place. Dandy certainly had that reassurance.

How long did I have him? I am not sure but long enough to have the new experience of being happy, not impersonally as with music but happy in a youthful, spontaneous way. Dandy and I rejoiced together. Then one night at dinner my mother said, "You have to get rid of that dog." For a moment I was too stunned to speak but when I found my voice I certainly spoke up strongly. "Take him out on your bicycle tomorrow and lose him," my mother said. "No!" I cried. "I won't do it! I have to have him! I love him and he loves me!" "That's just the point," said my mother. "You have to learn not to love."

I wept and stormed, nearly or perhaps quite hysterical. "You will take him out tomorrow and lose him," was all my mother would say. By the end of the evening she was showing her terrible face, the face I assumed to express almost uncontrollable hatred. It was still her face in the morning and so I had no other choice, I did take Dandy away and lose him, betrayed him by riding down a long steep hill faster than he could possibly run. He tried; as I turned at the foot of the hill and looked back for a last glimpse of him, he was stretching his legs as he raced to keep up, with the wind flinging back his ears.

For my betrayal of the little trusting dog there would be no comfort of any kind, no comfort at all, ever. To lose him was no way of learning not to love. I never saw him again but much later his bark, an echo, would save my life.

Dr. Isaacs considered this the saddest episode of my childhood. She said that some children would have killed themselves over it.

o

Mrs. George Forsythe, my music teacher in Kansas City, helped to get me back on the track. She assumed, as I did myself, that I would become a concert pianist and she was more practical than my Cleveland teacher about the need to develop technique. I still tried to hear the music in advance of playing it but there was a new project now, to become very familiar with, and play with lightning speed, the scales, all of them, major and minor. Studied in succession they proved to be fascinating, full of serenity and logic.

The sober practicing went ahead — I was beginning to practice the Beethoven Sonatas — and there was another musical outlet in accompanying a Kansas City violinist. We only played locally but the experience was good and proved that I would not be intimidated or fluttered by audiences. In this experience there was an element that seemed slightly mystical because of the discovery that an accompanist can have an extrasensory perception of what the soloist is about to do. I "just knew" in advance when she would retard or accelerate, or want less or more volume from the piano, and it was interesting to be aware of these coming demands and adapt to them. The violinist thought I should plan for a career as accompanist but I had bolder ambitions. Composing became less and less of a concern. To compose even a sad song requires a certain soaring of spirit which I didn't have at that time.

o

The situation at home continued to be distressing. I was treated with scorn because of the mythical disgrace of the park event. Soon then, without explanation, I began to be served with half portions at every meal. Dinner: a tablespoonful each of potato and another vegetable, a piece of meat little more than an inch across and no dessert. When, hungry, I would reach for more bread my mother would move the plate away. "You may have only one slice from now on," she would say. Breakfast was almost nothing. I started to school every day feeling starved and shaky.

Because I was not very strong and was spending five or six hours a day at homework for school and practicing, I needed at least the average amount of nourishment. Now I was ravenous all the time. I had been objecting to the new rationing and one day when my protest must have been shrill, I was told the reason for it: "You have to learn to control your appetites."

I had never paid much attention to food, just ate it and forgot about it, but now I thought about food all the time. To be deprived of it was no way to curb an appetite. With all my libido expressed in music, I was not aware of any other kind of appetite though I vaguely sensed what my mother meant. She was not specific. All the new emphasis on sex was conveyed in dark hints, vague enough but identifiable as, in her mind, foul. In addition to some physical nausea, emotionally I was filled with a sense of revulsion and finally vomiting and light-headedness made it necessary to call for a doctor's help.

He was not told about the new mealtime program. After a series of tiresome tests the decision was made that I was anaemic. A familiar remedy at that time was arsenic, several drops a day in a glass of water. I took them before dinner at night, measuring out the amount with an eyedropper. While I was doing this my mother would stand and watch, working her eyes in a way I found terrifying — she did the same thing at some other times when she wanted to be intimidating. Now she stood in front of me very slowly closing her eyes, opening them to greater than normal width, closing them, very slowly opening, closing them, while focussing on the bottle of arsenic. I thought, she wants me to put in too much and kill myself. I was very careful. But then I began to worry about additions of arsenic to my food. The portions that I was given had returned without comment to normal amounts but, wondering then about what else they might contain, I always tried to be in the kitchen when any individual portions were being put in the dishes. I thought that spinach and prune whip would disguise the flavor of arsenic most successfully. For the two years while the bottle of arsenic was around, I tried to observe the food I was given. For all that time I was convinced that I was in danger.

In the several years before I was twelve I had grown to feel fairly safe, having no illusion of being loved but believing my mother would only attack in a flare-up of temper, and that I could prevent that by being very cooperative. But after the accusation of being an Alice there seemed a colder possibility. Since she assumed that I certainly would disgrace the family, might she not decide that it would be better for all concerned if I were out of the way? It appeared significant that she had carried the near-starvation to illness, for I still was not very clear about "appetites" and the need to subdue them. If she had not weakened and called the doctor, might I perhaps have died? And would she not then have been glad?

From today's distance it seems questionable that she had had any such plan, but some time later she did say, à propos of nothing, "It is likely that many people who seem to die natural deaths have in fact been poisoned by their families." If she never had that intention, the thought may have been there, even the temptation. And my fear of her may have reflected partly a guilty conscience, because at that time I resisted her every wish and suggestion. Besides her dread expectation of future disgrace there was the daily provocation of having a child who was full of resentment. It must have been a great strain for a woman whose life was in other ways, too, filled with frustration.

One winter day I slipped on our icy stone steps and gashed a knee rather badly. While dressing it the discovery was made that there was no pain in it, not even while I was painting it with Mercurochrome. Curious. Was I in some way blocking the feeling in it? I "allowed" it to hurt — and pain flooded into it. I also found I could stop it again.

The next week I went to the dentist to have a tooth filled and made an experiment. I could stop that pain too. I could not have told how: I could just do it. A fine trick! But it seemed related to a state that was not as convenient nor as controllable — a kind of blankness that felt part emotional and part physical. Nothing seemed sharp any more, not the sense of free-flying lightness in watching blowing clouds, an old pleasure, not the beauty of falling snow, not music even, at least not much. This was a sort of empty living, and besides a diminished sensation in hands, feet, and skin, generally there was a very uncomfortable fogginess in my head. These are symptoms well recognized by the psychological experts now. They are called "numbing," or more technically, depersonalization, a condition that is accentuated by acute or prolonged stress. In those troubled days of my youth, it was actually a shield against emotional suffering. For my father was rarely there, nor my brother usually, since he stayed out with his friends when he wasn't in school. I had no friends of my own and only my mother for company, and she treated me with the same contempt that had been her attitude towards her father. Under strains like that one is apt to break down in some way, and I don't know what would have happened if fate had not intervened — as fate sometimes does in emergencies.

4

As amazing as miracles was a morning in June the year that I was fifteen and woke up in a tent on an island in Canada. We had arrived by lake steamer the previous night and, tired after the long trip from Kansas City, had gone straight to bed. Now it was daylight. I got up quickly, quietly and slipped out to see this new world.

The tent was a short way back from the shore with a path leading down to a little dock. I walked to the end of it. Ripples were gently rearranging the pebbles along the beach but the lake was smooth. Its wide and beautiful surface, delicate silver-blue, steamed with a mist that disappeared as I watched, for the light of the early sun, splintering on the tops of the mainland evergreen trees, was starting to fall on the mist and dissolve it. Curiously the lake's level surface seemed to be moving in alternate glassy streams, right and left, an effect that sometimes occurs on quiet water, I don't know why.

The bay in front of the dock was framed by the shores of the mainland, which curved together from both sides to meet in a point. At that vertex another island, rocky and tall, rose from the water. It looked uninhabited; and although a few cabins were scattered along the mainland, between and behind them was unbroken forest. It was my first sight of a natural wilderness. Behind our tent too, and several other tents here and a house in their midst, was the forest. Over everything, as pervasive as sunshine, was the fragrance of balsam firs. It was aromatic and sweet and I closed my eyes and breathed deeply to draw in more of it.

Voices from some of the tents meant that others were stirring. At the house wood smoke rose from the chimney, another redolent fragrance mingling soon with the smell of bacon frying. It is a combination familiar to everyone who has known woodland mornings. There would be talk at breakfast, the meeting with strangers — a loss. The sunrise across the wild northern lake seemed a kind of holiness that human chatter was bound to destroy a little. The water, so still and lucent, beyond it the dark mystery of the forest, and the firs' fragrance: for this sacred experience, enjoyed alone, I would get up at dawn every day during that summer.

We would be here for three months with my father joining us for July. Neither of my parents had been here before but friends, the Wymans from Painesville, had written to say that they knew of this island in the Muskoka Lakes and suggested our spending some weeks there together. After three summers in Kansas City, where the temperature day and night can stay above ninety, we were going to get away somewhere, and since my father had not been back to his native Canada for some time, the Wymans' idea appealed to my parents.

On the island were five or six visiting families. Some had children, of whom only one was a girl near my age. She would turn out to be very lively, never happy unless she was engaged in some boisterous game. I thought of her as an enemy. The family who owned this tiny resort were named White. They had several grown sons and a daughter. One of the sons, Dalton, nineteen, was just back from Montreal where he had won the junior world championship in canoeing. He was dark-haired and tall, with a puckish smile, to me that year probably the most glamorous youth in the world. One could never, of course, hope to be friends with him.

At the back of the house were a large vegetable garden, two or three sheds and an old boat with grass growing up through its timbers. Past them one reached a thicket. I pushed through it that first afternoon, into the woods beyond.

The brush was thinner here but the trees grew densely. I wandered on, memorizing some landmarks: this boulder, this berry bush, this fallen log. I looked back. All had disappeared! It was a different grove when one turned around.

The house was no longer in sight and my heart beat faster. I was lost! But one couldn't get lost on an island, although this one was large, three and a half miles long. It was only necessary to find the shore, mostly rocky and wild, and follow it back. But I still felt lost and curiously afraid.

The trees, vaguely and strangely, were menacing. Not in any park, cemetery or pasture had I ever been so entirely enclosed by trees. These were massive, like giants. One surrounded by them felt helpless. They spread above, forming together a cavelike dark. They were presences. *Which way had I come* — where was the shore!

Fear of trees is an old reaction, still a familiar emotion on primitive levels. Eskimos camping among trees, found along Northern rivers, dare not settle down beneath one for the night until they have stood off and thrown a knife into its trunk. Many other tribes have been awed by trees. If a branch has been broken off, if its bark has been damaged, or in the case of having to fell it, an apology would be made to a tree. The blood of a slaughtered animal was brushed onto it, or it was given a drink of water. In the Punjab, a former province of India, human sacrifices were made to a certain tree every year. Trees and groves in many parts of the world have been considered sacred.

In the Canadian woods I didn't believe consciously that a tree might be hostile. I was just strangely uneasy there in the eerie atmosphere of the grove. One can name this dread and call it claustrophobia, which probably is an ancient fear. A prehistoric man might have felt trapped in dense woods, and recently Sir Frank Fraser Darling, the eloquent conservationist, has said that many modern people are afraid of a wilderness, which is why they are so willing to see it destroyed. Anyway I was slightly alarmed by that island forest, and although I was rather eager to know what was there I couldn't force myself to continue farther.

My going and coming were noted, for I met Dalton on the way back and he said, "You didn't stay in the woods very long."

"I was getting lost." He smiled with amusement.

There were always three or four canoes pulled up on the beach. One day I got one of them out on the water and was floundering around in it when Dalton came down to the dock. He called, "Try to bring it back to the beach and I'll show you how to paddle." I sat in the bow facing him as with his strong, quick stroke he shot us out onto the lake. There he gave me the first lesson, demonstrating the right way to hold the paddle, how to turn it so smoothly in pulling it back that a canoe doesn't vary its course by an inch. "Line up the prow with some tree on the shore," he said, "and don't let it swing either side off the trunk." In shallow water again we changed places and awkwardly I tried to put into practice what he had demonstrated. A skill, a start in learning a new skill — inspiring prospect

— from this young man who himself was dedicated to perfecting a skill: was it possible that we might have something in common?

The Whites had a piano. It was in the sitting room of the house and I could no more stay away from it than I could have gone without food. My frequent playing must have been a trial to some of the other guests, especially a violinist who practiced several hours a day in his tent (a situation I didn't remind him of when I met him years later in San Francisco where he was teaching the young Yehudi Menuhin). But Dalton enjoyed my music. He used to come and stand at one end of the piano with his elbow on top, listening and watching.

He gave me more paddling lessons and after a while I too could hold a canoe's prow on the trunk of a shoreline tree. In the afternoons I went out with him in his racing canoe, as ballast he said, while he kept up his training. His canoe was a little sliver of a thing with graphite all over the outside to make it slip through the water faster. In Montreal he had paddled a mile in four minutes and seven seconds, a record which probably has been beaten many times, but when he dipped in his paddle, his canoe leapt away like a dolphin.

He landed us on the mainland one day and said, "Let's take a little walk." With a companion one could enjoy a forest. Besides, the trees here were of varying heights, they didn't form caves. It was an intricate scene, everything was prolifically growing — and dying. The ground was a litter of brown leaves and fir needles and sticks. It was unkempt compared with a park but fascinating.

All around us was limber movement. The grasses and wildflowers bent quivering in the flow of the breeze and the trees above were a green ruffling commotion. Their leaves, as they tossed and swung, seemed to be cutting the sky into bits, to be scattered as scraps of sunlight along the ground.

Birds were lacing the air, in and out of the trees and bushes. One on the ground was jumping forward and scratching back through dead leaves and one, also searching for insects, was spiralling up a tree trunk, pressing its stiff, short tail on the bark as a prop. At that time, in June, most of the birds would be feeding young, Dalton said, and they had to work all day catching insects for them. Besides this bright movement of wings, then, there must be thousands of tinier creatures doing whatever insects do on a summer afternoon: a world everywhere *alive*.

Dalton seemed to have realized that I knew almost nothing about what was here and was showing me things: a porcupine's tracks, a bee tree, a fox's burrow. He knocked on a tree and a flying squirrel poked its little head out of a hole. It was all wonderful, even exciting, but strange.

We came out on a small elevation. Below was a meadow brimful of yellow-green sunlight. Perhaps this was the pleasantest way to enjoy a forest: with trees and brush at your back but a wide escape if anything should approach from behind. Unmentionable were wolves, bears. (They may have been there in fact. That forest is now built up but resorts not far away advertise that guests can hear wolves baying.) Dalton had brought his rifle. Was he just thinking of shooting something for fun, or was the gun for protection?

The thought of escape was still there. Compare a park: only a few, spaced-out trees were allowed to grow, their dead branches were pruned away, the flowers were all in neat beds, the grass was kept mowed, never allowed to become weeds or "grasses." All controlled, therefore safe.

Here the plants grew their own way and the animals went their own way — one might appear anywhere, any time. No one knew what might happen — did happen, for there were dead broken trees among the live ones. Everything was wild — naturally. That was the meaning of forests of course, that they were wild. Therefore un-predictable.

Yet the wilderness was a beautiful, even enchanting place with its graceful movement and active life. Even underfoot if one scratched away the brown leaves as the bird had done, one might come upon small, secret lives. But might there be things that would bite? I had heard of tarantulas. With a feeling of cowardice, shrinking back, I wanted to leave, to return to the wide placid lake. And then I did something which made it seem that, on nature's terms, I had no right to be here at all.

Dalton said, "Look!" Pointing: "There's a porcupine in the crotch of that tree over there." One of the wild inhabitants of this forest, only medium sized for an animal, sat on the branch, his back a high curve, with his quills raised and bristling. He might be lying like that to let the sunshine come into his fur, warm down to his skin. He looked sleepy. Dalton handed the rifle to me and said, "Let's see if you can hit it."

He showed the way the gun should be held, braced against my shoulder, how to sight the target along the barrel. "Now pull the trigger back with your right hand — slowly, just squeeze it." I pulled the trigger and with astonishment saw the porcupine fall to the ground.

Dalton was full of praise. "Very good! I didn't think you could do it." We went down along the side of the meadow. Beneath the tree lay the porcupine, limp and still. Even his fur and quills were flat, lifeless now. Looking smaller, this was the little creature who, a few moments earlier, had been up on the bough wrapped in sunshine, enjoying life. I burst into tears.

Dalton went over alone the next day and drew out the quills and brought them to me to decorate the basket of scented sweet-grass that I, like all the women, was making. I gave them away.

I never returned to the mainland forest alone, but by midsummer I'd made my own a small peninsula on the island. Paddling along its shore one morning I had tied the canoe to a tree overhanging the lake and sat in its shade doing embroidery. The point — it was the southern tip of the island — was narrow, not more than fifty yards wide. Through its trees I could see across to the bay on the other side and the center was open, with a thin cover of grass and wild-flowers among sun-warmed rocks. It looked perfectly safe and I went ashore to investigate.

There was no trail leading away from here, the point seemed pri-vate, peculiarly mine, and it pleased me very much. I came back the next day and then other days. Sometimes I walked about but more often sat under one of the trees, which were firs and quivering as-pens, listening to the songs of the birds and watching them and a squirrel who was always there. I had a wonderful feeling — I had had it too with the chipmunk — that I was acceptable here, that I was liked, for they made little overtures even before I started feeding them bits of bread. Perhaps it helped that I talked to them.

Gradually, a few moments one day, more moments the next, being there in that small safe woodland began to seem almost the same experience as making music, as the way, when I played the piano, I *was* the music, my physical body feeling as if it dissolved in the sounds. I could say my dimensions then were those of the melo-dies and the harmony that spread out from the piano in all direc-tions. I had no consciousness of my individual self.

Tenuously, imperfectly that Canadian summer, the same thing happened when I would walk around the peninsula, unafraid. It was not a wide going out and out, as with music, but again of losing myself — this time by becoming identified with whatever I was es-pecially aware of. It happened first with a flower. I held a blue flower in my hand, probably a wild aster, wondering what its name

was, and then thought that human names for natural things are superfluous. Nature herself does not name them. The important thing
is to *know* this flower, look at its color until the blueness becomes as
real as a keynote of music. Look at the exquisite yellow flowerettes
in the center, become very small with them. *Be* the flower, be the
trees, the blowing grasses. Fly with the birds, jump with the squirrel!

Finally I spent every morning there. No one knew where I had
gone.

o

Before long it seemed clear that Dalton did not seek my company
just because I could play runs and arpeggios. He found me whenever he could spare time from his chores, I believed just because we
felt so comfortable together. It was a happy relationship, possibly
like the ease that the members of a loving family feel for each other,
and yet it was rather more because we were not together acciden-
tally. I knew Dalton would come and I didn't have to make any
particular effort, no attempt to be brighter, more gay, more interested than I felt naturally. I had only to be myself and whenever he
could he would just be there.

We didn't talk very much. Talk wasn't necessary. I didn't, of
course, tell him anything about my difficulties at home. What conversation we had was about what we were doing, going out on the
lake, swimming, playing Parcheesi. In a way the most remarkable
thing about the friendship was that it didn't seem at all remarkable,
not to me although I never had known a simply comfortable relationship before, not with anyone of about my own age. I just took it
for granted, except once when I wondered if knowing Dalton could
be the reason I didn't feel numb any more.

Almost every week a regatta was held on the lakes somewhere.

Since Dalton's championship had brought renown to the region, he was always present, as a referee, not competing. Recognized as "his girl" I was with him. Sometimes we went in his racing canoe; more often the organizers of the regatta would come for us in a luxurious launch. During the races we sat in those launches, amid polished brass and mahogany, at the finish line.

Dalton received with modesty the homage of his Muskoka neighbors, of the other young men, the worshipful little boys, the shy country girls and the summer visitors, who knew that he was a champion. The visitors tried to flirt with him. They were sophisticated, experienced in their flattery. Towards me most of them, being older, were inclined to be patronizing but Dalton, in unobtrusive ways, made it plain that I was the one.

And it still seemed perfectly natural, even inevitable, that I should have come to this kind of happiness.

Every night he was expected to paddle across to the mainland to pick up the mail. He took me with him, a situation that was a very cliché of youthful romance: water glassy-smooth, moonlight making a path that came straight to us, and silence except for the drip from the paddle and sometimes the cries of loons. At the other end we both left the canoe and climbed a sloping bank to the cabin post office, picked up the bag of mail and went back, with little delay since the White family and all the guests would be waiting.

In those hours we were drawn closer together, an intimacy only expressed by a touch now and then, tender and sensitive. But in the distance there was a roll of drums — anticipating what great event? — like the drums that preceded the high swinging of the trapeze performers I had seen at the county fair. In the distance only; Dalton, undoubtedly more experienced than I, though perhaps not much, was not taking advantage of my incredible innocence. He was not even deliberately trying to waken me from it. He was still a protective friend.

The relationship was profound and stirring but it progressed at a moderate rate. It could be gradual partly, no doubt, because it was not stimulated by anything whatsoever outside ourselves, since we had both been isolated in childhood — I for various reasons, Dalton by living up in the Northern woods. The new knowledge dawning for me was dawning at nature's own pace, not prompted by any of the external information that now speeds the awakening of young people artificially. I doubt whether any girl in the civilized world today could know an emotional growth so entirely from within.

It seems to me now that what I experienced in that summer was something like humanity's lost original Eden.

On the way back to Gravenhurst, homebound to Kansas City, I stood at the stern of the little steamer, salting its wake. My mother, walking around the deck with my brother, stopped to say with contempt, "You little ninny" — a ninny because I was weeping, she assumed, for Dalton though I wept as much because the emotional ease of the summer was over. Being with other people, she had restrained her ill feeling. Now there was no longer need for such caution. But — a ninny? Anger exploded within me and I faced her squarely. "A ninny I am not! And I am not an Alice!" With amazement her eyes opened very wide and then she and Jack walked away. There were no more tears. I watched without seeing the white frothy lips of the green wake as the engine kept thumping *Not an Alice . . . Not an Alice . . . Not an Alice.*

I believe the bold outburst, after all my appeasement, surprised me more than it did my mother. Those words fell out, without previous thought, as the words of some of my little poems had done.

I was not an Alice!

Of course I was not. That clear and lovely assurance took shape and became firm with every hour spent on the gritty little train to Toronto, the New York Central to Chicago, across Chicago in the Parmalee coach, then the Santa Fe Railway to Kansas City. By the

time we were in our own house I was sure at last I had nothing to
fear in myself, sure because after knowing not one boy at school,
after having to buy my own tickets to basketball games — always
humiliating; after never having been to a dance, never in Kansas
City having been sought out, teased, flattered, or talked to playfully,
I had been attractive to the world champion Dalton White and had
kept my head. I had kept it without any particular effort just because that was the way I was, and if I needed proof there had been
that nice Mrs. Graham, another guest on the island, who had a baby
girl and said to my mother, but smiling at me, "I'll be satisfied if my
baby turns out to be as sensible as your daughter." As sensible —
no other praise could have pleased me as much, and at first I believed that the welcome words, as well as the steadiness that my
mother could have observed, would banish the Alice image. They
didn't. Not for my mother. Once back in our house she resumed
her accusing attitude. It no longer mattered! The cock had crowed
for my dawn.

iv

PROXY PARENTS

SOON AFTER the Canadian summer a series of substitute parents presented themselves. Some of them tried to give what they guessed was lacking at home. One simply wished to bring sociability into the life of a girl too solitary. Others wished to instill their own enthusiasms in a responsive listener. And a few of the most helpful were between the covers of books and printed on sheet music.

Jeremy's volumes had always given their pleasant colors to a wall of our living room but I hadn't read many of them until a day when I reached for one in the long row (the Edinburgh Edition) by Robert Louis Stevenson, a random choice, and it opened onto a page which read:

"The excitement of a good talk lives for a long while after in the blood, the heart still hot within you, the brain still simmering, and the physical earth swimming around you with the colours of the sunset."

A good talk — talk so needed, so long discouraged: "You can pass days in an enchanted country of the mind, live a life more arduous, active and glowing than any real existence; and come forth again when the talk is over as out of a theatre or a dream, to find the east wind still blowing and the chimney-pots of the old battered city still around you."

Oh, to run away from my own life and join Stevenson and his friends in their enchanted country: "If we love talking at all, we love a bright, fierce adversary, who will hold his ground: sell his attention dearly, and give us our full measure of the dust and exertion of battle." In his two essays on *Talk and Talkers* Stevenson described a number of conversations with his actual friends. They all seemed to be men. Were women not acceptable talkers? He took up that point. There are few, he thought, except those "well sunned and ripened, and perhaps toughened, who can thus stand apart from a man and say the true thing with a kind of genial cruelty." His Tiger-Lily? Between men and women "the desire to please, to shine with a certain softness of lustre and to draw a fascinating picture of oneself, banishes from conversation all that is sterling and most of what is humorous." A door opening into an enchanted country to be closed then to me because I would be a woman — but wait! "It is not till we get clear of that amusing artificial [drawing-room] scene that genuine relations are founded, or ideas honestly compared. In the garden, on the road or the hillside, or tête-à-tête and apart from interruptions, occasions arise when we may learn much from any single woman."

Learn much? I did not want to teach but to share ideas. Talk, said Stevenson, was permissible for single women, talk even perhaps for a girl? I wondered whether my talks with John Craig had been Stevenson's kind. Partly yes. We had not been bright fierce adversaries but a genuine relationship had been found. I had not talked very much with Dalton White, a thought that brought a smile as I suspected that we had preferred silence because in it we had drawn nearer to love. Stevenson was not talking about love in this essay but of friendships, about which I didn't know very much. Now though I wished to learn and quite suddenly came on the elementary truth that to have a friend one must talk. And so talk I would! I would come out of my silence.

I talked to anyone who would listen. I talked in school, I stayed
after class and talked to the teachers, I talked to girls in the corri-
dors, I greeted the school janitor and the school cleaning women. I
talked to my brother, I even talked to my mother and when she got
up and walked out of the room I followed her and continued talking. She must have wondered what on earth had got into me, but
finally she listened with what seemed a slight degree of interest. I
suppose she began to realize that she didn't know this daughter at
all.

To her I talked about the news in the morning *Times* and the
evening *Star*. She read them thoroughly, being interested in current
events and somewhat in politics, and to have something to talk
about I too began to read them and on this wholly impersonal plane
our life brightened up quite a little.

I could talk with the teachers about subjects we studied, most of
which I enjoyed, and from those subjects sometimes went on to others. The chemistry teacher had a good sense of pupils as persons
and treated us with an agreeable lack of condescension. He was a
radical, and while we waited in class for our materials in retorts and
test tubes to make their transformations, Mr. Hepworth sprawled
over the top of his desk, running his fingers into his limply wild hair
and throwing out his electrifying ideas. He told us with glee that he
was painting his house himself and one day the principal came
along on his way to the Public Library next door, and saw him and
asked Mrs Hepworth to call him down. When he was back on the
ground the principal said, "Do you think it adds to the dignity of
our science department to have the head up on the roof straddling
the ridgepole?" One of the boys asked Mr. Hepworth if he had
stopped painting the house and he laughed and said of course not.

Mr. Hepworth's world was a different world from the one that
our newspapers wrote about even though the same events happened
in both. In Mr. Hepworth's the population was composed of work-

ers and bosses. "The workers" absorbed as much of Mr. Hepworth's thought as acids and alkalies did and far more emotion. But wasn't everybody a worker in one way or another, even a beautiful wife? Not to Mr. Hepworth, who put cloth caps on all workers' heads and had them snatched off if a boss came along. The development that would allow the workers to keep on their caps or even wear hats was socialism. I believed him absolutely and meanwhile bled for "the workers."

Free love, as it was then called, was another exciting subject. The great thing about free love was not any promise of tenderness or delight but the fact that it would free women from their subservience to men. I tried to square this with the only marriage I knew much about, and my mother did not impress me as being a slave. Still. Worth thinking about. There were other controversial subjects and it suddenly seemed that the world was full of greed and injustice. I was one of Mr. Hepworth's most attentive listeners, and frequent questioners, and soon was doing some questioning on my own.

The first target of my new critical attitude was our church. With profound sixteen-year-old cynicism I saw my mother's spirits rise each week as Friday approached when, looking as nice as could be, she would set out to spend the day at the church, sewing with other women for charity. Sometimes her church committee would meet at our house for luncheon: on the table the best lace doilies and party food. I was always expected to play for the members after they had transacted their business, and I didn't mind that, but was this religion, finding one's way to God, or were these Ladies' Aid meetings just social occasions and therefore an arena for social maneuvering? I am chagrined at the memory of this youthful judgment, for at this distance it seems as if church involvement would be an ideal way for newcomers like ourselves to make friends, especially if a family had been authentic churchgoers in the past, as we had been.

Worst of all, it seemed, was the custom of renting pews. Every fall the church members were given charts of the pews with the prices, just like seats in a theatre, and when they had been bought up for the following year, one could look over the congregation and know where each family stood financially, or so I imagined.

In the cheapest pew sat an especially nice family, the Stanleys. At least they were in the main part of the auditorium until the year the price of the pews was raised. For the Stanleys that meant that they had to move farther back, under the balcony. They were the only ones there and a wide aisle and several empty pews separated them from the rest of the congregation. There they sat every Sunday, alone in the dark and the draughts, and their isolation seemed all the more poignant because they apparently didn't sense any humiliation. Indeed they so enjoyed coming to church that their faces lit up the gloom — the mother, a woman endowed with naturalness like a talent, and the father, an unsuccessful insurance salesman but not thereby deprived of contentment. With them were always their four intelligent children, and when we passed them and turned down to our pew, on one side near the middle, I felt every time that we had insulted them.

As a protest I refused to go to that church any more, a defection that caused a slight stir and appeasement was offered in the form of responsibility for choosing and arranging the flowers for the pulpit each Sunday. I enjoyed doing that but disapproved of the baiting and since nothing was changed for the Stanleys, I arranged the bouquets and then, as the organ rolled out the first hymn I always strode sternly and stuffily home.

My next flurry of idealism didn't work out well either. Having heard about a pathetic old woman with cancers all over her face, I undertook to visit her once a week with flowers or fruit. But she received my calls coldly, offended, I can imagine, by my ill-disguised pity and perhaps my incipient nausea at the look of her face. So that effort was given up and I turned to stuffing envelopes for a civic improvement group that interested Mr. Hepworth. It was obvious that he thought I was a likely convert to liberal causes, for sometimes he would bring his tray and sit with me in the school cafeteria and continue his talk. I was impressed and announced at home that I was changing from the family's Republicanism to become a Democrat. I was still five years from being of age to vote.

At the clang of the school's eleven o'clock bell we left Mr. Hepworth's stimulating influence and went to the Latin class, and again to propaganda but of a most gentle and philosophical sort. Mr. Otis, the teacher, was one who had taken too seriously perhaps Seneca's comment that there is truth in wine. I don't think we ever saw him entirely sober but if this was drunkenness, I used to think, then the world needed more of it.

·Mr. Otis did not bother to defend the study of ancient languages, for it was only in a secondary sense that we were being taught the language of Latium. He made sure that we learned the practical details, vocabulary, sentence structure and the like, but he put his emphasis on the thought that the Roman authors expressed. Besides our daily assignments he used to write on the blackboard Latin quotations that he thought would impress us with their relevance to our times. Some were these:"We must be careful that the child, not being old enough yet to love his studies, does not come to hate them. Education must be made an entertainment." By Persius A.D. 34–62 and what a congenial mind that was! He also wrote, "Oh, but it's a fine thing to have a finger pointed at one and to hear people say, That's the man!" Having read that, our basketball heroes studied their Latin with a little more gusto.

And there were other quotations slanted to the boys in the class: "I know the disposition of women: when you will, they won't; when you won't they set their hearts on having you." (Terence), and: "There is nothing more silly than a silly laugh." (Lucretius).

The boys of course thought that referred to girls' giggling. But the girls weren't neglected:

"Let no woman believe a man's oath, let none believe that a man's speeches can be trusted." That by Cicero who also wrote: "Lack of adornment is becoming to some women."

And the timeless poetry: "The broad ease of the farmlands." "Steep thyself in a bowl of summertime."

There were two which seemed to have been written specifically for me: "Leave thy home, O youth, and seek out alien shores. A larger range of life is ordained for thee." And absolutely the best, this bit of dialogue written by Seneca:

"*Nurse:* The Colchians are no longer on thy side, thy husband's vows have been broken, and there is nothing left of all thy wealth.

Medea: Medea is left."

"Does it seem marvelous because it was done long ago?" It seemed most marvelous that Livius Andronicus had that particular thought two centuries before the birth of Christ.

The worldwide travels of today's footloose young are of course giving them a wide respect for the human qualities that are independent of national boundaries. They know from their own experience what young Terence (he died at twenty-six) wrote 2100 years ago: "I am a man, [therefore] nothing human is alien to me." In this greater knowledge of shared humanity may lie our only hope for future peace and our species' survival. I too have crossed many boundaries and have friends of various backgrounds but a humanizing influence even more deeply effective came from recognizing congenial minds that have sent their thought down from distant ages: "Being acquainted with grief I am learning to help the unfortunate." We, individuals, suffer; the ancients, individuals, suffered and by suffering we have all learned compassion. Latin is not a matter of memorizing rules of grammar; it is a way of coming to sense the larger humanity that includes ourselves. That I absorbed from Mr. Otis's teaching in high school. "For mortal to aid mortal — this is God." (Pliny the Elder, A.D. 23–79.)

Actually Mr. Otis's deepest and richest feeling was for Greek, not only the language but every aspect of the Greek civilization. Sometimes he read bits of those classics to us, and loving Latin so much, I thought that if there were anything better I had to know about it. Mr. Otis, like Mr. Hepworth spotting a convert, told me that if I could get twelve pupils to sign up for a class in beginning Greek the school would be obligated to offer the course. I got my signatures and then, being ill, was not even one of those in the class. But I had talked. It took quite a little talking to arouse enthusiasm for Greek in sixteen-year-olds.

"It is likely that many people who seem to die natural deaths have in fact been poisoned by their families."

Our first-year Latin was not taught by Mr. Otis but by Miss Lash, a woman so extremely passive that she had a kind of perverse charm. She was quiet to a fault, even her lips scarcely moved when she talked, but the most attractive boy in class hung around her: an embryonic cartoonist, Burris Jenkins, Jr., whose talent would later bring him national fame. Hoping for an introduction to him, I also hung around Miss Lash, with the unexpected bonus that she invited me to lunch one Saturday, at the home of the married sister with whom she lived. Perhaps warmed by my admiration, those pleasant extroverted people took me in and soon I was having lunch with them every Saturday. A daughter, age twenty, was engaged to a handsome Australian giant, in Kansas City to study stockyard management, and the flirting and the playfulness that went on were a language beyond English and Latin. It did seem to fall into place in my temperament, somehow, and trying not to seem inquisitive or intrusive I absorbed every gesture and glance. Catherine had blond curly hair and she let me watch as she did it up, with only a twist and a couple of pins, in the most fetching way. She made her own clothes, never starting till afternoon the gown she would wear to a dance that night, and something else that I learned from her was that carelessness can be lucky.

There was another daughter, younger than I but much more aware of new popular songs, clothes, hobbies, and fads. She and Catherine must have thought I was pretty strange but they did talk to me and I learned to talk to them and at last, then, even to girls at school. That most natural kind of sociability had so far been beyond me. What did girls say to one another? From Miss Lash's nieces I had found that a good way to open a conversation and indeed to carry it on is with questions. "Did you make that pretty dress yourself?" "How do you manage to look so cool on a hot day like this?" "Did you get what you wanted for Christmas?" At last I had a casual acquaintance with several of my schoolmates, but not much more. I can't remember the face or name of a single one.

Questions became my personal social technique, developed further when I was adult, for with them one could avoid saying anything about oneself, and about me I felt there was seldom anything I would wish to say. But when I went to the arctic to live with the Eskimos, I found that their social customs forbid asking questions ever — because your companion may not want to answer. "How is your mother, is she getting better?" Perhaps she is getting worse and no one would want to say that. "I see you got back from your fishing trip. Was it successful?" If it wasn't the fisherman would not wish to tell you. One should not even ask, directly that is, for a piece of impersonal information: "Do you happen to know what kind of nest the phalaropes make?" The man may not know; and by asking any of these questions one may either embarrass the listener or force him to lie, either of which is discourteous. It took a surprising amount of effort and thought to change my social tactics to the Eskimos'; and then when I came back into civilization again I was quite at sea. The ability to carry on a spontaneous conversation naturally is learned early in childhood, under normal circumstances. If not then it may take a lifetime to pick up the knack.

The fourth in my quartet of teacher-friends was Miss Trotter, the English instructor. I had been expecting that English would be my favourite subject but it proved a great disappointment, partly due to my fault and partly to hers. My fault was in spoiling myself for a grind by following my fancy in Jeremy's library; hers in overestimating what high-school children could take in of her special enthusiasm for eighteenth century England. I wanted to go on reading about romantic gatherings in the Raffles Hotel at Singapore; she wanted us to share her obsessive interest in Joseph Addison. She was fond of quoting Samuel Johnson: "Whoever wishes to attain an English style must give his days and nights to the volumes of Addison." I wished to give my days and nights, what was left of them after music, to chemistry, Latin, French and mathematics, to Jeremy's novels by Jane Austen, the Brontës, George Eliot, and the poetry, particularly of Keats — that ravishing melancholy! — Wordsworth, and a book of ballades, by whom I don't remember. Dickens was there in a beautiful edition but illustrated by Gustave Doré with scenes so horrendous that they put me off reading the Dickens novels. There were books of essays, the best, I thought, by Robert Louis Stevenson's bright, fierce adversaries, Sidney Colvin and Edmund Gosse. Most absorbing of all were the memoirs of travelers, of the restless Englishmen who had gone out for adventure and knowledge to the most remote dangerous places. From my father's tales of his roving aunts I still had the impression that this was what, in our family, a woman did and so I went all the way with the travel writers. And not always in danger. There was that party under the flowering frangipani trees in the garden of Singapore's Raffles Hotel, and such is the tendency of dreams to realize themselves that I would sit in that garden myself one night while my escorts from the ship collected a lapful of fallen blossoms from the grass and my nose would balloon and my eyes stream with tears for I would be desperately allergic to frangipani pollen. (Fate likes to correct an attitude that is too romantic.)

One small volume of Jeremy's, light blue with a rainbow-colored border, was an abridgment of the third century philosopher Plotinus. Its words were so beautiful and congenial that I took the little book to my bedroom and often would read a few lines and then put down the book, letting the words run through my head for a day or two as a melody will. I was approaching a period of religious doubt when I would remember particularly Plotinus's thought that "God is an atmosphere." That was an appealing idea at the time when I was rejecting the certainties pronounced from pulpits: "God requires us to . . ." "God becomes angry when . . ." "God says we must . . ."

Instead, God is an atmosphere . . .

Returning often to Stevenson I had found his essays on the art of writing and understood as never before that the use of words could become a skill. A skill: magic thought! For in acquiring a skill myself, music, I had discovered the joy of creative effort, a dependable source of both energy and delight, what G. K. Chesterton called an indwelling excitement. That excitement was like an electric charge in everything Stevenson wrote about "the remarkable art of words."

Words themselves: "Restore them to their primal energy, wittily shift them to another issue or make of them a drum to rouse the passions."

Form words into patterns: "It is imperative that a pattern shall be made . . . To be ever changing, as it were, the stitch, and yet still to give the effect of an ingenious neatness." "Each sentence shall first come into a kind of knot, and then solve and clear itself."

Most enticing, rhythm: "Each phrase of each sentence should be so artfully compounded out of long and short, out of accented and unaccented, as to gratify the sensual ear."

Fired with all those exciting challenges I could hardly wait for the chance to write themes in the English class, and the class had an auspicious start because it took no more than thirty minutes to discover that Miss Trotter's admiration for England matched in ardor my own. But it soon became clear that Miss Trotter's England was in the past: the eighteenth century Age of Enlightenment. That was the world she talked about — its politics, social customs and the writers who commented on them. The class, therefore, rather than reading such enchantments as Stevenson's *Travels with a Donkey*, were deluged with Dryden, Milton, Swift and Addison, the hopeful eyes of the pupils being made to focus on:

> *Fly envious Time, till thou run out thy race,*
> *Call on the lazy leaden-stepping hours,*
> *Whose speed is but the heavy plummet's pace.*

In the themes Miss Trotter assigned us, (Describe Swift's divided loyalties; Re-state in your own words any ten lines of Milton's; Describe the early influences on Dryden's style), there was no inspiration to try to write sentences "so artfully compounded . . . as to gratify the sensual ear," and my compositions were among the most leaden-stepping in all the class.

Miss Trotter should have been in some university, for we were too immature to absorb the historic attitudes she was trying to teach. We needed encouragement to love books we could understand and we needed drilling in punctuation, sentence structure and even spelling. I had cause to regret her over-reaching ambition when I was a freshman at Wellesley. By that time, having read a fair number of books for my own pleasure, I had a good-sized vocabulary and a few ideas about what I wanted to say; and after the first theme I turned in, the English Department decided that I could skip freshman English if my second theme showed as much promise. For that second theme I chose a rather adult subject: Outgrown Heroes, and its thought was considered favorably, but I would have to take freshman English after all because I "apparently didn't know anything about punctuation." Punctuation! To lose that flattering chance to surge ahead with more advanced writing in order to learn where to put *commas!* My resentment against Miss T. knew few bounds.

She had singled me out for friendly conversations however, mainly about the possibility that a concert pianist might have time also to be a writer. She was surprised that I knew so many English books, if not of the eighteenth century, and she told me fascinating details about the land for which I yearned — so many that when a Wellesley psychologist was giving us free-association tests, he discovered that my strongest response of all was to the word "England."

None of these high school teachers knew anything about my problems at home but they helped by giving me an escape into other interests. For any child this first contact with adult minds on something like an equal footing can lead him into his own age of enlightenment. For me they were more and I remember all those teachers with gratitude.

2

In a restaurant where we all occasionally had dinner we met an intelligent little woman of fifty, Mrs. Ely, a pianist. She and her unmarried daughter came to our house sometimes and I went to hers, the friendship being more between Mrs. Ely and me than my mother. She was encouraging my musical progress and when I called on her we would play for each other. One day while she was playing a Chopin *Etude* she lifted her hands from the keys and without looking in my direction said, "At the earliest possible moment you must get away from your mother." Then she went on playing and at the end of that piece began a discussion of it. She was not inviting confidences nor intending to say any more. I was fifteen and that was the first time anyone had intimated that my situation at home had been observed.

But about the same time there was another, Mr. Harry Nicolet, Financial Editor of the *Kansas City Star* who, with his wife, played bridge at our house at the infrequent times when my father would be at home. One evening, in everyone's hearing, he said, "There is an old adage that there is never room for two women under one roof." My mother responded with a sharp laugh, saying to me: "Shall I leave or will you?" "I'll be going some day," I said. But to make sure I would, Mr. Nicolet often referred after that to the time when I would be out on my own.

I saw him more often on Wednesday evenings, when we all had dinner at the church. Since I rebelled against going to the prayer meeting afterwards, and Mr. Nicolet didn't go either, having made it known that he was an unbeliever, we used to sit and talk sometimes in the Sunday school room.

He called me Mouse, a bit of propaganda because he was trying to persuade me that I would have a happier life if I would aim for obscurity rather than fame. "If you insist on being conspicuous," he would say, "be the big frog in a little pond." It didn't occur to me then that he might be doubting whether my piano playing was of concert caliber but perhaps he was. Being a writer himself he talked knowledgeably and often about a writing career, tactfully easing out of the conversations anything about concertizing. Or did he simply understand me well? I live very obscurely now and have found that that is the way I can be most contented.

He often gave me advice. Sometimes it was allegorical but then there would be something pointed and personal in his manner which made it likely that I would recognize its intention. One night he told me that he was making a study of luck. For ten years he had played cards every Saturday afternoon at the University Club and had kept a record of all his hands and the outcome of all the games. He had found that the cards he was dealt were poorer than average but "by thinking strenuously" he had been able to win more than half the time. This was a message, in case I should feel that I was unlucky. He also said more than once, "Press your luck when you have it."

He had a great interest in nature and once I told him about the Canadian wilderness and how disappointingly timid I'd been. The conversation took place on one of the Wednesday nights and during a towering thunderstorm. I had always been terrified of violent storms, and I was then, and Mr. Nicolet said, "Let's climb up in the belfry where we can be right in the center of it."

We went up the narrow dark stairway to the top where we came out at one of the open archways. In the air at that height — we could look down on the tops of trees — the crashes were overwhelming. One's mind was smashed flat for an instant, only recovering to see streaks of lightning snake towards the belfry. The lightning and thunder were coming almost together, meaning, I knew, that we were literally in the center of the storm. I am not sure that this was the safest place we could have been, but Mr. Nicolet kept murmuring, "Wonderful! Marvelous!" letting a tone of exhilaration come into his usually unemotional voice. I actually caught the excitement and only understood later what he was suggesting about the way to overcome timidity.

Most of us have seen children whom we suspect of not being treated lovingly by their families. With only a little thought almost anyone may spare them the ills that result from a sense of inferiority, since what they lack is the feeling of being cherished and we can provide it for them. Otherwise most of these children will have an exaggerated urge to justify their existence, but even if, later, they gain prominence in some field or other, they may not be convinced inwardly of their worth. For psychologists have made clear that it is essential to be respected *before* one has proved by achievement the right to respect. One must be cherished, that is, for oneself before being cherished for what one has accomplished. In most cases that reassurance can only come during youth. Normally it will come from families, but if the families fail in their loving, others can give immense help by singling out the child for special attention, for signs that he is found lovable. We, the outsiders, can in a small way become proxy parents.

There will be difficulties. The real parents, often with unconscious, or perhaps conscious, guilt, are apt to resent any interference in a distorted relationship. Jealousy too may enter, for the child, responding to the unfamiliar evidence of warmth, may show an unwary amount of affection for the new friend. This may bring down on his head an even greater amount of abuse. The problem is to make an unhappy child feel that someone fully approves of him and to do it without encouraging too much response.

Besides these several adults who made me feel acceptable there
was one whose interest was more generous still, and yet so adroit
that, even though she was one of my mother's closest friends, in becoming my friend she never at any time betrayed that first loyalty.

One way she made me feel cherished was by invitations to spend
frequent weekends at her house. The excuse was that she had a
Steinway concert grand piano and it would be an advantage for me
to practice on it since I expected to play on such pianos in public.
Actually I didn't practice there although I did play for pleasure, and
there was an ominous discovery that the stiff action of a concert
grand was fatiguing. My hostess was rather formal with me, I think
in order to keep the conversation away from my situation at home,
something of which she had heard from my mother; but if our talk
was impersonal, there were a dozen ways in which I was made to
feel welcome.

Those were the years of the Alice myth, the white dog, the diminished meals and the ominous arsenic; and I left the atmosphere
where I was treated like a delinquent and at the other end of a
streetcar ride was a pampered guest, given an elegant tea, company
dinner in candlelight, flowers in my bedroom and, best, the companionship of a hostess with sensitivity and an aristocratic mind who actually seemed to want me to talk. This "Aunt Caroline," Mrs. C. R.
Woodworth, was a widow, with a daughter younger than I who
went to bed early, and then Mrs. Woodworth and I would sit in
front of a grate fire and discuss music and books, for she gave me
books and every year a subscription to the *Atlantic Monthly*. I told
her about my classes in high school and the stimulating ideas of
some of the teachers, but most often we talked about Wellesley,
since she was a Wellesley alumna, and how it wouldn't be long before I would get on a train and ride away to that beautiful college.
And after college a new life. At her suggestion I read Dante's *La*

Vita Nuova; and would there be romance perhaps, even for me? Like Mr. Nicolet she was keeping strong and real in my mind the promise that some day I would be independent and free.

I hadn't been long at Wellesley when my health broke down and Mrs. Woodworth crossed half the country to bring me her help. She called in a Boston specialist who persuaded the Wellesley physician to lighten my program and excuse me from sports; she arranged for me to have a private dormitory room and, the first essential, talked the college authorities into letting me stay rather than sending me home, as was the threat. All that, while she gave me her friendship with so much tact that my real mother could have been present at every one of our conversations. Mrs. Woodworth apparently realized what an escape it had been for me to leave home, and I think she probably understood very well what the problem was: that delusions of a limited type were responsible for my mother's gloomy view of my future. She could disagree with that view herself without losing the warmth that she felt for my mother. They were very fond of each other.

Modern parents, with their tight nuclear families, do not always find it easy to share their children. In times past, when other relatives usually were present, it was probably taken for granted that a wider exchange of affection was normal. The benefit to a child seems obvious. Eskimos go even further. They accept as natural and desirable that there should be special friendships between children and outside adults. All grown-up Eskimos love all children — a man will stop his work, perhaps building a kayak, to play with a two-year-old not his own; a woman cleaning a tubful of salmon will be surrounded by children admiring her skill. There are no age groups, that limiting concept, except perhaps at the courting stage, and in the usual intermingling it is inevitable that a child and a grown-up will sometimes feel a special affinity. Then the child may

spend half his time at the house of his older friend, he may sleep
there frequently, and his parents welcome this enlargement of his interest and affection. Perhaps one reason that Eskimo parents can be
so generous is that the children are never driven to seek a proxy
mother or father because their own are unloving. Eskimo children,
almost without exception, have a secure sense of being cherished
within their own families. That is not to say they are never cor-
rected. They are carefully guided from babyhood towards becoming
courteous and considerate; if they weren't, their relationships with
their adult neighbors would not be so good. When the special
friendships do spring up, it is not because they are needed to fill a
lack, rather to develop further the happy congeniality found at
home. And it seems likely that the generous, caring spirit which is
typical of all the members of Eskimo communities has its origin in
the affectionate caring of the children for a wide number of people,
the encouragement to be fond of anybody to whom he feels at all
drawn. A loving attitude can become a habit, and when it is
planted so firmly in early years it probably would persist through a
lifetime.

My own devotion to the adults who were giving me help was in
most cases a cause of further antagonism between me and my
mother. She was reproachful, since I was letting each of those
grown-up friends be a powerful influence, at the same time ignoring
or actually rejecting any advice at home. What mother would not
want a daughter to come to her for guidance, especially in adoles-
cent years? I don't remember ever asking, "Should I do this or the
other?" yet I know now that my mother made various good suggestions, regarding clothes, speaking correctly, and learning the elements of pleasing manners. I came to many of her precepts myself
in later years. Having discovered what an advantage it is to understand the norms of well-bred behavior, I can hear echoes of my

mother's voice telling me this long before. But I didn't give her the satisfaction of listening. In fact I thought consciously that her advice could not be trusted because I assumed, from her dislike of me, that her motives were hostile and therefore that what she was telling me would be harmful. We had gone beyond the point, if there ever had been such a point, at which we could reach each other.

3

The doorbell rang one afternoon and my mother answered it. Standing there was her father, long assumed to be dead. He was dressed in a new black suit, with new luggage, but with a dyed mustache which seemed to my mother a symbol of all the cheapness that she detested. He came in without a word, found the comfortable chair by a window, and sat looking up with a brightly defensive face. Not a word had been spoken.

It was a very tense time. My father was not there and my mother had little to say to this man who, she believed, had betrayed all the Harden ideals. My grandfather, leaving the guest room at breakfast time, would spend the rest of the hours by the window, silent mostly, while day by day one could see his morale crumbling. On the fifth day he left, almost as suddenly as he had come.

Although he had been sober, he was a broken man, anybody could see that. And two months later there came word from a Cleveland official that he had died in a hotel there. Had he known when he came to us that this would happen? Had he wished to die among relatives? What lonely adventures had filled his life in the eight years since my grandmother died and he disappeared? There was no funeral but arrangements were made to have him buried beside my grandmother. It is with loving sorrow that I remember

PROXY PARENTS
121

him, and with regret, because I don't think that when he came to
see us in Kansas City I "acted pretty" with him.

Just at that time my mother had started to read the books that
were always lying around in my bedroom. She didn't approve of
them. In Joseph Conrad's *Victory* and Richard Le Gallienne's *The
Life Romantic,* illicit love affairs were described without apology,
and she assumed that I read them to be sexually titillated. In Gals-
worthy's *Forsyte Saga,* which she admired extravagantly, there is
plenty of sex but of course it is treated with disapproval and counter-
balanced by the almost frenetic emphasis on family prestige. I had
tried *The Forsyte Saga* and found it dull. Were not my tastes, then,
depraved?

The shock of my grandfather's sudden appearance threw my
mother into a state of anxiety in which she combined her suspicions
about my preference in books with the old fear that I had inherited
her father's weak will, and so I was treated once more as an outcast.
For five months she only spoke to me through my brother. At dinner: "Tell your sister she looks like a freak with her hair conjured
up like that." My brother did not repeat these remarks but they
made things difficult for him. It was obvious that I was in some
kind of disgrace, I believe he didn't know what, and undue friendliness on his part would have been frowned on. He solved the problem with the adroitness typical of him: he devised a code for communicating between us by knocks on the wall that separated our
bedrooms. It was a kind of talk, and as in many cases during those
years, he was a bright sane element in a gloomy house.

I was seventeen years old and that year, in the spring, I was com-
pleting the study of Beethoven's *Appassionata Sonata.* I was not
playing it well. When I played separate sections of it they seemed
satisfactory but there was a slack of some kind when I put them together. The sonata was memorized. I had the luck to be able to

memorize easily; as soon as my fingers could handle the notes I would know any piece "by heart" and it is only then, when playing without any thought of the score, that the deepest musical impulse can be released. There seemed to be some physical source of such playing, not quite in the heart but for me somewhere behind it. I could feel the source of the impulse *there*. When playing the *Appassionata* this source of energy failed.

In April Josef Hofmann, the famed Polish pianist, was coming to Kansas City to play with the symphony orchestra. I would be in the audience and it promised to be a great event. For Hofmann was going to play Bach's *Concerto in D Minor,* one that represented a pinnacle of achievement for all pianists, as Mrs. Forsythe had told me. Some day I too would play that concerto and with an orchestra. This occasion would be like a vision of the future towards which I was traveling.

The orchestra played a short warming-up selection and then the conductor left to escort the soloist onto the stage. Now here they were, Hofmann not tall but impressive with his well-rounded muscular figure and, more, his commanding presence. He bowed to the applauding audience and seated himself, taking time to wind the piano bench down a little. For several seconds longer he waited, no doubt to gather his emotional forces. I knew about those pauses but never had felt in myself the sense of authority that was in Hofmann's bearing.

He began to play. The first movement of the concerto, *allegro,* begins mildly, not crashing into the listener's consciousness but allowing him a few bars to prepare for the tumult to come. Flung, then, with Hofmann's immense vitality onto the keyboard was a breathless interweaving of the piano's voices, a mounting concord of runs, arpeggios, melody, harmony that spun and whirled and flew, the notes spilling forth as if from a boundless source — as indeed they were, from Bach's boundless invention . . . and on and on, the plunging speed accented forcefully by staccato beats in the bass, but the soaring and flashing right hand also sharpened the rhythm, creating a tension which became almost desperate as the notes raced ahead, with a brief slackening now and then interrupted quickly each time by a return to the same sweeping tempo: what Erik Smith has described as daemonic energy in that movement.

The second movement, a darkly minor *adagio,* had almost a deathlike stillness. It was the saddest theme I had come across in any Bach composition, a theme which seemed to express despair, and I listened, limp with more than the ceasing of the *allegro's* speed, with submission to the mood of the melody so without hope. A later choral adaptation of the theme carries the words, "Through much affliction shall we enter into the Kingdom of God." One could believe that much affliction was in Bach's mind when he first wrote the *adagio.*

There is no gentle approach to the torrents, cascades of sound in the third movement. We are swept into it on the opening notes and through to the close there is never a break in the urgency of the sounds. This movement seems very Italian, like a hot-blooded dance that would continue its agitated speed until the performers dropped. Even more than in the first movement the beat is emphasized with crisp, bouncing staccatos, like stomping heels. And like a dancer himself Hofmann flung his hands up and down the keyboard at almost a manic pace in which, again, the listener had to sustain an almost unbearable tension. There is a limit beyond which unrelieved speed cannot be endured, an ultimate in suspense that Bach seemed to reach in the *D Minor Concerto.* Finally then, after a false pause and a last whirl of notes, came the cadence that brought the music to a harmonic close. The audience responded with a stampede of applause and cheers, many having been brought to their feet by Hofmann's virtuosity and the magnificence of the music.

I will never be able to play like that.

Mechanically I stood up to let other listeners in my row of the balcony leave for the interval and unseeing, watched the last orchestra members walk off the stage. The music had been an assault, for as soon as the stimulating sounds died away I faced the defeated thought: I will never be able to play like that. Hofmann had dominated the whole orchestra of — how many? Eighty players? To be a first-class pianist one would need to have all that power, one would need to have shoulders like his, his muscular arms and hands. The clue to my limitation in playing Beethoven's *Appassionata* must then have been physical strength. It was not enough to understand and to feel and to care: sheer massive energy would be required to tear from a keyboard the sounds of ultimate musical truth. And anything less than that truth would be nothing. As a pianist I would be nothing. I was not strong enough, I was not *large* enough. Why had I not been warned? But I had been. I would remember later much oblique dissuasion by adult friends. Stubbornly I had refused to hear it.

It did not occur to me on that fateful day that music could give welcome pleasure with less than the ultimate technique. A minor talent should not be despised. But a minor talent was so much less than I had visualized that it was not worth considering. I walked home from the concert in the smoky afterglow of a sunset, many blocks, uphill for my feet, steeply down for my spirits. For I faced the fact that muscles were not all I lacked. Something else was not in me: true greatness of musical concept, authority, the ability to play and *know* that this was the way the composition should sound. People said that I played delightfully. That was far less than strongly, and I could not play with complete assurance until my judgment became self-sufficient, which could take forever.

I ignored the meal left on the dining table and went up to my room, there to lie awake until morning while waves of sickness rolled up from the foot of the bed.

4

I said nothing about this revelation, practicing less and less though playing as many hours for consolation. My music teacher was puzzled but I did not explain. Rudderless days; and my health broke down under the combination of strains. After a start as acute sciatica, a low fever, which kept me in bed, continued for almost a year. When the sciatica left, the illness was diagnosed as some obscure kind of tuberculosis but later was thought to have been only a stress fever. It seemed a relief at first to be resting, and I found ways of amusing myself, among other things painting sexy paper dolls which I sold to a bachelor friend of the family for five dollars a set. He said that he played with them in the evening, a paper harem, though perhaps he was just being kind. I sewed and read more of Jeremy's books. Sometimes my young brother stopped in for a few minutes of playful talk; Mrs. Woodworth came and the doctor. Though my father was not at home, in the beginning the days were not really unhappy. But my mother's distress at my illness, perhaps a reproach for her five months of silence, was causing a new and growing tension. The future was problematical, since no one knew why I was running the fever, and would I be there, so inescapably *there,* indefinitely? I recognized her emotional anguish, although days would go by without my seeing her. A maid brought up my meals and cleaned my bedroom and, although I could not go downstairs, I could take care of myself. The atmosphere had the charged sultriness that precedes a thunderstorm.

My doctor remained convinced, in spite of no concrete evidence, that I had tuberculosis of the spine and so decided to put me into a rigid cast. To make it he and an assistant strung me up by the neck to a broomstick which was laid across from the top of the medicine cabinet in the bathroom to the shower rod, with my feet not touching the floor. In this way it was hoped to make the cast fit a straightened-out spine, but the plan didn't work because I fainted immediately, a rather gruesome example of the effectiveness of being hanged.

A few days later my mother came into my room with her sewing basket and started darning a sock. She sat down by the window as if she might stay for a little while, a thing she had not done before. But after a silence she said in a tense, hard voice:

"Perhaps you should know that — up to this time — you have cost us altogether seventeen thousand, five hundred and forty-nine dollars."

It took me a long moment to absorb this information. An account of everything I had cost: did it go back to my complicated birth? No doubt, and included all the illnesses, and the music lessons, the schoolbooks and concert and theatre tickets. And my railroad fare whenever we went away, my part of the summer board — and also a fourth of the cost of our meals at home, and of running the house, a fourth of the coal bill, ice, phone, electricity? And of the garden and maintenance work? Ah — and the gifts? I found my tongue and asked,

"Does that total include my birthday and Christmas presents?" I think the question surprised her but she said,

"Why — yes, naturally."

I asked if she had kept an account of everything my brother had cost. She didn't answer that but said:

"And this illness you are having has cost — so far — eight hundred and eighty-nine dollars." She let that sink in and finished, "If I had an undiagnosed illness and I knew that I was nothing but a burden and an expense, I would kill myself."

Then she gathered up her sewing and with her most terrible face left the room.

That incident disturbs me less now, when I know the explanation of her unloving attitude, than it did at the time. Even then I had realized for so many years that she wished me out of the way that the new move was only a moderate shock. At least the suggestion of suicide left the matter to me, and I just said to myself, Well, I won't do it. But I did realize that my continuing presence at home had to end, and I beat down the fever, almost by will power, and soon got up out of that bed and was well and bending all thought and effort towards preparing for college.

o

So the vicissitudes of my childhood ended, and after those months with plenty of time to think, I had a clearer view of the part each of us had played in the saga of our American family. Like many other families, I am sure, ours appeared to be happier and more secure than it really was, but we were all working out ways of living that may not have been ideal yet had compensations.

It was simply fate that my father had been given that large responsibility for developing a vast and distant territory; fate too that his assistant in Kansas City was so efficient that my father could be away for as long as six months at a time. His company must have been satisfied, for they raised his salary each year. And was he himself satisfied with the arrangement? Did he accept emotionally a routine that kept him so far from his family?

I think he probably did, for his relationship with my mother had deteriorated badly. I know she believed that he could have come home more often if he had wished, but did her suspicions arise before there was any real excuse for them? Or had she been patient beyond the point of reason? Before long it was true that when he did come it was not to any warm and affectionate welcome. My mother's defensive weapon was always ridicule, and as I remember the times when my father was with us, she made fun of everything that he did, of the way he walked, talked, laughed, told a story. She spoke slightingly of his family and of himself, of even his trait of friendliness, which she considered undiscriminating. He did have a few small awkward mannerisms, but it seemed evident to me even then that they were aggravated by her scorn. He was vulnerable, as she knew. She called him sensitive and would make that quality sound like a weakness.

He was a man who always had lived with bright expectations and with confidence in his ability to bring them to pass. But when he went out of the door after one of those infrequent weeks at home, the light would be gone from his eyes and his Gladstone bags appeared to be heavy. All his success in that job depended on having belief in himself, and how then did he recover his confident manner? Did he argue himself back into awareness of how much he enjoyed his work, how much satisfaction it was to be putting the cheer of fresh, light colors in grim institutions; or did he make himself neutral, emotionless for a while so that his natural resilience would rise up again? Or was there someone in Texas who had a restorative influence? Not necessarily the last, since he had a spontaneously buoyant temperament, but there may have been someone who fostered it and provided encouragement.

One year we all went down to spend Christmas in Dallas. A view of the world into which he had disappeared: and what kind of people did he associate with there? He introduced us to three good friends, frequent golfing companions. They were all university professors, and his manner with them suggested a freer, more self-confident self than we ever had seen in Kansas City. I think my mother was shaken a little.

There had come to be almost no direct communication between my father and me. He had been warned that I was sure to disgrace the family eventually, and the poor man would look at me with affection but now with sorrow — and bewilderment, for like most fathers, I imagine, he did not doubt a mother's judgment. He had become gently reproachful without being specific enough so that I could defend myself. Besides, what defence is there against misdeeds that still lie in the future? One can't categorically deny a doom.

He was such a modest man, my father, it may never have occurred to him that in addition to supporting us well, he himself was needed and missed at home.

Meanwhile my mother maintained the house. In a setting she always ornamented, new furniture, tastefully chosen, was added from time to time, and the flower boxes were filled each spring, the lawn was kept trim, every summer the coal and wood were got in and every autumn the gutters were cleaned and the screens repainted. I don't think I ever saw a tool in her hands but she always knew whom to call in emergencies and they always came promptly. The house was never less than immaculate and she had a most tactful way with help. The laundress used to speak of her "sweet step" overhead. Add to all this the fact that we had gourmet meals and it will be seen that she did everything and more that could be asked of a woman in keeping house.

For her the great consolation was my brother, who already showed signs that he would become, as he has, all she admired in a man — successful and witty, with beautiful manners, a substantial citizen in the most graceful way.

In temperament he is a very interesting example of the mix that parental traits can produce, traits which seem contradictory in my brother's case and yet have worked out very well. His career has been a male expression of his mother's social achievements, for in both business and local government he has been an important influence in half a dozen cities around San Francisco Bay. Yet he has gained these positions with none of the show of force, none of the overbearing aggressiveness by which many men reach the top. There is no hint in him of attempting to push others aside, rather a reticence that suggests his father as much as his blue eyes and the shape of his face do. Such a modest manner might seem a handicap in gaining prominence, but he has proved that intelligence and tact are just as effective as bombast, if one has the knack for them.

It could be said that my brother was, and is, elusive. Even at age three and four he was very much his own man, and by the time he was ten he had developed a light and clever playfulness that allowed him to keep out of reach. He lived his own life, explaining his doings with stories whose very outrageousness was disarming. At fourteen, to his distraught mother at 3 A.M.: "You'd never guess where I've been. I was coming home at eleven-thirty and up here at the corner there was a Pierce Arrow with its engine stalled. A countess, she was wearing a long red velvet dress, she was standing out in the snow wringing her hands and the chauffeur was trying to fix the engine. I asked if they would like to have me take a look at it and they said please. It was simple enough. I found the trouble right away, and the countess insisted that I go back with her to the Nelsons' [William R. Nelson, former publisher of the *Kansas City Star*] — she's staying there and we sat on the floor and played dominoes and ate sausage sandwiches." What could you do but laugh if the storyteller was a delightful son? His very elusiveness probably made him more interesting to her. He and his offspring were the perfect element in his mother's life, the only one but many people make do with less.

My brother and I never were sober and matter-of-fact with each other. We communicated with a mad kind of nonsense good for both of us I should think. Like most jesting it hid inner lacks — in me the lack of mothering and in my brother perhaps the lack of companionship with his father. His work had taken him away from us before my brother was five years old, and after that they only saw each other at infrequent times, during which my father became more and more like a stranger. My brother never was treated cruelly but he probably felt deserted. When he was still a young boy he said that when he grew up he wanted to have "a big house and a lot of children," reminding me of how I said on my ninth, unhappy birthday that "Some day I'll make it up to a little girl of my own." Did my brother also think, consciously, that he would make up to a lot of children for his own lack of fathering? He has, in fact, been an infallibly loving and generous parent, rewarded by his children's affection and that of the grandchildren who now romp through his big house. He at least could have felt he belonged in the Kansas City house, but for him it may not have been a real home without a father in it.

It was not a home for me because I was not welcome there. But I was fortunate in the other interests I had a chance to develop. We were not an outstandingly affluent family and yet I could buy all the books and sheet music I wanted, see all the plays, hear all the concerts and operas, and study music under the best teachers available. When my mother met one of my college professors, the professor spoke of my background as being more favorable than that of many girls, and my mother said, "We have only wanted to open the doors for her." That remark did not make me feel cynical — rather especially grateful that, being unloved, I still was given those good compensations. And most grateful of all that I had been sent to Wellesley.

This summary is a little more coherent than I would have been able to make it while I was lying in bed trying to understand human riddles. But essentially this is what I concluded during those hours of illness. What I didn't do was to try to see myself in that family, or to see myself at all. If I had tried I would have found that in my own eyes I was a kind of non-person.

I can hardly guess what others thought of this girl soon to set out to lead her own life. As for me, what indeed was I? Not a musician. Not a member of a family in the sense of knowing what shared affection is like. Not one who had friends. Not one anybody would miss if she were absent. Not one who had any conscious ambition or purpose. Not one who had any confidence in the future, beyond a certain knack of coping with momentary challenges — not the ability to plot any long-term advance. I did have sympathy for those who in any way were unfortunate, and it was obvious that I responded with a degree of intelligence to the arts. But responding is not the same thing as initiating. It is a non-person's talent.

On the day I departed for Wellesley, and looked out at the dreary railroad yards as the train pulled away, I had a strange little attack of homesickness — for a haven that was not there in Kansas City, but for a home somewhere. Out in the world for which I was bound, would I be able to make or find a home? By the time I did find one, it would be a good thing if I had found also a self to live in it.

v

"LIFE AS IT REALLY IS"

ONCE WHEN Bertrand Russell and Julian Huxley were dining together, Sir Julian described the habits of an obscure amphibian. Lord Russell, so great a mathematician-philosopher, listened with humble absorption and at the end said, "It is nice to know things."

Indeed it is. Knowledge, familiarity with the thought and experience of the human race, should be the birthright of everyone born — as much so as light and air. But until fairly recently most kinds of knowledge had been withheld from the feminine half of humanity. Even a hundred years ago there was much opposition to letting women know things. It was said that their minds were too weak, they would break down if they tried to take in the knowledge given to men in all civilized lands. In England some of the most stubborn resistance to education of "females" came from that little hen of a woman, Queen Victoria, who was content to let her adored Albert function mentally for her.

There had been exceptions. Plato believed that women were capable of the highest philosophical thought and admitted some of them to his academy; and a few women had been recognized as intelligent even in China and India, and of course Rome. But there never had been provision for making knowledge available to all women until the last century, when various "female seminaries" began to spring up in Europe and the United States.

Wellesley was established in 1875, at a time when there was a ferment to secure better conditions for women: to gain the right to vote, to own property, to hold office, to earn wages the equal of men's, to have legal status as persons. Mr. Henry Fowle Durant, a Boston lawyer, had great sympathy with these campaigns. He might have been expected to work for more liberal laws but instead he wished to give knowledge to women, believing that if they could talk to men from a background equal to theirs in information and understanding, they could no longer be denied the rights that are obviously due to a fully developed intellect. He said, "We revolt against the slavery in which women are held by the customs of society . . . the subordinate position, the helpless dependence, the dishonesties and shams of their so-called education." And so he founded Wellesley College, where the education offered to women was to be as advanced as that in the best of men's universities. Before 1900 Wellesley had laboratories for experimental work in physics (1878), chemistry, and physiological psychology, and soon a salt- and a fresh-water vivarium, an arboretum and an astronomical observatory. There were also intensive studies in the humanities and the arts; and since Mr. Durant wanted the girls to be strong in bodies as well as minds, he built a gymnasium.

Remarkably, all the faculty in the beginning were women, including a woman president (where did Mr. Durant find a woman to teach experimental physics in 1878?), but this arrangement soon gave way to a mixed faculty, although Wellesley has always maintained a high proportion of women instructors. Mr. Durant had said, "The real meaning of higher education for women is . . . the assertion of absolute equality. All our plans are in out-spoken opposition to the customs and prejudices of the public." By the time my class was graduated, in the 1920's, the original spirit of revolt had given way to a more easy acceptance of women's capacities. We were no longer proving to the public, or to ourselves, that we need not be subservient and helpless. We were treated at Wellesley as having no handicaps in intelligence and we went forward with the wholesome attitude of using our brains instead of proclaiming them. The impression of women's equality with men was simply in the air and we learned to live by it. We recognized that we would not find acceptance of that idea everywhere out in the world, but we prepared to make our contribution, intending to cope with opposition, when we would meet it, by relying upon the brains so rigorously exercised at Wellesley.

We learned to work very hard, to demand a great deal of ourselves, and that, I think, has turned out to be an effective way of combating prejudice. For the willing and dedicated performance of a job does not arouse the resentment which is sometimes received by protesting militants. This is a bold claim but supported by the achievements of my own class. A large number have been directly or indirectly associated in their husbands' work; others have been doctors, psychiatrists, musicians, painters, editors and writers. But there is no tone of inordinate pride in their reports of their achievements; rather, what seems to be a feeling of, This is what Wellesley taught us that we could do, and so we have done it.

Today the faculty offer many chances for discussion of women's place in society. Specific courses take up this subject; in others a new emphasis is given to women's accomplishments, or sometimes unfortunate lack of them, in history, literature, the creative arts and the sciences, with the professors listening more than imposing beliefs. The Wellesley graduate should be well equipped to help think through the vast present confusion about women's role.

When I was there we were happy in a very youthful way, which is not to say with delayed maturity. The letters I wrote to my family were saved; I have them and they make merry reading. The escapades, the pranks, the sheer ebullience seem to be largely lacking now, at least it appears so to visiting alumnae who remember the days when our intense studying was relieved by mirthful relaxation. The girls of today, growing up faster, in a world more grim and disheartening, must have a new kind of stamina to withstand so soberly the academic demands.

The supremely beautiful campus was and remains an idyllic background for students: 400 acres of sweeping tree-shaded lawns, slopes and dells, a brook and a pond as well as serene Lake Waban, where we swam, went canoeing and skated in winter, and on whose shores we walked and lunched and dreamed and sought privacy with beaus. In the first letter I sent from Wellesley I wrote, "The lake is worth all the tuition and effort to get here." No doubt a surprise to my parents. "This morning the lake was calm in strips, rippling in others. All the bright-colored trees (they are already turning) were reflected in it, the white slim birches standing out among dark green and red and yellow masses of foliage. I went down and sat on the shore, where water-lilies and rushes grow in the shallows. The sunshine was so gold it was like a mist over the lake. And there wasn't a single jarring human sound — only the insects' droning, an occasional bird note, the cawing of a pair of crows, and always the lazy lapping of the water."

I was so grateful to be at Wellesley that I thought of the college rituals with a kind of reverence, no less enjoyed for that, especially the step-singing. In the cool dusk near the shore of the lake we gathered on and around the chapel steps for a brief choral interlude. Our voices rose unaccompanied in "America the Beautiful," written by two Wellesley professors, Katherine Lee Bates and Clarence G. Hamilton; in folk songs and carols and two or three college songs, some quite witty, and finally a chant that ended with a briskly sung "Wellesley!" The word echoed against the hills across the lake and came back with perfect clarity but a diminished volume which suggested the tenuousness of youthful innocence and hope. Step-singing has recently been abandoned, no doubt because the present-day students found it sentimental.

After I returned at the start of my second year I wrote that "my greatest joys in being back are, in this order, the campus, the girls, and last, of course (*sic*) the classes." Girls had come into my personal life for almost the first time ever. Today when it is thought important for children to learn "social skills" in kindergarten or earlier, it might seem a disaster to go to college without ever having had friends of one's own kind, friends in a "peer group," as the sociologists say. How could one ever break out of such isolation, how discover so late the way to approach others?

It's quite simple: one casts aside all of one's pent-up loneliness in a day and rushes headlong into the joyous discovery of what companionship is. Finally to laugh, to chatter, to smile and know the warmth of responding smiles, to feel somebody's arm on one's shoulder, to put one's arm through another's in walking along, to have allies, supporters, to be wanted, sought, joined gratefully, left regretfully, to be liked, to be loved: with such a rich experience suddenly proffered, why should earlier solitude be a barrier? To have friends at last, after so late a start, is socially to be born!

A college is an auspicious atmosphere for such a blossoming because some of one's classmates will be homesick, reaching out for just what one wants to give. (I told my family I hadn't been homesick, not for one minute, and what did they think of that?) And then, other Wellesley students may have been somewhat lonely as I had, perhaps because some would have been "the serious type," as children said of the girls who had an eager longing to know things. Two of my friends had been absorbed in studying music, and two had had illnesses which had cut them off from young comradeship.

But most were just normal girls who already knew how to establish relationships. I learned from them. Before I had been at Wellesley three months I sent back word that I had "twenty-five *best* friends." My social success, such as it was, must have been partly due to the fact that I was so happy. Happiness attracts. Others borrow one's joy.

There was, at that, a barrier of sorts. The girls talked about their families and the events of their childhood, and on those subjects I had little to say. One could build pictures: "I have the kindest, most devoted, most dependable father in the world. And my mother is very beautiful and dignified and gracious." The boastful claims could be elaborated, though perhaps not very convincingly, and I am not sure the others believed them. I could describe my brother with more sincerity and he wrote me amusing letters which were passed around and gave my earlier years some reality. (I paid him a tenth of a cent a word for them.) But I kept most of my conversations to questions and jokey comments. One girl said, "You are so easy to know on the surface, but pretty soon one senses a wall."

About letters, a wonderful thing happened while I was at Wellesley. Those I sent back to Kansas City were forwarded to my father and he was so pleased with them that he began to write to me regularly, something he never had done before, and was sending me money and candy and Texas pecans. I think he must have decided that I was not going to disgrace the family after all, and being in truth a kind, loving father, he welcomed the chance to express himself again freely. His letters were such an outpouring of affection that they re-created the relationship we had had before I was six. When I went back to Kansas City at the end of my sophomore year, he, alone, was on the station platform to meet me and something like a new era began in our family relationships.

The delight of my escape into the Wellesley world was made undiplomatically explicit in the family letters:

"I am wildly happy! Be glad!"

"I walked back along the lake shore. It was bright moonlight and the water reflected every tree on the shore, a thing I never had seen before at night. I almost laughed out loud, I was so happy."

"You wouldn't know your gay, affable daughter. The sociableness here gets into my blood."

"Dinner is the happiest time of the day, there is so much laughter in the air. When I look around the dining room I feel as if I were out in warm sunshine after having been shut up in the dark for a long time. Rejoice!"

I was stupidly slow, well into my second year, before I realized the effect this exuberance was having in Kansas City. My mother did not rejoice. But I learned that it was safer to exult in the classes, genuinely so stimulating, and in my friendships with two or three of the faculty members.

All the courses I took helped to free me from my embattled self. Even mathematics proved interesting when one discovered that its higher reaches approach philosophy. In zoology it was moving to see the tiny lives in a drop of pond water, spinning around trying to get what they wanted just as I was trying, in peering into the microscope, to get what I wanted. It was moving but in a less pleasant way to dissect a cat, but the course was a good grounding in comparative anatomy and would prove invaluable later. Psychology was disappointing. Already knowing a little about the theories of Freud and Jung I had hoped to learn very much more but instead had to study the mechanics of sight. Biblical history, a required course, was undertaken with flailing protests but developed into one of my favorite subjects, due to the intellectual challenges of the professor, "Dutcher the Magnificent," who had a romantic apartment in Boston's Trinity Court and sometimes invited students to Sunday night suppers. She had a grand piano and she and I played for the others.

Of all the courses, however, the most illuminating was English

Composition. For, with the first paper turned in, I made the unexpected discovery of a new talent, a discovery as momentous to me as my first discovery of music.

Why did this come so late, why, throughout my childhood, did I write only the little poems? Perhaps because all my libido was being expressed in music and in only a minor way in the poems of which I made songs. With the collapse of any further ambition in music there was the year's illness, and then I was in a Wellesley class where the English instructor, Miss Katharine Liddell, was as inspiring as Mrs. Bunce, my first music teacher. Her encouragement, her assumption from the start that I was destined to be a writer, was a great impetus. Much more important, because it came from within, was the revelation that a mysterious source of ideas could be tapped at will, that some unsuspected voice had begun to speak through my pen and was there to be called forth at any moment. In describing this curious faculty I feel completely humble, since it is not related to anything I can claim credit for. A writer's flow of words is something that simply happens, as explained in the memoirs of many authors. The words that go down on paper are often quite unexpected, unrelated to any previous conscious thought, and a large part of the pleasure in writing is the suspense in turning on this obscurely based current. Creativity has been called a functioning of the subconscious mind, implying that subconscious minds have a store of forgotten observations and experience (and perhaps the archetypal experience of the race, as Jung believed), and that so-called creative people have no more than an unusual knack for gaining access to their subconscious. That explanation seems convincing to me. The sudden appearance of unexpected ideas comes to workers in all the arts of course, and just as fruitfully to creative scientists. I am sure that it also functions in people who have a talent for human relationships. And is it a talent too of those with a daemonic aptitude for evil? Until we understand more about it, that possibility cannot be ruled out.

At the time I began to write, a whole culture, perhaps even a civilization, had been destroyed by the revelation of human brutality which had occurred in the First World War. Most of my Wellesley professors had clear intimations of this loss. They were even more aware of the destruction of sentimentality that had come about through the new scientific outlook with its emphasis on objective facts. Science had brought in a new world, and new means of expression had to be found that would be compatible with it. Finally they may have sensed the desolate belief among artists of every kind that an historic era of artistic expression had ended. In writing, Yeats had declared, all the nuances had been explored, sensitivity had gone the whole way and there was nothing else to be found down that path. In music and painting too it was felt that the old techniques had expended themselves.

My Wellesley professors were conscious of all that must now be unlearned in the arts. This understanding had not yet reached most of the students but our instructors were intent on giving it to us. "Realism" was the key word. We must be taught to see clearly and think realistically — a daunting task, for most of us had been ignorant of the revolution in attitudes. We had absorbed the largely Victorian approach of our parents and we had to be shaken out of it. This was done most effectively in the English Composition classes, where writing methods were treated as of less importance than what was thought and expressed.

Because I did have a little technique, from extensive reading and study of Stevenson's *Art of Writing*, I could produce fairly acceptable themes (except for punctuation) from the beginning; but what impressed and pleased the English Department was the tone of disenchantment. They were surprised to find a student who seemed already to have absorbed the new mode of thinking and they used my themes as examples of the attitude they were trying to instill in their charges. But no one was more surprised than myself at the tone of those essays. I had not known that I thought like that. Unless I was sitting at a desk putting down words on paper, I didn't think like that then.

And yet here came the cool and disillusioned words in themes one after the other. The first, the one called "Outgrown Heroes," described the way further experience takes the bloom off childish devotion to various individuals. Miss Liddell wrote on that theme, "There is no question about the strength or reality of this piece of work."

We could choose our own subjects and my next essay, flying high without embarrassment, asked, "Is Democracy Possible?" I concluded it wasn't, because too many citizens are not interested in public issues and will let inferior men run the country for their own corrupt purposes. In the next I asked, "Did Henry James have a sense of humor?" It was something of an emotional stretch to claim that he didn't, because he was my current hero. His books were feeding my galloping wish to become sophisticated, but I wrote that, however witty and subtle his mind, it lacked cleverness of a playful kind.

Still more disloyal was a paper on Stevenson, the idol of much of my adolescence. Was his bright and spirited temperament inborn, or was it actually a compensation for his tuberculosis, indeed a symptom of illness? The question seemed realistic all right, and pleased the professors. What they didn't guess, nor did I very clearly, was that I was asking the question about myself: was my own euphoria a compensation for childhood disasters that I had not, actually, assimilated?

The euphoria, by that time, was puzzling my faculty friends. I had been rather taken up by some of those generous women —

mothers to minds, was having frequent meals at their houses, was being treated as someone pretty mature — because of the themes. And what they were learning from knowing me personally was that I was one of the most misty-eyed of their students; that far from seeing my present circumstances realistically I considered Wellesley the most perfect of ideal colleges, all the girls as paragons of charm and intelligence, and the faculty at once brilliant in their specialties and concerned about the students with utter selflessness. Even regarding themselves they disapproved of such uncritical judgments. It was Miss Liddell who began saying, "When you get out in the world, you must try to see life as it really is." Others in the department took up the refrain, and my themes became less realistic because I was trying too hard and too self-consciously to sound disillusioned. I wish I could have explained to these helpful instructors what had planted the disenchantment in the deep layers of my mind, and why an escape from the early events had filled me with an ecstatic gratitude. But I didn't and probably couldn't.

I was not able to stay. At the very start of my freshman year the college health department had threatened to send me home until Mrs. Woodworth came and persuaded them that the disappointment would be cruel. But the heart problems began to creep up and the next year they could not be ignored. At Easter the Boston doctor told me that when I went home in June I should plan to rest for a year and then finish at a less strenuous college. When I heard this crushing news I relapsed into an extreme attack of the old psychic numbness. For several hours my mind was just blank. When it cleared I could recognize that to push beyond the felt limits would mean a breakdown — inevitably; and for several years I had recognized that to fight the inevitable is simply to throw away strength.

I am not sure that the effort required at Wellesley was in fact the reason why I could not keep up. The college physician and her assistants, the dean and instructors all tried to lighten my work, and I was not being pushed any more than I had been in the last year of preparation for college. I probably brought on the difficulty by being so happy at Wellesley. For a heart specialist told me afterward that "elation puts as much strain on a heart as worry does."

But what a lot I had gained in those two years — best, self-confidence, the quality on which Mr. Durant had put the most emphasis when he founded Wellesley with his liberating hopes.

Alma (Lat., *food giving, cherishing*) Mater (*a mother*).

2

I don't know whether my father came home specifically to welcome me when I returned. He may have. He planned to go back to Texas the following week but enough days intervened to show that affection was reborn between us. During the years when he had accepted my mother's judgment that I was worthless, he had been on her "side." Now he showed with a pointed tenderness that he regretted the time of lost faith in me.

I had hoped, naively, that my mother too would find me, at last, acceptable. For two years I had known the approval of very intelligent people. That was made plain in my letters, and seeing me now, changed as I was, so much more self-assured, surely a mother would welcome me? In that expectation I was not seeing life as it really is, for few mothers would be able to admit that they had misjudged a daughter throughout her whole childhood. She did admit it though, in a negative way. The day after I arrived she and I were sitting out on the porch, reading the two sections of the evening *Star,* which had come half an hour before. Suddenly she jumped up, throwing her part of the paper down on the floor and saying with blazing anger, "You think your childhood has been a tragedy and that I am to blame for it." Without waiting for my reaction then, she strode in the house.

I wouldn't have put it so plainly but, yes, I thought, she was right.

I had already realized that my rapturous letters from Wellesley must have reminded her that I would have missed all that happiness if I had followed out her suggestion and killed myself. Had some such thought made her uncomfortable, was that the reason why all her letters to me had been so down-putting? I had dreaded getting them. Sometimes I left them unopened as long as a week.

Another thing she said in the first few days after I returned was, "Read Robert Louis Stevenson's story of Dr. Jekyll and Mr. Hyde. There are people like that." She could acknowledge responsibility for my troubled years, but not remorse, which could have been expressed by no more than a little sign of affection. But if anything her revulsion had increased while I was away. She could not face the prospect of being alone with me there in the house again. And so she did the logical and dramatic thing: she left. With only a few hours' warning and with no instructions about keeping things going, she got on a train and rode away — to California to visit her brother, she said. And for how long? She just shrugged her shoulders and laughed.

My father decided that he would remain for a while at the headquarters in Kansas City. And I tied on an apron and went into the kitchen, where the only things I knew how to make were fudge and tea. My brother, curious at the new developments, hung around the house, and my cousin Will, Alice's son who was then living with us in Kansas City, sat back and watched, looking amused.

Three men depending on me for three meals a day: I would have to learn fast. I floundered along, slowly finding out what most women know instinctively: that five o'clock in the afternoon is too late to do the day's marketing, that no two kinds of food take the same length of time to cook, that soufflés and omelets fall and custards and mayonnaise curdle. We had hot biscuits with every meal for I was determined to learn how to make them, but mine had to be broken open with knives.

Emergencies overlapped. The laundress demanded an unexpected vacation, the roof developed a leak, moths were found chomping away in my father's best suit, the car's rear axle broke down, and my father acquired a pain that was diagnosed as either a gallstone or indigestion. Indigestion perhaps, due to his great anxiety. For what was the meaning of these troubled days? Had my mother incredibly left us for good? I didn't believe that she had but my father was not so sure. If she had, what would we ever do? We couldn't go on this way, at least he could not. Two of the main-office salesmen were quitting; he should be taking new men out on the road for training but felt that he could not leave. And the Texas branch? He was not very explicit about the problems there but he made it plain that he had to be getting back.

We did hear from my mother, though not very often, and she said nothing about coming home. She was certainly needed, but could anyone fail to admire the cleverness of her getting away from me and at the same time retaliating for being alone through so many years? She had run the house virtually single-handed; now the rest of us could take charge.

She must have known for some time what she was going to do, for no vacation plans had been made. Every summer since the one spent in Canada we had got out of the Kansas City heat, but this year the question had not come up, and we seemed to be stuck in temperatures that went up to 105 degrees every day.

Somebody at the factory told my father about a fishing lodge on

Lake Taneycomo, down in the Ozark Mountains. We left the next afternoon.

It was an artificial lake, made by damming the White River which winds through the mountains of Oklahoma, Missouri and Arkansas. Its water now partly filled what once was a valley, where officials had visualized a chain of profitable resorts on the shores. Let those who are tempted to promote similar projects note that men cannot make a lake as well as, for example, a glacier can. An attractive feature of many natural lakes are the beaches of sand and gravel, torn from a glacier's bed as it moved along and deposited where the lake was formed when the glacier melted. The pebbles and sand are pleasant to sit and lie on, and walk on when going into the lake. If this light-colored rock material lies all over the lakebed, the surface looks bright and is apt to reflect the sky. At Taneycomo the gaunt trunks of dead trees still stood in the shallows. Eventually they would die and fall; some stumps were already down and partly or wholly submerged. On the shores were no pebbles or sand, rather the water-soaked mud of what had been wooded slopes, and the bottom was mud and ooze, so dark that the upper surface was murky brown. Only children enjoyed going out in it.

The surrounding steep ridges formed valleys with almost vertical sides; therefore the sky was not spacious and light as in most outdoor places, but could only be seen in strips. Though sunshine did reach the lake, its rays disappeared into the turbid depths. I didn't feel timid, not as I'd felt in the more inviting Muskoka, but was repelled because the Ozark lake seemed so false. It was a scene rather gloomy and weird — fittingly, for it was here that I first had a chance to observe life realistically, and the people that I would meet were in several ways bizarre. But that was not until early the following year when I would be back, surprisingly earning my keep as a fishing guide.

We were in Kansas City again at the end of summer, for me to resume the routine of meals and housework and try to cheer up my father. By then he was deeply depressed, not only about his neglected work but as much, I think, from a sense of how badly his marriage appeared to be failing. He was another who did not always see realistically, and until that year he may not have fully faced the near-breakdown of his relationship with my mother. From his mood one could believe that he was remembering how triumphantly he had won her and how happy the earliest years together had seemed; and that he was contrasting their spikey sparring of later times. Being a humble man he would take to himself too much of the blame. At home now he seldom talked and never smiled. He seemed like a dreamer bewildered by a harsh world into which he had wakened.

After my mother had been away for about six months, my brother skinned his knee playing baseball. Proud flesh (granulation tissue) formed around the wound. It looked wicked and so we took him to a doctor who said it was nothing to worry about. I reported this to my mother, but she set out for home on the day that she got my letter.

I would be the next one to leave: she took care of that. Before I left however, there was a strange little talk. When I expressed an interest in what she had done while away, she said that among other things, "I spent a weekend at one of the foothill resorts near Los Angeles. It was the off-season but an interesting couple were there. They were both married but not to each other — attractive people, and it was evident that they enjoyed being together." She smiled, and her voice trailed away on an indulgent tone remarkably unlike the one she had used in speaking of Alice and Jeremy.

It was obvious that I needed, now more than ever, the rest that had been prescribed when I had to leave college. My mother had no wish to see me languish around the house and suggested that I should go back to Lake Taneycomo. As the plan worked out I was given a quasi-job there and set out on my first expedition into the adult world.

During the summer I had been out on the White River frequently with a young man who had taught me some fine points of fly-casting. While recovering from tuberculosis he was spending all his time fishing, usually at Rocky Mountain resorts but he had been at Lake Taneycomo before and knew its shores and the river well. From him I learned the local lurking places of fish, and surprisingly it developed that I had a certain knack with a fishing rod — as Robert told the proprietors and they could note from the number of bass we brought in at the end of each day. Our catch could feed most of the summer guests. The following winter, therefore, I proposed that they give me a cabin and board and in exchange I would take out, as guide, the businessmen from St. Louis who often came down for weekends of fishing. The owners agreed.

To the men it was a novelty to have a girl as a guide and the plan worked well. Another reason it did was that most of them were not very experienced fishermen. They had bought what they had been told was the proper tackle, and when they got down to the lake and didn't know what to do, it was probably less embarrassing to have a girl show them than if the guide were another man. I was lucky, for if they had been men with more skill they would have shown up my own poor qualifications. I was reminded of them later when I lived in New Hampshire, where men would come up from the eastern cities to hunt during the deer season. Many of them never had had a gun in their hands before and they were a terror to local people. One shot a farmer's horse, another entered the country store when I was there and excitedly told his friends, "Four, five miles north of here there's a bunch of deer standing right alongside the road!" He had shot one, which was draped over the hood of his car. It was a Hereford calf.

I found it no problem to see my fishermen at the lake realistically, but the game warden was puzzling. He came in his motorboat from the nearest town, ten miles away, ostensibly to catch poachers but he didn't do any police work, he just fished. He stayed at the lodge two or three days a week and when I didn't have customers, took me out in his boat with him — a chance for me to pick up some more hints about fly-casting. But for a man of the natural countryside there was something curiously artificial about him. He was pleasant enough but guarded, seeming very carefully even-tempered and mild. He never raised his voice, never smiled. At night in the cheerful dining room, eating the fish we had caught, he still didn't relax.

One day I asked him what he did when he was not fishing and he told me: he was an undertaker. His manner was understandable then, and he did have one liberating talent — he liked to dance and he danced superbly (but when I touched his hands I always wondered how recently they had been working over a corpse). After dinner he always wound up the gramophone in the lounge and we danced until bedtime. I've met other excellent dancers in wilderness places and suspect that their expertise may be somewhat due to their being uncomplicated men, not trying to dance for effect nor in a trendy way but for conscious pleasure in their finesse, such as they have in casting their flies. I had had little practice in dancing myself, due to my sober girlhood, but from that unlikely teacher, an undertaker in the remote Ozark Mountains, I learned enough so that the next year in Hollywood my newly acquired skill opened up a glamorous opportunity.

One day we went farther up the river than usual and passed a large rustic cabin. When we had gone by he said in his usual dead-pan voice, "The couple who live there aren't married. She was a famous actress and he financed one of her shows — what's called an angel, I've heard. He was married but he fell in love with her, so they had to go away ———" the speaker took that for granted, and, "They came here fifteen years ago and have never left since." He rowed along for several minutes and then, "He's a lot older than she is, maybe sixty by now. He's not very well. Stomach ulcer." Another pause. "My father's got a furniture store and one day I had to go to their cabin to deliver a mattress. Her dressing table had fifteen or twenty bottles on it. Not medicine, I guessed. Perfume maybe."

I met that pair several times, for they walked through the woods from their cabin to buy butter and eggs at the lodge. The actress, simply dressed, usually in a dark-blue sports coat and dark-blue felt hat, was attractively unaffected and forthright — later when I saw Ingrid Bergman I was reminded of her. On her hand was a huge diamond ring. It was odd to think of the man as her lover, he seemed so old, with a tense and petulant manner. He had a graying Vandyke beard, wore a tweed jacket and carried a walking stick with a silver knob. Was she happy? What did she think about when she woke up in the night and remembered that she had given up being a star, a woman admired by thousands, in order to spend her life in these distant woods with a man who had become so tiresome? If he didn't live very much longer, maybe she could go back and play on Broadway again. But while I was there he died suddenly from a stomach hemorrhage, and six days later the actress married the undertaker.

Once a month, on the night of the full moon, the valleys were filled with a splendid, heart-stirring music as native families went up to the tops of the ridges to yodel to one another. They were so isolated, living in single cabins scattered among the mountains, that they had little chance to see neighbors, but they could sing their greetings and many of them had developed impressive skill. Did they themselves discover that yodeling has great carrying power, that they could fill the valleys with music in which falsetto notes and chest tones alternate in sounds like the bouncing of golden balls; or did some yodeler from the Tyrol teach them?

"It is likely that many people who seem to die natural deaths have in fact been poisoned by their families."

The most interesting people I met at the lake were a young native couple, Alf and Ernie, who lived half a mile from the lodge. I didn't think either could read or write, though their one-room cabin was papered with illustrated pages from mail order catalogues. Neither had ever been out of the county. They had no money except what Alf earned by working one day a week chopping wood at the lodge, and most of that went for food for their horse, for their clearing was small and the horse had grazed off most of the cover. They had a vegetable garden and Alf fished and hunted wild game. They kept a few chickens.

Each of them seemed to have only one garment, a pair of overalls for Alf and for Ernie a gingham dress, and neither wore shoes. In the cabin there were a bed, a table, two straight chairs and a stove — that was all. When I went to see them, as I did fairly often, Ernie and I would sit on the steps of their cabin and watch while Alf worked in the garden, or he might be mending their rowboat, which he had made himself. He was not efficient by civilized standards. The vegetables had to compete with stones, though they seemed to grow all right; their rows weren't straight, and the horse was fenced out with a single strand of barbed wire, haphazardly strung between trees. The boat leaked. But no one could feel superior to Alf and Ernie. They got along well enough and were refreshingly real and gentle.

What did we talk about? Usually nothing. It was enough, the

physical presence of each, to make the others feel more contented. I was down in the Ozarks to rest and the resting went along best at that primitive cabin. Ernie was pregnant. She would not be having a doctor. There was no way to call one and besides, they didn't have money. Alf came to the lodge one day and told the woman there that the baby was coming. She went back with him and the birth took place quickly, without complications. The next day Ernie got on the horse and rode eight miles to show her mother the baby.

The hours I spent with the fishermen, hours with nothing to do but lightly press on the oars to hold the boat over the lairs of the bass, gave me plenty of time to think. And what I thought about was the future, what I should try to make of my life. Of course I would be a writer, a prospect I didn't question, but write about what? I still believed that "life as it really is" was the only acceptable subject, and did that mean characters like these fishermen here in the boat? They were certainly lifelike but were so similar and so undramatic — what could I say about them? I would prefer to write about Alf and Ernie.

Well, why not? I remembered how sympathetically Willa Cather had described her prairie neighbors in *O Pioneers!* and *My Antonia*, books I had loved. She had shown them as people close to the earth, living by elemental, eternal values which gave them a rich significance. Everything that such people did would be worth observing. I had enjoyed noting Ernie's flexible toes, how they would curl down over the edge of a step, how Alf would stop work on his boat to watch migrating geese in the sky, how his hand touched her hair as he passed going up the steps, how her eyes followed every move that he made. Their actions all seemed to have individual meaning and to reveal the deepest truths about human beings. I was idealizing them of course, but they were what represented "life as it really is" to me at that time.

Soon after I had decided to make Alf and Ernie the subject of my first writing, the fishing lodge owners said I would have to leave; they needed my cabin for summer guests. I didn't, as yet, have nearly enough material for a book about living as mountaineers, but I would come back. In the meantime another subject was right at hand: I would go out to the prairie country of Willa Cather. Her pioneer neighbors might not be quite as colorful as I found Alf and Ernie, but they would have the same earthiness. They too would have their bare toes in the soil and therefore would have absorbed nature's soundness and wholesomeness. They too would be artless and genuine.

Willa Cather had written about Nebraska, but Kansas ought to be similar and I had a promising possibility there. I would go to Emporia, where a country newspaper, William Allen White's *Emporia Gazette,* was owned by a good friend of a good friend of mine, Mr. Harry Nicolet, who no doubt would give me a letter of introduction. Mr. Nicolet had said that the *Gazette* was read throughout the United States, just news about local people but so well written that it was almost literature. Mr. Nicolet had even told me that material in the *Gazette* was sometimes comparable with the stories of Willa Cather's. I had heard that Miss Cather had left her own state. I would take up her torch!

I was sure Mr. White would find my appreciation of Kansas people congenial. So I would go to stay. A writer ought to be able to type and I could; my parents had given me a new Royal portable and two months at a secretarial school, and with those I set out, as well as my entire wardrobe in luggage — and most importantly, Mr. Nicolet's letter. I think I was actually confident that I could have walked into Mr. White's office and have been welcomed without credentials, but the letter would be a clincher.

The train was one of those gritty M. K. & T. locals that wound

through Kansas, Oklahoma and into the Texas Panhandle.
Absorbed in the latest *New Yorker,* I had not noticed who sat on
the red plush seat facing me till a twangy voice said, "My daughter's
hands aren't as white as yours but I'll bet she can do more with
them." I put down *The New Yorker.* The man was a rancher from
Canyon, Texas, a born talker and he presented a vivid picture of
Canyon and of ranching in the spacious country of Texas. His vast
herds — he had just brought a trainload of them to the cattle market in Kansas City, he said — were tended by cowhands who, when
they were pasturing near enough, came to the ranchhouse for chow,
which was prepared and served by his wife and daughter. But his
daughter was just going to be married to one of the cowboys and
why didn't I come to Canyon and live with his family? He promised that I too would soon be married and have a ranch of my own.
Anyway, why not come down and pay them a visit? He threw in
some names of other Panhandle towns, as bait probably: White
Deer, Muleshoe, Matador. Canyon was on a river, the Prairie Dog-
town Fork. I was fascinated by his descriptions but not enough to
consider spending my life peeling potatoes for twenty or thirty cowhands. Mostly I was fascinated because, only an hour after setting
out into the great unknown, life had flung me such an adventurous
opportunity. It was a thrilling omen.

Checking my bags at the station I called at the office of the *Gazette* and learned that Mr. White was working at home. I bought a
copy of the paper and scanned its main stories as slowly I walked towards his house. A store had changed hands and the new owner,
who came from the East, planned improvements and innovations. A
youth with a shotgun had tried to hold up a movie-theatre box office
but an alarm bell had called the police. A bank would start enlarging its building soon. A state senator would be in town the next day
and address a businessmen's club. Work was completed on the re-

pairs to the leaking roof of the railroad station. And yesterday's school picnic had been a great success, the largest gathering ever, although it had been the hottest day in seventeen years.

I proceeded more slowly. Willa Cather's prairie pioneers? On the shady side of the street some Emporia residents sat on their wide pleasant porches fanning themselves. Certainly none was barefoot. Most of the women had marcelled hair and wore light pretty dresses. Two boys passed on the latest type of expensive bicycles. Several cars were parked at the curb. A young voice was singing "I Wonder Who's Kissing Her Now." If I wanted to write about illiterate primitives, who papered their houses with pages of mail order catalogues, I had come to the wrong town, in the wrong state, and at least a generation too late. Five minutes away from Mr. White's house I suddenly realized that Willa Cather's books had described the people and places she'd known in her *childhood!* A world of forty to fifty years ago. I left the *Gazette* in the crotch of a tree and went on without having the slightest idea what I would now say to Mr. White.

Mr. White sat in a large darkened room with wide-opened windows. He was talking to two men visitors when I arrived and during my wait Mrs. White took me into another room for a glass of iced tea. Fairly recently the Whites had lost their only daughter in a riding accident, and as Mrs. White talked, kindly, courteously, a flood of tears poured down her cheeks. Yet her voice was calm and her face did not crumple with grief. Such restraint was impressive and for the moment I forgot my dilemma. Originally I had planned to approach Mr. White with a smile and what I hoped would be an irresistible "I have to come to Emporia to work for you," and then launch into a few long-considered words about sharing his respect for the earthy virtues. The amended impression that Emporia had made — that essentially it was a small Kansas City — had undercut my whole program and I was humbled further by Mrs. White's self-control. When the men left then and she took me to Mr. White I presented Mr. Nicolet's letter with what must have been a poor imitation of confidence.

"I don't need anybody," said Mr. White, handing the letter back. I told him I thought I could add enough to the worth of his paper to pay my salary. "And what did you think you could add?" Quickly doing a mental somersault I said, "Well . . . sophistication." I hope that I had the grace to smile at the outrageous suggestion, but I'm not sure I did. I remember him as large (was he or did he just have a strong presence?) and somewhat disheveled that very warm day. He looked as any man might at home on a Sunday morning. His eyes were humane but sharp.

"You see —" I went on, obviously assuming that Mr. White never ventured beyond the outskirts of Emporia — "it is very exciting to be in the East these days. The War has put our country much more closely in touch with the rich and ancient cultures of Europe. It has extended our boundaries so that now they include London, Paris, Rome, and we are becoming a much more thoughtful and sensitive people. But I know from living in Kansas City that this marvelous wakening is only beginning to reach the Middle West. I can help to bring it to your Emporia neighbors."

I have wondered sometimes how Mr. White heard this absurdly youthful speech without laughing. He did not even smile but simply said, "We like the people of Emporia the way they are and we write about them the way they are. Your kind of sophistication . . ." a slight satirical pause, "would ruin our paper. Nothing could induce me to let you write for it."

Life in Emporia as it was in that year, not in some romantic past, must have been exactly what the Wellesley teachers had meant when they advocated realism so fervently. "The new clarity of vision, the new honesty": my early recognition of what they had meant had dimmed, but it blazed out now in "We like them the way they are and we write about them the way they are." I was very depressed as I unpacked my luggage in Kansas City. For I had not only observed life as it is that day; I had experienced it.

vi

DREAMS AND NIGHTMARES

DURING THE TIME I was down at the lake, my father had been ne-
gotiating to form his own company. The thought was proposed by
the president of a lumber company, a friend who had interested two
other friends in what, essentially, was an investment in my father's
proven ability. The three men, plus my father, put in equal amounts
of money, although the firm was to be set up as a partnership of
my father and the bachelor who had bought the paper-doll harem.
The start wasn't auspicious because the two men were not really
congenial; still it had promising aspects and soon after my trip to
Emporia the formal documents were made final. My father offered
to make me his secretary.

It was a great satisfaction to have him at home all the time, and I
could be helpful in many ways — handling most of the company's
correspondence, buying office supplies, writing their advertising and
designing their labels. It was certainly not a glamorous job; the
building they bought was old, in a manufacturing area stifled by
stockyard odors. Nevertheless I was happy there and my father relied on me more and more. But at home a familiar crisis was boil-
ing up: the great stress that my presence was causing my mother. I
could have moved out and still worked for my father, but that possibility did not occur to any of us. And so I was already half prepared

for my mother's suggestion that I should go out and visit my uncle's family in Hollywood. I agreed, and perhaps for fear I would change my mind, she hurried downtown herself to arrange for my transportation. In my bedroom I took it out of the envelope. It was a one-way ticket.

Western Kansas rises into the foothills of the Rocky Mountains. After my train had crossed them we reached the base of that ridge of stupendous peaks, the spine of the continent. Six of the peaks in Colorado are more than 14,300 feet high, six others are more than 13,500 — eight times the height of the mountains we'd seen in the Ozarks. The peaks march along the horizon, their snowy whiteness making them seem even more towering in the distant sky. From Denver I could see some of them and my rapt intuition said, *This is my kind of country!*

It took two powerful locomotives to pull the train up and over the Continental Divide. I was asleep when we reached the top some time in the night, but I woke when we stopped and I looked out into a snow covered scene where the railway crew, their breaths steaming, were taking off the superfluous engine. We would be starting down now but would be in the mountains for the rest of the night, in the Royal Gorge and the canyons of other rivers, as the train swung its way westward over the tracks of the "Denver and Rio Grande" — a commercial name but it stands for a soaring of spirit for countless Westerners. At six o'clock I awoke again. Towards the north was a snowclad peak touched with the first rays of the early sun — a cone of rosy light standing out in the sky that still held the nighttime dark. Later I heard that the Indian scouts used to rouse their tribes at daybreak by running through the camps crying, "Look! The sun is coming down the mountain!"

The Indian word was Idaho.

The train entered a valley again. On the rim above, two horsemen stood in the fresh morning light. They ignored the train. One was pointing to something far off on the mesa. Freedom and space and exhilarating wild country: *this* is where I will stay! I flew into my clothes, rang to call the conductor and said that I wished to get off at the next station. Without comment (how many passengers had the same impulse?) he left, and with the berth made up I sat waiting. The next station came several hours later — Salt Lake City lying out on a flat, bleached plain. I decided to go on to Hollywood, but the view of that high, spectacular land had become a destiny. I would be back.

My twenty-four hours in San Francisco also became a destiny. Mr. Nicolet's son Charles was there, telegraph editor of the *San Francisco Chronicle*. He took charge of my evening. We had dinner at the Casa Beguine, one of the city's, indeed the country's, most famous Bohemian hangouts, no basement den but a brightly lighted and spacious room whose walls were divided into large panels, some white and blank, others decorated with murals of bacchanals. Charles said that every time two of the artists were married their friends painted a panel. One was half finished.

Surrounding us were the Bohemians themselves, relaxed, thoughtful or high-spirited men and long-legged, attractive girls who seemed marvelously released. Both men and girls wore nondescript clothes but unquestionably had style. And were beautiful — they were beautiful *creatures,* as birds, cantering horses and dogs in action are, or as I now would say, deer, mountain lions and wolves. And how easy appeared the relationships, men and girls spontaneously enjoying each other! There was no sign of maneuvering here, none of the artificial charm calculated to win a husband or wife. Charles said that these were the city's outstanding painters, writers, musicians. He didn't seem to know anyone, we had only come because this was a spectacle, one of the city's sights. But what it meant to me was the view of a life to which I passionately felt I belonged. Dismayed, though, to realize that I could not have sat down at one of the tables and have fitted into that company. I had too many inhibiting, conforming habits, of both mind and emotions. Could I ever be rid of them, could this ever be my way of life? I wanted to leave. I did not want to come to this feast as a tourist.

From the Casa Beguine we went to the Geary Theatre and saw Jane Cowl in *Romeo and Juliet,* a performance almost unbearably poignant, and afterwards walked down Market Street to the Embarcadero and out to the end of one of the long wharves, where we sat with our feet hanging over the water and watched cargo being loaded into the glowing hold of a ship. It would sail tomorrow, the foreman told us — to the South Seas. Around the piles below us lapped the ripples of the dark wide Bay, overhead there were stars and on our right rose the romantic heap of the city, its interfolding hills defined by myriads of lights, with the long, straight chain of lights that was Market Street running west towards the Pacific Ocean.

"I am going to Hollywood but I'm coming back! I am going to live here!" I said. One day that would be true.

o

For an American scene Southern California felt strangely foreign. This did not seem to be American nature: palms, pepper and eucalyptus trees, desert plants, cacti, yucca, and Joshua trees and great masses of brilliant exotic flowers. The houses, with pink, blue, yellow or lavender walls, looked to an inexperienced eye as if they belonged in the tropics, or as something only imagined, as unsubstantial as if they might blow away. A few months after arriving I was a guest in one of those houses. I was being taught by the more sophisticated guests how to blow gin fumes out of my throat when suddenly there was an automobile in the living room with us. Being by then more than a little dazed, I thought the car was an alcoholic illusion — but no. It had jumped the curb and come through the wall which, thus broken, proved to be made of chicken wire, covered on the outside with a thin layer of stucco, on the inside with plaster and wallpaper — a wall altogether not more than an inch thick. But most exotic of all in this country was the dreamlike quality of the air. It was not the torpid atmosphere of a hot summer day in the Middle West; it was only pleasantly warm but sleepy, inducing a sort of trance, a mood so relaxed that one wished for nothing but a chance to sit still in the sun and smile.

The relatives urged me to stay. I was only mildly interested until through a cousin's acquaintance I heard of a job with a play and casting agent — call him "Mr. Dudley" — for whom I could act as receptionist to his actor-clients and also write movie adaptations of stage plays. It was not the kind of work I had set out to find, but it was writing, and life in Hollywood still must be life and therefore worth knowing about, so I thought.

The job came to seem like fun. One of his offices was a large living room which he had furnished to attract the actors we had under contract, and Mr. Dudley liked to see them sitting there, hours at a time, all that potential income, when he breezed in and out. He could drop hints of possible jobs coming up and thus try to keep them tied to us, for periodically their contracts with us ran out. "We're writing an adaptation of a play that will have a wonderful part for you, Myrna. I'll try to sell you and the play as a package." Myrna was Myrna Loy, discovered recently by the photographer, Henry Waxman. She was so obviously attractive that Mr. Dudley had established her starting salary as $200 a week. He didn't put anyone under contract who would earn less, and a few who were stars earned more; two were Belle Bennett and Warner Oland. Mr.

Dudley wished also to interview pretty girls, not yet in pictures, who might become starlets. His interest in them seemed logical for a while.

I was supposed to help keep the actors' morale bolstered up. It was acceptable, even desirable, for me to sit for hours listening to their life stories. Many were so fantastic that they could not have been used even as movie plots. At first I discounted them as the imaginings of a childlike people. Later I learned that they did go through terrible times — and it was disturbing to find that they seemed almost untouched by them. In Hollywood this would always bother me: that the actors could live out the most melodramatic tragedies and seem hardly more changed than if they had watched those events in a theatre. They were willing to tell the most intimate details to anybody they thought they could trust. I probably was the only one who knew that a department store executive was giving a minor star $1000 a month, which she was splitting with a more desirable lover; and he was splitting his $500 with a more attractive starlet who was keeping a youth just arrived in Hollywood from her home town.

As an agent, Mr. Dudley had in his files the scripts of more than a hundred plays. I was expected to read them, choose the most promising, make résumés of the plots, and describe any colorful scenes that might make a studio editor want to consider buying the play for a picture. It was fairly outrageous for me to even attempt that work, for I'd never had time to become much concerned about movies and I had no idea what would make a good picture plot. But the dramas! To me a new kind of writing, and what could be more intriguing? I read them for hints of speech rhythms, regional differences in expression, and dialogue as revelation of personality. Especially the last: I increasingly looked for unconscious confessions and then, since our actors, some of them always there waiting, gave a chance to hear natural talk, I spent more time in conversation. Dialogue, both real and in plays, became so absorbing that I neglected to describe our plays in terms of visible action, which of course was the thing that would sell them to scenario editors. One day this awakened interest in dialogue would be valuable to me, but at the time I failed Mr. Dudley. We didn't sell even one play in the time that I worked for him.

2

The job settled into a routine. I thought less and less about San Francisco, more and more about the big pictures coming up, possible roles for our clients, the studio gossip, the shifting fortunes of the important "picture people." I had begun to identify with the make-believe world but was snatched out of that element by some dramatic events of my own.

One day on Hollywood Boulevard I ran into a college classmate, Rachel, a girl who had not been one of my friends at Wellesley, but I was glad to see her. We went into Musso Frank's for lunch, during which she said that she lived in Los Angeles, her husband was out of town, and on Sunday night she was going to a party, not of picture people, on the heights behind Hollywood. Would I come?

It was a night of thrashing rain when she called for me in her car and we wound up a wooded road several miles to a secluded but conventional sort of house. Other guests, six or eight men and women were in the living room when we entered. They were a few years older than I and I thought not very promising. Wallflower types mostly: ill at ease, unsmiling, making labored efforts at conversation. The hostess was prettier, a tall dark-haired girl with a serious face.

One by one the guests disappeared. Rachel too left the room without explanation. I was sitting alone on a sofa wondering what was going on when the hostess came over and said, "You can take off your clothes upstairs in the room on the right."

The stairway rose from a hall where we had left our coats. I got mine and quietly left the house.

This probably was a nudist group, I thought, perhaps naively — members of a cult that was just starting up at that time. But why had Rachel not told me? And why indeed would one be a nudist? I had plenty of time to think about that on the long trek back to Hollywood, in rain that was still pelting down, running into the neck of my coat, down the back of my legs, into my shoes, high-heeled shoes, and I kept turning my ankles on rocks, for the road was not paved. But I was hardly aware of being uncomfortable, so provocative was the thought, why would one be a nudist? I tried to imagine those self-conscious people, now naked — would they be back in the living room, sitting in the same chairs, with crossed legs no doubt, and wouldn't the whole occasion be more awkward now, in that chilly house with rain dismally falling?

Why did they do it, were they attempting to lose inhibitions, which they seemed obviously to have? And was that such an un-worthy ambition? I too had inhibitions, and I wished to be rid of them. Should I have stayed and tried the experiment? No, it would seem a violation to try to shed them by deliberate, cold self-expo-sure. There must be ways to lose them with greater integrity. I knew, anyway, that I could not have stepped, finally, out of my pant-ies and bra and walked downstairs to face with my bare body the roomful of sober strangers.

But inhibitions, yes: accept the fact of them. Accept the need to do something about them. I never had been so sure about that be-fore. It had not been a lost evening.

By morning I had my solution, a simple one: I would take danc-ing lessons. I picked a name out of the telephone book and enrolled the next day. My instructor was black-haired, tall and in no way ro-mantic looking. One could imagine him teaching mechanical drawing, or as manager of a swimming pool — rather faceless and unambitious. In that first judgment I was not being perceptive how-ever, and I soon learned how he came to life when he danced. He was one of those artists who save themselves for their creative ex-pression.

"Let's see what your natural rhythm is," he said and put a one-step roll on the player piano. "No, that's not it," "A fox trot?" That wasn't my natural rhythm either. Nor a waltz. A tango? "Ah! Now we have it!" above my head his rather plain face broke into a smile. For an hour we tangoed, towards the end with some intricate steps. This was total release, freedom from gravity it seemed, for my feet hardly touched the floor. And freedom too from constraining tensions, a vast expansion of spirit. A religious conver-sion could scarcely mean more.

I had two lessons a week at first but soon one each night and from then on without charge. For it developed that the instructor had an offer to return to the Orpheum Circuit, on which he had danced be-fore, if he could find an adequate partner. In me, unbelievably, he thought that he had one. At his urging I also took ballet lessons, from a teacher who told him, "Her muscles are those of a child of ten." But limber muscles were not the magic, it was my utter de-light at this new form of expression, the sense of complete libera-tion. It almost was flying, literally, for my partner had devised an adagio tango for us, in which I was some of the time in the air.

We moved as one, no doubt a result of the training that I was having, since for part of each lesson I had to dance at least two feet away from him, not touching and yet following even elaborate and unfamiliar steps. I am sure many dancers can do that — and yet how is it possible? With some kind of subtle communication, it seems, and I remembered the violinist I used to accompany and how I "just knew" what she was going to do next. In learning the aerial passages of our tango routine I would have to follow an action I'd never seen and he never explained: he just tossed me up and somehow I came down to him in the way he had planned.

Our dance portrayed a sexual kind of harmony, not merely a routine, rather a unison re-created each time. It was a rather sensual dance but idealized, with frequent attitudes of great tenderness. And yet surprisingly not tenderness that we were feeling personally for each other. He took me out in a boat in Westlake Park one night, a test I am sure, to see if there were anything personal in my response to his leading. There shouldn't have been and there wasn't. It may be hard to imagine that we could perform that intimate tango and still be quite cool and unemotional towards each other, but professional dancers will understand how the passion is all felt for the dance itself, not the partner.

We danced in public sometimes, again a test no doubt, to see whether I would be popular, and I did not fail. Suddenly I who had had such a sober childhood, a girl who had had to buy her own tickets to basketball games, now had a flock of suitors. Champagne days! I went to one private dance with seven escorts and being so new in this role, was surprised and hurt by the chilly reaction of other girls. I was sure that most of the men were not in love with me, with only my dancing feet, though I had a more interesting friendship with two or three.

One was a mandarin Chinese who had a Ph.D. in physics from Yale and was the Hollywood correspondent for an Argentine newspaper, writing in Spanish. And one was a young Colombian architect who had recently taken his degree in Madrid and had been

given a year of travel before settling down in Bogotá. Juan seemed
genuinely troubled with the fear that my being out in the world
alone and a dancer (unthinkable in Colombia) would give people
the wrong impression that I was not respectable. On Sundays he
walked me up and down Hollywood Boulevard pointing out the
clothes in shop windows that he thought I should wear — staid, almost middle-aged styles (I remember a shapeless tweed hat).
Sometimes I rebelled at his criticisms and yet his concern seemed
flattering. He had tangoed since boyhood, and on Saturday nights, if
I wasn't dancing professionally, we went to places like the Ambassador Coconut Grove where we danced for hours and on those occasions the harmony was more personal. At the table he always buttered my bread.

Finally came the occasion when my instructor and I were to
dance for the Orpheum Circuit executives. The tango went well and
the men left with a single comment: "We'll prepare the contract."

There was a little delay of several days before we got it, during
which I wrote to my parents ecstatically about this bright opportunity, bright indeed, for the Orpheum Circuit at the time offered the
best opening anywhere in the country for a performance like ours.
And strangely, as in my friendship with Dalton White in Muskoka,
it seemed natural and inevitable that I had come to this happiness.
It only fulfilled what I always had felt: that somewhere, sometime,
I would reach a great blossoming of joy. The present had often
been rocky and dark, but ahead (how could it fail?) I would find—
the sun! And the promise, I thought now, had obviously been my
talent for dancing. It was even more truly my natural self than the
talent for music had been, because it was expressed more easily. In
adagio dancing the small heart defect, curiously, seemed no disadvantage at all.

With no foreboding, then, I awaited my parents' reaction. But my father was not at home and so the response came from my mother alone. She wired: ABSOLUTELY FORBID YOU TO GO ON DANCING STOP IF YOU SIGN THAT CONTRACT I WILL PURSUE YOU FROM CITY TO CITY.

The telegram filled me with indescribable rage and frustration. For the chance to become a professional dancer actually had been more: a chance to escape from the inhibiting doom of her hatred. I had thought wondrously that at last I was well out of it, but the release was foiled. For I knew that she certainly would do as she threatened, hound me from city to city. It might seem that I should have gone ahead anyway but if I had had to cope with that dreadful emotional conflict I knew I would not be able to dance effectively. Gone would be the new sense of physical liberation. Again I would be a lost girl.

I tried to explain but could not make my partner understand why my mother's attitude was so serious. He could not believe that my airy weightlessness and what he said was infectious rhythm were in literal fact an escape. They were the physical celebration of freedom after a long imprisonment . . . but I was caught again now. Not surprisingly he was furious and at once discarded me out of his life.

My bitterness was unmanageable and I stayed drunk for two weeks. But from a later perspective I can see that my mother's motive was mixed. Part of it was her old wish to destroy, but it also is true that women of her generation considered that any stage personality was déclassée. Believing that respectability was the supreme value, she always had felt that the chief role of a daughter's mother was to guide the daughter into a safe social milieu. That she might be trapping the daughter there she had never recognized.

All my luck seemed to desert at once. Up to that time I had been heart-whole, but now I was to be humbled. It happened suddenly. One day in my office Purnell Pratt, the stage actor, was telling about a role he had played on Broadway. In it, to point up a moment of heightened drama, he was twirling the cord of a window shade when another character came through the door — a significant entrance at which Pratt let the shade fly up with a snap. He demonstrated the bit of startling business with the shade on the office window and then continued to play with the cord, idly, for he couldn't have guessed that he soon would be snapping the shade for me. But a stranger came in, very tall. Sitting down as I was, I let my eyes travel up the row of brown leather buttons on his tweed waistcoat; they reached the top, then his face — his eyes! Purnell Pratt recognized the impact and let the shade fly. He left and Geoffrey said, "Where shall we go?"

In his open roadster we drove for several hours along the coast, scarcely talking. After a late dinner in Santa Monica he took me home and in parting said, "I'll be back tomorrow, of course."

For two weeks we spent every evening like that, silently driving and then having dinner, during which we did talk. I learned that he was an English actor and although still in his twenties, he had played Shakespeare for several years in England. Also, as I otherwise knew, he had been starred on Broadway and had been brought west to play the same role in a film. Not once had he touched me, not even when we were separating. And then suddenly I no longer saw him. No word, no sign. I asked my doctor, a fatherly friend, if he could explain such a strange relationship. "He will come back," he said.

Geoffrey did. One afternoon he was there again. He said that he had been ill. We went to the beach as usual but returned to my flat rather early. Geoffrey sat halfway across the room with his back to a window. He did seem unwell, very white and his nearly black eyes looked wild — like the boughs of a tree outside, which were thrashing about in the wind. He said, "This is the last time we'll see each other."

My thoughts flew to the logical explanation? "Your wife ——"

No, he told me, he was not married. He went on, in a tight voice, with what I thought was a planned explanation: "Of course I would wish that we might be married. We can't. And I can't even tell you why. But — Trust me. I am being honest with you. There is . . . a rather sad reason why that kind of happiness cannot be, for us. I can't say more than that."

This was an odd way to tell me he didn't love me, I thought. Puzzling. Why was he so distraught? I said — apparently calm, as one can seem to be in such situations, "It's all right. I understand."

"You *don't* understand!" He was vehement. "You haven't any idea what I am talking about! But I'll tell you this. If we should be married I'd wreck your life — in the same way, for the same reason, that my father wrecked my mother's life. Her health and her life. I am not going to do that to you."

I was not catching on very fast and I suppose Geoffrey thought he had to erase, in some way, my look of bewilderment. He said something about his father's being a sadist, and, "I've inherited his temperament. I throw things." He made the obstacle sound like insanity, and perhaps that, insanity of a particularly unpleasant kind, was what actually he meant, but I didn't consider that possibility until later. It all seemed so preposterous that I almost laughed. "What kind of things do you throw?" I asked.

"Oh — dishes." He looked around the room. "Vases." And then, "Listen to me. I can't stay here and keep away from you and so I am leaving. I am taking a ship to Tahiti tomorrow and I'm not coming back." But his contract, his promising future in pictures! I assured him that he should not give it all up on my account (such an amazing idea!) — I would not try to see him. There was no chance of his changing his mind, he said.

He got up to go. I walked down to the door with him and he left without any melodrama. He did not kiss me goodby. That was the last time I saw him, and he did go to Tahiti. There was much talk about this, about his breaking his contract, and everybody was mystified. So was I until I saw my doctor again and told him all these details and a few more.

He was convinced that Geoffrey had syphilis. It was very prevalent then in Hollywood, he said, especially among the actors who had come out from New York. He guessed from Geoffrey's comment about his father, and his father's wrecking his mother's health, that this father had had it too. Perhaps Geoffrey had watched him disintegrate and anticipating a similar fate for himself, he had already planned that he would abandon ambition and hope when he recognized ominous signs in himself. The doctor said that Geoffrey probably went to the South Seas because that was a well-known refuge for syphilitics. (This was before antibiotics made their fate less desperate.) When I mentioned that Geoffrey had told me he had been ill during the time that I didn't see him, the doctor said the disease would have been aggravated by his being strongly drawn to me sexually, and that could have brought forward what he might have intended to do ultimately. He said I was fortunate that Geoffrey had acted so responsibly, and he respected him for that. In spite of the episode's sordid overtones, the doctor made Geoffrey seem a friend well worth grieving for, and I wept until the old familiar numbing had blurred the ache.

But — what if the recent events suggested a pattern? I was very much concerned about fate at that time and was trying to read my future from past and present happenings. They were not auspicious. I wondered if one could be born under a crooked star. While I was growing up I sometimes had thought that I was born under a dark star, that romantic dark star of a doom. Now, after the shock of Geoffrey's leaving it seemed to me that the events of my life had an element of the grotesque. Every promise of a bright happiness had been snatched away, as it appeared, arbitrarily. There was mockery in the way that fate treated me. Perhaps a mother's hatred was so unnatural an emotion that all one's future would be distorted by it: the crooked star. Perhaps the hatred could even reach through space and exert a destructive power. I had become superstitious and was almost engulfed in hopelessness.

There was still the job, however — bizarre enough but amusing. Every day in that office seemed to produce some drama. At least the conversations were always diverting, and so I must not lose heart. I had good luck along with the bad. Didn't I?

During all the time that I worked for Mr. Dudley he had been interviewing the pretty youngsters he called possible starlets. They came in late in the day, most of them saying that they had met Mr. Dudley in going around to the studios and he had told them to be at the office about five o'clock. When he returned at the end of the afternoon he would talk to the girls in his private room. To me some of them didn't seem very promising — pretty but without personality. What they did have, all those he told to come in, was fear in their eyes. Many had arrived in Hollywood with little money, believing that they would "get the breaks" by the time of the final emergency. When they didn't, when they were down to their last few dollars, their desperation was evident. Mr. Dudley would talk to them and in most cases I never saw them again.

Why always the frightened ones? Was he being kind or taking advantage of them? He didn't seem like the philandering types I had met in books. They would not be so brusk and knobby, so energetic, so indifferent to the impression they made. He had a bristling mustache which he used to push out when he was annoyed. Most unattractive.

One day a girl slightly older, perhaps twenty-three or four, was sitting on the stairs when I arrived in the morning. As I approached she began to babble incoherently. It appeared that she blamed Mr. Dudley for something, but the name that she kept repeating, and with a look of something like horror, was Harry.

I went on in the office, closing the door, and was wondering what to do when Mr. Dudley came in. He was disturbed and angry and said, "Call the police and get that girl out of here. She's escaped from the bughouse." Three days later she was again on the steps.

One thing that made the episode seem especially distressing was Mr. Dudley's unfeeling attitude. He was so cruel towards the girl, one couldn't help but suspect some guilt. I sensed that something was going on here that I, being in charge of the office, was unpleasantly involved in, and after dinner a few evenings later I went back to get my forgotten handbag. Mr. Dudley was there with several hard-faced men and rather more of the little girls. And the very day after that, curiously, I met one of the free-lance scriptwriters in a restaurant and sat down at her table. During the meal she said, "Have you discovered yet that Mr. D. is a pimp?" I resigned from the job without giving notice.

Few girls anywhere, surely, would be easier targets than the ones at that time who had fallen prey to the frenzied ambition to be in movies. Like all obsessions it was a form of madness, but it was stronger than most and not only with girls. The casting offices were besieged by the young and also by women, and even men, in decline. Many of the women had left husbands and homes to come to Hollywood in the belief that they could get at least character parts. Or they came because they were infatuated with some movie actor. Hundreds, perhaps thousands, of them drifted around the studios, refusing to go back home even when the remittances from their families stopped. It was well known that some were starving — poor creatures, victims of what was plainly a widespread mania. The young and pretty usually made their different adjustment. They at least had enough to eat but for most of them little chance of success in the movies. Some were supported by minor studio employees, assistants to directors and cameramen, by electricians, grip boys, even porters, who would persuade a foolish girl that they could introduce her to a director; but the directors seldom picked their casts from this floating source of inexperienced talent. More girls probably found their way into the clutches of operators like Mr. Dudley and then onto the couches of the Los Angeles businessmen.

My closeup of all this induced physical nausea. Was this what the Wellesley advice had meant: "Try to see life as it really is"? How fit together in the same world the college idealism and the mad girl on Mr. Dudley's stairs and the frightened ones meeting the men in his office? How endure it if the professors had been defrauding us and Hollywood was the true adult life? But hadn't I always known of that split? When I had stopped on the way home from school to feed the swans, to talk to them and look into their wild black eyes that stirred inexpressible thoughts, like music, and then go home to . . . what was at home. Hadn't I always known that life was a contradiction?

I would do now what I had done as a child — I would turn away. I would go back to San Francisco! I wished that I had a little more money, but with my energy in full flood because I would be so happy there, I would be able to get a job quickly, some writing job now that I'd had a little experience. Everything would be possible! My trunk was half-packed when a telegram came from my mother: ARRIVING SATURDAY SEVEN-FIFTEEN P.M. SANTA FE.

Saturday was tomorrow. The trunk was unpacked.

I was stunned by the news. Why was my mother coming? I lay awake most of the night, absorbing this new situation. She had sent me away from home because she could not stand it to have me around, and yet she was following me. Would I never be rid of the

Myself at two, still with the "smashed-in" face of the birth injury.

My mother two months before my birth. "She would never again be so beautiful."

My mother after the first twelve disturbed years . . .

. . . and at seventy, herself again when my distressing presence was gone.

Proud husband and loving
father of newborn daughter.

My brother, Jack, and his two
children, Janice and John.

My father
in his last
year, with
grandson John.

The champagne
days—myself in
Southern California.

Dr. Carl Renz,
compassionate giant
who gave me a *vita nuova*.

The rim of the rock, seen from the North.

Beetle Rock and beyond—there was the feeling that one "could walk right out into the sunny sky."

The white firs of Sequoia National Park, with the giant sequoia trunks at right.

Sooty grouse in his
courtship display.

Myself with
a lodgepole
chipmunk.

The cabin
at Beetle Rock.

The torn-eared buck who lay for hours each day under a very large sugar pine. The belligerent bear appeared from behind these trees.

A little spike buck, one of our company at the cabin.

The chickaree who was so insistent
on justice—and myself, "home at last."

incubus of her hatred? At least I would not go to San Francisco, not with the possibility that she would go too. San Francisco would be my last chance of escape — sometime. I would just have to wait for it.

Ever since my mother's reaction to the dance contract I had sent family letters that revealed nothing about myself, nothing of course about Geoffrey or the happenings at the Dudley office, and so she didn't know I was out of a job. I must get another, and quickly. I did know of a vacancy, at the Metropolitan Studio. I went there at nine o'clock Monday morning. The manager, William Sistrom, thought my experience was just what he wanted. I had been concerned with both actors and scripts, the combination that was required. I started the following day and as far as my mother knew, that was where I had been all along.

At first when my mother arrived I was afraid she had left my father permanently and intended to live in Hollywood. At the end of the second week I found out that she had come for a different reason. At my doctor's office for help with renewed numbness I heard:

"So your mother is here. She came to see me about you. Did she tell you?"

"No!"

"She came to find out if you're leading a virtuous life. I straightened her out on that, and I said that she should be giving you credit, because the pressures in Hollywood are probably greater than anywhere else on earth. Here you are, into your twenties, and she goes to such lengths to check up on you. I let her know that I didn't approve."

I was almost speechless with anger and perhaps the doctor saw that I was, for he went on: "But . . . in view of her age, middle life, is it possible that she is not quite her normal self?"

She was being her usual self, the self I had always known, but was that self normal? I began to observe my mother with more curiosity. In the hotel lounge: how she must try to charm every other guest, except one. This was illogical, because these people didn't mean anything to her. Why make so much effort, why so intensely? Was my mother, even yet, unconsciously trying to overcome a sense of inferiority left from her childhood?

Among the guests were an elderly English couple. The husband had few of the little flattering ways with his wife, pulling out her chair at the table, stepping back to let her precede through a doorway, that are typical of American husbands. The lack of these outward forms of respect enraged my mother, it almost seemed on behalf of all womanhood. I suggested that there might be different customs in England; perhaps all English husbands walked through doorways ahead of their wives. That remark didn't ease her attitude and was this not the explanation: that her whole view of marriage, especially her own, was a reaction against her inadequate father? Her mother had had few of the traditional courtesies from him, and for several years he had deserted his family. Therefore my mother was tense about any treatment that so much as hinted of a husband's neglect. My father was always kind and there wasn't the slightest chance of our lacking anything it was in his power to give us — except his company; and the indignation with which she took his absence surely did nothing to shorten it. I was sorry for both of them and I began to see her own problem more clearly.

But her treatment of me was as much a puzzle as ever, for I was still trying to figure out logical reasons for it. I couldn't, though I believed at the time that its effect would be lasting. That prophesy came one afternoon when I was on one of the big red Pacific Electric streetcars. I was sitting on one of the front, lengthwise seats and was watching an aging mother and younger woman, obviously from her features a daughter. The daughter was haranguing the mother with so much venom that I wondered what her attacks would be like when the two were alone. The elderly woman was not replying. She looked straight ahead and her mouth was firm though her eyes were troubled. When she could endure no more she got up and went to the front of the swaying car where she stood holding onto the rail that encircled the motorman. There were empty seats, but one could guess that she wanted to get as far away as she could from her daughter. The daughter, chewing a lip, turned her face to the window.

I felt, in what was almost an hallucination, that I was seeing what my own life could become if I ever should have a daughter. Family traits sometimes skip a generation and my mother's granddaughter could inherit her temperament. Then, when I was old and frail and not well able to hold my own, my life could end as it had begun.

It wouldn't. That was one situation I could avoid. As I got off the car I said to myself that the happiest marriage would not be worth the risk of having a daughter. It was a fate to which I never would come. The faces of the two in the streetcar are as clear today as they were at that moment. They could not have been a reminder more permanent if they had been burnt into my flesh with a branding iron.

There is one other memory of the ten or twelve weeks that my mother remained in Hollywood. Juan, the Colombian architect, was still there and one night he took us to the Coconut Grove for dinner. The orchestra leader, who recognized Juan and me, played a tango and Juan and I danced. As sometimes happened the other couples left the floor to watch. My mother was pleased. When we went back to the table she said with an airy smile, "If I had known how well you dance, I would not have opposed your signing that contract."

3

The confusion between the actual world and the dream world of films applied all through Hollywood — in the house on a clifflike hill where I had a flat, for example. It looked like a movie set for *The Three Musketeers,* with a living room that had wrought iron grilles over the windows, a red tiled floor and twisted columns of plaster; and there were a large bath and a dressing room and an un-covered balcony but nothing prosaic such as a kitchen. No matter on weekdays when I ate at the studio. For Sundays I brought in cold meats and bread and boiled vegetables in an electric coffee pot.

When I got home from the studio, about 2 A.M., I used to lie out on the balcony till I had rested a little. Below was a sheet of lights, jewels on a plain ending abruptly at the dark sea ten miles away. Here on the hill the air was dense with the fragrance of mimosa, honeysuckle, petunias, geraniums and the pungence of eucalyptus trees. Mockingbirds sang in the boughs, New World nightingales which had learned the songs of other fine-throated birds during the day and threw medleys of them into the scented night.

From this excess of romantic atmosphere I went indoors but not always to sleep for often, towards morning, a neighbor came out on her terrace, faced the town below and sang Rudolph Friml's "Indian Love Call" in a contralto voice of great carrying power. After five or ten minutes a sports car might, or might not, come roaring up the steep hill, and fully awake and resentful then I would think, She could have sung it into a telephone.

By that hour the mockingbirds would have become still but the "Indian Love Call" would rouse them and they would resume their singing. Seeking some sanity in the heavy emotional ambiance, I developed a chant that I would repeat to myself, a series of mundane words: *hardware store, oatmeal, muddy road, coal, notions department, chicken house, hardware store, oatmeal* . . . and someone else on the hill felt that a balance was needed. He was a pianist and his own antidote was to get out of bed and play Bach. Music cool and true would flow down among Moorish walls, the imported trees and the perfumed gardens — music perhaps too complex to be imitated by mockingbirds for they would fall silent again. The street lights at last would be flickering out. Dawn would have come, gray and matter-of-fact between the moonlight and the languor of the California sun.

I was due at the studio at ten o'clock in the morning to start sixteen hours of work, six days a week, an inhuman schedule that no one questioned — it was the normal day for personnel in a picture studio. I was called a production secretary, which meant being eyes and ears for the manager, who could not keep track personally of the progress made in all our fifty-two pictures a year, one completed each week. In the story conferences: how were the plots developing, were there big scenes for the stars? What preparations were being made for each oncoming film in the art, prop and wardrobe departments? On the sets: were the scenes going well, without too many retakes, were the stars happy; were the chief cutter and his assistant at work? They had recently become lovers and often deserted to go to the beach.

Love affairs, waxing or waning, were to be watched for. Erotic involvements, especially between stars or between stars and directors were taken into consideration as analytically as the expenses allotted to individual pictures. An affair in full swing could be the most important element in a film's success; one declining could make a film fall apart. One of our units included a top director, a very skilled woman writer, his mistress for years, and his cameraman. The trio had made the most profitable pictures to come out of the studio but the director had tired of the writer and told the cameraman, who told me, that he would have to seduce the writer or lose his job. The cameraman, a happily married husband with several children, talked the matter over with his wife and they sadly agreed that he should give in. It was amusing, though disturbing, to watch the cameraman's rather subtle advances and the writer's yielding.

While Mr. Sistrom and I ate our meals from trays on his desk, I reported how things were going. That took care of the day. In the evening we ran other studios' films, I being there to make notes of any effective details it was thought we might want to copy. (Dorothy Parker said that the only ism Hollywood believed in was plagiarism.) About midnight the rushes, prints of the scenes shot that day, were delivered and for two hours were run and judged by a group in the manager's private projection room. This was where acting and camerawork, costumes, sets, lighting and cutting were found pleasing or were rejected. By that hour everyone would be drunk with fatigue and otherwise but was sure that his judgment was unimpaired. I sometimes wondered if I myself were sober, so bizarre was the conversation. For these movie men had no home life, due to the abnormal hours they worked, and no social life outside the movie colony, and in trying to make the pictures believable they argued at length about questions that could have been answered by anyone stopped on one of the nearby suburban streets. Do farmers wear long underdrawers in the summer? Do children wash their own hair? Would a bride be wearing her wedding dress when she and the groom arrive at the honeymoon hotel? Old people cry a lot, don't they? Would an electrician kiss his wife goodby in the morning? And this, my favorite, when a woman undresses to go to bed, to sleep, does she take off her shoes before she puts on her nightgown? Men who were making entertainment for millions of American families were baffled by matters as simple as these.

The Metropolitan Studio was owned by Cecil B. De Mille, a man totally without humor, and Al Christie, producer of slapstick comedies. The coordinator between these polarized temperaments was Sistrom, an engineer from the Eastman Kodak Company, perhaps put there by George Eastman, said to be a third owner. Only in Hollywood could anybody imagine that three such men might co-operate, but Sistrom's influence worked around most of the difficulties.

He was an Englishman who looked frail but had excess energy which he disposed of by always humming intensely on one note, like a bee on an urgent mission. I suspected that the whole enterprise and his part in it seemed quite mad to him, for his laughter used to burst up from profound and sardonic depths. He especially dreaded emotional tantrums by stars — such as Joseph Schildkraut who once jumped up and down on his handsome hat because someone else had signed for the projection room when he wanted it. Mr. Sistrom threw his telephone at him but the cord was too short and the phone fell to the floor and broke. Mr. Sistrom laughed first.

He was not really a showman and sometimes his decisions had unexpected results, as when Vera Reynolds was scheduled to be starred as a girl jockey. She absolutely refused to get on a horse, of which she was terrified, and so the engineer, Mr. Sistrom, had the prop department construct a plaster horse with an up-and-down gallop and also a mobile eye, which kept rolling back as if to share a huge joke with the rider. It was the funniest picture Metropolitan ever made but it was never released.

De Mille, Christie, and Sistrom produced the pictures but the men who financed the making of them were in New York, bankers mostly. Every spring they came out to approve the next fifty-two, or rather the titles. Pictures were sold on titles, even more than on stars at that time, and the bankers believed they knew best what titles the theatre owners would buy. They believed further that they were as good as anyone else at devising them, and so there would be a two-day session with bankers, producers and studio writers throwing salacious titles into the ring to see which ones would get the most ribald laughter. It was a stag meeting and I was not there but was told that it was an orgy of verbal sex. Scheduled for the night of the second day was an authentic orgy, cornily Roman, produced by De Mille at his country place. Described for me: how the men were provided with couches on which to dine, surrounding a dance floor on which strippers performed, and how afterwards trays of expensive jewelry with genuine precious stones were passed and each guest chose what he thought would appeal to the girl most attractive to him. The girls came back and paraded and the guests bid for them with their jewels. Beyond that the narrative did not go.

This was the movie high life for which, as much as for business, the money men came to Hollywood. Then they went away, leaving the studio with the problem of fitting sexy titles to stories, it might be of a boy and his wild pony, or a family cast up on a lonely island, or a mountaineering thriller. But theatre audiences already knew that any similarity between plot and title was apt to be coincidental. It was a situation at other studios as well as at ours. A famous example was the first picture that Eric von Stroheim was making for Carl Laemmle. Von Stroheim wanted to call it *The Pinnacle* but Laemmle said that the public wouldn't know what a pinnacle was and anyway, "There are more blind husbands around than pinnacles, so we'll call it *Blind Husbands*." And they did.

De Mille was absorbed in making spectaculars, Sistrom, the manager, kept the wheels turning over, and Christie made most of the decisions believed to attract the audiences. They had liked the comedies he had produced at his Sunset Boulevard studio, but when he bought into Metropolitan it was for the chance to express new and grander ambitions. He wished to make serious films but didn't recognize that they called for some different techniques.

He was a very large man and unlike most men of his size was quick and excitable. As each of our films neared completion he held a stop watch and if the suspense was not well established in ten minutes the picture had to be cut, re-shot or scrapped. Throughout every scene as it was made he kept muttering in the projection room, "Come on, come on, let's get on with the plot." Speed had been an important ingredient in the farces on which his success had been built, but the tempo of *Charley's Aunt, Up in Mabel's Room* and *Getting Gertie's Garter* was not the pace of real life, and if one can't believe in what's happening on the screen, why care?

Few other movie producers had much understanding of true acting ability. What they wanted was only a repertoire of facial expressions turned on at a moment's notice. A director would call them forth by the word "register." "Register jealousy." "Register love of children." "Register devout religious feeling." George Jean Nathan was scathing about such acting. In the 1930's he wrote: "In Hollywood wistfulness is something you do with the neck." The minor players and sometimes even the stars would not know the plot. Many directors preferred that system. They liked stars who were passive and malleable, and the instructions were so minute, the directors would say, "I am the one who does the acting."

Tears were the plum in the cinema pie. Any girl who could turn them on at will, at ten o'clock on a rainy Monday, was assured of a steady income, for audiences were no longer deceived by glycerine; they wanted to see the tears *come,* and some actresses found it hard to produce them. In that case many directors resorted to cruelty, telling a star she was hopeless, she probably would be replaced in the picture and the studio never would cast her again. When she burst out crying the cameras would turn furiously and at the end the director would say, "Beautiful, dear. I knew you could do it," but what she had done was not acting, of course.

Christie had even less understanding than most of acting as art and he confused quality with an excess of sobbing. We had under contract one of the world's most intelligent actors, the Viennese Rudolph Schildkraut, father of Joseph. In one picture he gave a carved box to a mistress who kept his love letters in it. In a later scene, when he was old and running a pawn shop, a stranger brought in the box and asked for a loan on it. The loan was made and the man left. Schildkraut stood behind the glass counter, looking at the box. He didn't touch it, his face hardly seemed to change expression, and yet all his poignant remembrance was visible there. It was acting of the most perfectly controlled, reticent sort, without sentimentality but so moving it brought tears to the eyes of our blasé group in the projection room.

The film was stopped and Al Christie turned to Edward Sloman, the proud director:

"What's the matter with you — don't you know a good thing when you see it? *Milk* that scene!"

Milk it, that is, for a bigger audience reaction. The next day the scene was shot again. At the director's sad insistence Schildkraut milked it and when we saw the new takes the scene was maudlin, sickening, but that was what Christie wanted and no one in the projection room could convince him that the acting was ruined.

If my job had required a large output of physical energy I would have had to resign, but about all I did for the sixteen hours a day was to sit and watch, though with sharp attention and that was wearing. Continuously I considered leaving and going to San Francisco. It was hard to save on my salary however, and I always thought that I needed more money. Besides, at Metropolitan I could observe many kinds of skills: acting, photography, cutting and especially the techniques of drama, and those were still interesting.

The most fantastic of these, the least realistic, was the creation of glamour. We have outgrown glamour now and are somewhat abashed to think we ever were taken in by it, but it seemed magical for a while and to watch it being produced, a process cold and deliberate, was like seeing a magician practice the tricks he will later perform for an audience.

When a studio mogul thought that an actress was promising, he had a superstructure built up that went far beyond her own inborn charm. In this choice the makeup artists were crucial. It is amazing what can be done. Alfred Hitchcock was in our studio frequently, at a time when he was interested in both stage and screen, and one day he said:

"Come to New York. I'll make an actress out of you."

I laughed and told him to look again: my features weren't good enough. He was scornful of such artlessness.

"The only thing that matters is the shape of the face," he said. "All the rest is done with makeup."

I didn't want to go to New York but I did know something about the magic of makeup. One of my early Hollywood friends was a makeup artist, then perfecting a skill in creating national types. He liked to practice on my face because its structure is rather neutral, and when he had finished an hour's work I would look in the mirror and see a face I would never have known — an Egyptian face, Spanish, even Japanese. One day he put on a Hungarian face. I wore it, with a new dress and a different hair-do, down to dinner at the small hotel where I was then living, and none of the seven at my table (not picture people), whom I saw every night, recognized the stranger. When I began to talk they were astounded. Experiments like that were made on the starlets. The constructed faces were studied and the one that was judged most alluring became the new personality.

Who was she now? The little girl born in Austin or Iowa City became a vampire, a home-wrecker, a sex kitten or an insipid girl-next-door, a travesty of herself. What, after all, had won the applause and the money — herself or this paper doll put together by showmen? There is nothing more dead than a myth that has dissolved, especially a myth of oneself, as it did dissolve for many a star with startling speed or a slower dimming. The only thing that could reassure her was flattery, and there was a tacit studio understanding that all of us should contribute praise. The stars reached for this help. My office was an anteroom to Mr. Sistrom's and when I was there the players, wishing to make their optimal effect on the manager, appealed first for a buildup of confidence. Behind my door was a mirror and when one of the stars came in she would close the door, study the mirror, give herself an enchanted smile and turn to me radiantly saying, "I look well today, don't I." That was the cue for me to say, "Marvelous. You were never lovelier." And she would sit down to wait, having grasped a little more firmly her purposeful charm.

The endeavor was catching. Nowhere but in Hollywood would there be such a charming group of bookkeepers as we had in our accounting office, such a charming gateman to turn away sightseers, such charming boys to handle the stage apparatus. Even the carpenters were personality boys and the seamstresses in the wardrobe department had the telling manner of character actresses.

Desirable femininity and to a less extent masculinity buttered everyone's bread and was discussed and assessed above all other interests. For we all, from the studio owners to the porters, were depending on the market value of sex appeal — the appeal of our stars.

"It's sexy, this melancholy look her new love affair's giving her."

"Why don't they start blacking his scalp? It's showing through."

"The dames will be noticing that his neck's getting fat."

"She shouldn't be cast as a fifteen-year-old girl — a woman of her age has the wrong kind of legs."

Those were comments about the studio's profits, for we all were obsessed by the price of seductive good looks. It was the constant subject of conversation, as cars are in Detroit.

There was one however who saw the whole scene as a spectacle of delusions — Bert, the projection operator. When he wasn't running a film he loafed in the sunny doorway of the projection room, watching the comings and goings, amused and disenchanted. The only way to get a response from him was to toss him a quip, when you were likely to get a better one back — Bert, almost the only one who stood apart from that manic world.

But I had my own defense against it, my chant: *hardware store, oatmeal, muddy road, coal, notions department, chicken house* . . .

I did have one other tie with reality, the director, Paul Powell, who was somewhat a friend. He kept urging me to leave Hollywood and we had frequent discussions about why it was false and ultimately degrading. He was one of the few directors who wished to present human truth and to inspire their casts to give thoughtful performances. Those directors were frequently out of work. Some observers said that the moneyed producers were jealous of talents they did not possess, but when a director was idle for a long time, as Paul had been, the rumor began going around that he had lost his luck, and in the superstitious atmosphere of the studios that was the same thing as saying that he was finished.

Mr. Sistrom respected Paul's work however and assigned him a low-budget film about pirates. Its locale was to be one of the uninhabited islands off the California coast and the plot concerned the hijacking of fishing boats. Paul, telling me but no others, determined to make it a real, believable human drama. He chose his cast to represent misfits rather than ruffians and planned to suggest plausible reasons why they had become outlaws. He was especially pleased with the girl, a newcomer in Hollywood, who, he said, was "not too pretty to be beautiful."

Through all the preparations I encouraged Paul in his wish to shoot the picture poetically, and as the scenes began coming back, brought each day by launch, I was sure they would reinstate him as one of Hollywood's finest directors. For no one could fail to applaud the visual art and the honesty of portraying the lawless characters as people deserving of understanding — but one could, Al Christie. From the first he was angered. This was not what he had expected. He talked as if he had been deceived, as in a sense he had, for he had not authorized a picture whose mood was realistic. But Christie had been disappointed in other films and had not responded so violently. Something in this one provoked an emotional ferment. Before the shooting was finished he called the company home and decreed that the film should be scrapped.

Paul Powell never was given another chance to direct a picture.

4

After that humiliation Paul, who lived in Pasadena, came to Hollywood only once. He realized that he had had his final chance to prove that he was a great director. I tried to explain Al Christie's perverse reaction, but Paul was sensitive and I think he felt, wrongly, that he had let Mr. Sistrom down.

On that last afternoon I walked with him out to the studio gate. In our mood, one of disillusion for both of us, we were silent. Then he turned suddenly and said something which had nothing to do with the time and place:

"If any man ever tells you what it is all about I will come and kill him." He said it so soberly, it was almost as if he meant it.

But of course I already knew.

I felt dismay and a sense of guilt for my part in Paul's failure. Even without my enthusiasm he might have shot the film as he did, or perhaps not, but I knew better than he did Al Christie's limited artistic taste, and if I had been more acute I would have warned Paul. And yet there was only one way he could work — by giving his best. He had been right to end his picture-making career on a note of complete integrity.

At least I knew now what I was involved in at Metropolitan. It was a crass and cheap enterprise (so I told myself at that unhappy time). It would always reduce art to the appeal of a fairground.

Why then stay any longer? Why, indeed? After I finally did leave and could measure my depths of exhaustion I knew that it had been reason enough for not pulling myself away. But I think the languorous weather may have contributed. A sociologist who grew up in Hollywood, but escaped, has said he thinks that the dreamy, subtropical climate has a peculiar paralyzing effect on the will. He believes many residents stay because they can't stir themselves to get out of the narcotic atmosphere. Then in summer a warm blue haze veiled the mountains, making them look like a gauzy backdrop The air was too soft, too still. One day I pleaded illness and went to Westlake Park where I rowed a boat out among the swans and sat with idle oars, looking away towards the misty mountains. I told myself they were a trap, and I never would get away.

It didn't help that our next film was so silly. A flippant young man kept as a pet a full-grown African lion. In the picture he would be taking the lion along a city street to visit his girl. The lion would go to sleep on the girl's couch and prove uncooperative when they wanted him to get down. We were going to use three different lions. In a few scenes the girl was to fondle the lion's head and for those the Selig Commercial Zoo was to furnish an old, toothless lion. A medium lion was cast for the scenes in which actors were on the set but not near him, and a savage one, filmed through bars, when he would be alone and provoked into showing rage. Having watched the third lion's fury, the audiences were expected to quail when the girl stroked what they supposed was the same animal.

On the first day of shooting we used the medium lion. I went to Stage 3 where the filming was going on. The scene was the girl's boudoir. The draperies were pink, the dressing table and even a wastebasket were flounced with rows of pink taffeta and a vase five feet high was spilling pink roses. The couch was on the left side of the room. It was covered with satin. On the right was a door through which the man and his girl would enter.

In front of the open-sided boudoir was the immense technical clutter, the cranes with their cameras and microphones and, below, more cameras, reflectors, lights, the big ones and baby spots, each with its cable. Cables were everywhere, festooned overhead and snaked all over the floor. At the back were some chairs, for the director, stars, script girl and myself.

The crew were standing among the equipment and on that day others had left their work for the excitement of watching the lion, about fifty closely packed people. As I found my chair the lion was on the set and the observers were quiet, absorbed, while the trainer tried to maneuver his animal onto the satin couch.

The lion was pacing from side to side in the frivolous feminine room. He seemed to know what was expected of him but did not want to do it. He would approach the couch but there turn, the whole length of his body, including his tail, following through with a beautiful but rejecting gesture. On the other side of the set he would turn again as if, also there, he were frustrated by the so-alien scene. At each step his feet made a backward flip as they might in pushing through fallen leaves, although he was walking on a white carpet. The muscles working beneath his skin plainly had massive power — held in check at what cost to himself, I wondered.

The trainer kept uttering wordless, strained, menacing sounds. The lion did not seem afraid of him but the glances between the man and the beast were not friendly.

Finally the lion did make a jump, as smooth as the flow of wind, up onto the couch. He let himself down but too far towards one end and although his head faced the cameras, the position was awkward and the trainer risked a quick questioning glance towards the director. The director motioned that they would start filming anyway.

Cautiously the two stars walked towards the right. The flood lamps came on. The cameramen and the rest of the crew stood at their posts. Would the lion stay on the couch? It was a time of tense waiting.

As the huge animal had walked back and forth it had seemed offensive to see his magnificent grace and strength in this farcical setting. Once he was up on the couch a thought clicked into place: that fate enters the lives of animals as it does of humans and that the most improbable of events had taken this dignified creature out of the world where he would have been king and had given him this ignoble role. The view of the couch with the lion on it dissolved into a vivid, imagined scene of his own high plateau, where the savannah was wide beyond scattered trees. Perhaps I remembered a photograph of that country and the lion's stride had brought back the picture with him in it now, almost as sharp as a vision. A quick pulse of sympathy rose: lion, that this has been done to you, that you never again will lift your head to sniff the informing breeze, never lie watching upon the sun-warmed branch or go bounding across the grasses ——

With a flying leap off the couch the lion was past the trainer, was streaming through people, equipment and cables to stop in front of my chair, his eyes not two feet from my face. My thought must somehow have reached him and he came swiftly, involuntarily, towards release, as if in my mind I had freed him.

At the lion's jump there had been a gasp on all sides — and then utter stillness. No one tried to escape. The human figures around us were frozen with one of the oldest instinctive reactions, to try to avoid being noticed.

Only the trainer moved. The lion's eyes held my own with intensity like a physical grip, but off at the side I was aware that the trainer was skirting around the set. The man made a frantic blurred passage across a bright open door and then was behind us. There he stopped, for he couldn't fire at the lion among all these people. Nor could he risk startling him out of his trancelike absorption.

For this brief time the lion was king again, in complete control. His head was up, his tail slightly swinging.

How long did he hold his gaze? Two minutes, three? Long enough for a blaze of light to come streaming into my mind. For that length of time I saw nature's truth, much more overpowering than even the clearest of human truth. From the lion's eyes I partook of wildness, so that now his truth was mine too. Briefly ours was the Africa where bees hum, ants sting, and the hoofs of wild an-

imals muddy waterholes. There the significant things were horned
heads flung up in alarm, tropical smells, sand, and the far-off cry of a
bird. In this Africa of the animals no mind ever deluded itself with
romance, none ever milked any situation for others or for oneself.
This was the ultimate reality, as rocks are real, dew, trees, mountains, and clouds.

The lion's gaze was becoming still more intense. I knew that I
must do something to break it. Not daring to look away I leaned
forward a little and quietly said, "I was thinking of your jun-
gle ———— "

The lion did not of course know the words but the tone had its effect. He relaxed. With an easing of all his great muscles he let
himself down on the floor, his hind legs under him and his forepaws
outstretched a few inches in front of my shoes. His head swung to
one side almost drowsily. If there had been any danger to any of us,
it was past.

The trainer stepped forward. In his shrill, clipped voice he ordered the lion back onto the set. The lion complied. He jumped up
on the couch at the trainer's first command, and the crew, breathing
again, turned to their cameras and other equipment. But as soon as
the trainer had backed away, the lion was off the couch and down at
my chair. He sank immediately into his attitude of repose, this time
lying beside the chair, not in front of it.

The whole episode repeated itself. As soon as the trainer had got
the lion onto the set once more, the director said urgently, "You
must leave!" I already knew that. I was moving away towards the
door.

As long as the lion worked on Stage 3 I did not go back. After a
few days the crew began shooting scenes on the studio streets where
the peach-colored stucco buildings were supposed to represent family homes. It was planned that the lion would walk down the main

street and enter the Administration Building ("an apartment house"), and those of us who had offices on the ground floor were evacuated for the time he would go in and out. We lined up to watch from behind a strong netting stretched across one of the side streets.

The lion headed obediently towards the proper building but as he reached the side street he turned abruptly and came to me on the other side of the barricade. There again he held my eyes with the same appeal as before. Now too the trainer got him back under control and started him down the main street but could not get him beyond the side street where I was standing. I left and was told to stay at home until the scenes with that lion had all been shot.

Before the picture was finished I had resigned from the studio and prepared to leave Hollywood. I didn't have enough money saved for a new venture and still was so tired that packing a trunk took a week, but there was no question about my going. The Selig Zoo urged me to come to work for them as a lion trainer. I was not tempted, although I did feel disloyal, as if I were failing a friend, for I had a great sense of gratitude to that lion. What I had thought of as human truth had always made it disturbing to live in the false atmosphere of Hollywood, but the glimpses of nature's much deeper truth had made it impossible to stay. I felt an emotional release, perhaps like the lion's, as the wheels turned under me heading towards San Francisco

vii

BECOMING A WRITER

THE FIRST DISTRICT of San Francisco I came to know — and it was all I saw for about two months — was the long straight beach south of the Cliff House. It was a cold spring and so there were no swimmers. Sometimes someone brought a dog for a run and it was a lift to one's spirits to see the dog explode with energy when he was let off the leash. He would go racing away to chase gulls or play tag with the breaking waves, he so bold when he dared them to catch him, then scampering back when the white teeth of a wave would come up on the sand to bite him. Sometimes the dog would return to his guardian for a touch of reassurance or praise and quickly be gone again, ears blown up and sand flying. None of the dogs were terriers but they made me think with a pang of the little white dog I had had to lose deliberately in Kansas City. Probably he was dead by now, the small friend I had betrayed.

More often I was alone on the beach, which was foggy on many days — only a strip of sand, the gray mist above, and the white curl of a gray wave falling over. Except for sleep nothing could bring a mind nearer to absolute rest. Day by day, week by week, Hollywood's false wild dramas receded and my own thoughts and emotions began reappearing, the thoughts and emotions that had been obliterated by the shocks and the killing fatigue of the last three years.

The walks on the beach had to be short and sometimes I could almost not make it up the four landward blocks to my room, a slight grade but too much. On the way I passed a small fruit stand and one day an empty orange crate was upended beside the door. I sank onto it gratefully for a little rest, and always after that an orange crate stood by the door and I was always glad to sit down on it, too tired for talk but I thanked the kind Italian fruit man with a smile.

At first I was so exhausted that I felt fortunate when I had lived from one hour to the next. The family that I was boarding with, an electrician, wife and son, had called a doctor for me. He was a vigorous hiker himself and prescribed exercise for most of his patients, hence the walks on the beach, but that was a mistake, actually, for I was having a heart problem.

It was a leaky valve that I'd had all those years. Such a leak will diminish the heart's thrust but the heart will compensate by pumping harder than normally necessarily. But if there is, in addition to the leak, too much stress or fatigue, the heart just gives up making the extra effort, it "decompensates" (the medical term), and then with the thrust so much reduced, the blood flows through one's body — and worse, through one's brain — sluggishly. It doesn't pick up its oxygen fast enough in the lungs either, and so one is breathless as well as listless. The thing to do is to rest until the heart resumes the task of its greater-than-normal push, and that was what I should have been doing instead of walking along the beach. But after two months I had recovered enough to ride on the streetcar down to the public library, and for something inspiring to do I began some research towards writing a history of music, as described in brief biographies of the composers who had carried forward music's increasing complexity.* It was certainly intuition which put me onto that

* I never wrote the book but I understand that someone else has published a similar history of music.

track, for the research was an undemanding and very enjoyable task, the best kind of therapy there could have been. And at noon, eating the sandwiches my landlady had given me, I would sit in the Civic Center Plaza, watching the fountain and feeding the pink-footed pigeons, who walked around with their soft step and anxious dignity until I tossed them a bite, when one would fly up and perch on my arm — for a moment this wondrous contact with a creature not human, not cruel; within a pigeon's limits, dependable.

"It is likely that many people who seem to die natural deaths have in fact been poisoned by their families."

o

After four months in San Francisco a day came when my financial backlog was down to 45 cents. I was not in a panic. I knew the rules of my new venture, that of becoming a writer. Those were the days before government aid to indigents and so it would not be comfortable to be without money. That however was part of the contract: anybody aspiring to write for a living must simply assume the burden of insecurity. Anyway I had a belief, almost unconscious, that writing was so much the right thing for me that in the last extremity luck would come to my aid. This was not a philosophy or the result of experience; it was just something I deeply felt, like the realization that illness usually gives way to returning health.

When I had started to look for a job I had moved downtown. And luck had taken me to ideal living quarters: a decaying mansion on Steiner Street where I had a one-room apartment overlooking the Golden Gate. That view, with its continual passage of ships and the smooth Marin hills beyond, helped to support my morale and the couple who owned the house had an almost parental kindness. The husband, a small, compact man with a naked and vulnerable face, was a science teacher. On the side he was studying bee diseases for the U.S. Department of Agriculture, and so we had a garden abuzz with diseased bees and I woke up each day to find a dozen or more swimming around in the air of my room.

The scientist was about five feet tall, his wife a foot taller. On her high world she looked out through a thicket of frizzy gray hair, a tutor of Latin students and a woman of sterling worth though a kleptomaniac. I lost many things to her but she always left something in return, and so when I came home at night and found part of a cake or pie at my door I knew that something inside would be missing. They weren't things of great value but sometimes, as in the loss of an alarm clock, I was rather inconvenienced.

The house was musty with age. Its shabby furniture had been the original owners' and had stood where it was on the dusty carpets so long, it looked as if it had grown there. But I was allowed to use the piano in the drawing room, and once when I left one of my poems in a library book, the songwriter who found it tracked me down and got me to write some lyrics. We composed the songs in the evenings among the drawing room's Victorian relics. I never made anything from that effort but for a while had an amusing time.

When I started out with my final five dollars to get a job it didn't turn up the first day, as I had expected. A week later, with the last 45 cents and still with youthful confidence, I was walking along Montgomery Street and looked up and saw on the wall of a building on Sacramento Street the painted sign, PACIFIC MARINE REVIEW. Well, I thought, I liked the sea and so maybe that was the publication that I should write for. In the dingy lobby of the narrow seven-story building I asked the elevator operator to take me to the editor's office. He stopped at the sixth floor and I went in a door labelled Edwards Publishing Company. I asked for Mr. Edwards. The girl at the desk said I would have to wait and she gave me a magazine: *The Coast Investor*. I turned its uninteresting financial pages and still had the publication in my hand when I went into Mr. Edwards's office.

He was a tall paunchy man who must recently have lost weight for his clothes hung on him loosely. His face too hung on him loosely, and he had a hound's sorrowful eyes and the aggrieved voice of a man much put upon. He opened the conversation:

"What do you think of that magazine?"

I, with amused airiness, "I think it's the dullest thing I ever read!"

"I suppose you could do better."

"If I couldn't I am not much of a writer."

It dawned on me belatedly that Mr. Edwards probably also published *The Coast Investor,* as was confirmed when he asked, "If you were doing an article for it today, what would you write?"

An idea, quick! I said, "I recently came up from Los Angeles on a bus and we passed so many large trucks that I wondered if the trucking industry isn't cutting into the railroads' profits." The thought actually had occurred to me, but the threat from road haulage was not generally recognized at that time and Mr. Edwards was pleased. He said, "Bring me the article Monday."

Then, at ten o'clock Friday morning, I knew absolutely nothing about finance but at ten that night, when the public library closed, I knew a great deal, for the techniques of research had been part of my Wellesley training. I knew, what I never had known before, the difference between stocks and bonds, and the way that railroads are financed, and their current standing (poor). I knew something about the way they had been showing a loss on freight revenues and from reports of the U.S. Department of Commerce that there was a proportionate growth in the profits of trucking companies. I was certain that articles must have been written on the subject I had proposed but I couldn't find them and plunged ahead with quite reckless assurance. I had bought grapes with 25 of my 45 cents and lived on those all day Friday and over the weekend. On Monday, a little lightheaded from hunger but stimulated by having tackled a hard job and finished it, I handed the article to Mr. Edwards. He read it while I waited and without comment wrote out a check for $50. All he said was, "What are you going to write next?" I had thought about that as I walked down from Steiner Street and told him, *Fashions in Frauds*. "Have it here a week from today," he said. I just made it to the bank before the 3 P.M. closing time and with $50 in my pocket took the cable car homeward. My spirits rose faster and higher than the car on the perpendicular California Street hill.

For the next three months I spent all my time writing articles for *The Coast Investor*. None was turned down, none revised. For material I was interviewing some of the bank and stock-brokerage presidents and had begun to feel that I knew a good deal about finance. It had even become rather interesting. It had turned out that the *Pacific Marine Review* was published by a different firm on the floor above ours, and it was fortunate that the elevator man had not taken me there, for that magazine was mostly about machinery, such an alien subject that I don't believe I would ever have become well-informed about it. Anyway, it would only have been a maverick like Mr. Edwards who would have welcomed a girl so unqualified and bluffing her way into unknown territory. He still was the one I saw with my manuscripts, although the magazine had an editor that I met occasionally — a tiny young man who got out a magazine with eight feature articles every month and numerous short pieces, most of which he apparently wrote himself. I assumed he was clever and he was, too clever, for one day when I was there four burly policemen arrived (why four?) and took away the miniature man. Somehow they had learned that he was receiving smart bonuses for recommending the stock issues that he described. Unprepared for that emergency, Mr. Edwards gave me the editor's job the same afternoon.

The ratty offices where we worked were a strange place from which to purvey information about how to get rich. There were three rooms, the small reception room where a typist-telephone operator worked (a new girl about every second month — I was soon to learn why), Mr. Edwards's paper-strewn office with its huge desk, and a larger room crowded with desks and files were *The Coast Investor* and another Edwards publication, *The Coast Banker,* were produced. *The Coast Banker* was a semiofficial organ of the banking community. Its contents consisted chiefly of statistical information compiled by a taciturn middle-aged man named Thompson. And then there was aging Miss Minnie, as tense and nervous as if the whole Edwards enterprise depended on her, as it almost did. She was Mr. Edwards's secretary, read proof, prepared the ads, pasted up the dummies and got out the advertising bills for both magazines. And last there was myself: only these three, working behind dirty windows and blowing the dust off anything that we touched, to give voice to the investment opportunities of San Francisco, indeed of California, for San Francisco was the State's financial pivot. Some of the material we published did have substance; our articles often were written by executives of the banks and stock and bond houses. Nothing was paid for those articles, which probably were written by the market analyst of the various firms but reflected prestige onto their supposed authors. To me they seemed unendurably dull and I tried to liven up the rest of the *Investor's* pages. In some months we didn't get any of these voluntary contributions and more than once I wrote all of our eight articles, using eight different names. It amused me to give certain individual traits to these imaginary characters. "Arthur Marshall," who usually wrote my bond articles, was full of platitudes, while "Ray T. Adams," the author of frequent *Fashions in Frauds* contributions, was jaunty, even facetious. I planned all the issues, only conferring with Mr. Edwards in the sketchiest way — this, four and five months after seeing my first words in print. No one outside our organization knew that I had so much authority. When I interviewed experts I always said that I was collecting information for the magazine's editor.

Now I had something more to add to my *hardware and oatmeal* anti-fantasy chant: *financial monthlies*. For nothing could have been less romantic than that dingy room where the only concern was money. And no one could have been better insulated against movie-type charm than the disillusioned Miss Minnie and coldly matter-of-fact Mr. Thompson. This utterly realistic atmosphere was refreshing after three years of Hollywood, but probably no one guessed that the very grime and the boring statistical charts were reasons for my enthusiastic devotion to the Edwards Publishing Company.

Mr. Edwards himself was realistic about what makes an article readable and from him I was learning to write. He had two rules for the material in the magazine: no word of more than three syllables, and every statement, if possible, should be made in terms of things seen and heard. The rules were not absolute; a word like *determination* would get by if it were familiar enough but not *anachronism* or *antecedence*. I tried strenuously to limit myself to the shorter words, not so much to make it easier for our rather unsophisticated average reader to understand but because I was discovering that the shorter words — usually Anglo-Saxon — were more forceful and they made for a bouncier rhythm. The style I was developing would be an asset when I was writing radio programs, where sentences addressed to the ear should not be complicated. But later, when I was writing books, my style would sometimes sound too simplistic. That danger was in the future. For the present I was learning something about making a sentence that had to be thick with abstract meaning catch and hold the eye. Tidbits of good advice fell my way, too, from Mr. Thompson. "Never start a sentence with 'There is' or 'There are,'" he said. "Just leave those words out." Occasionally it seems necessary to disregard that rule but I never do without realizing that the sentence is weak.

The first articles were a challenge but they took desperate effort. When I wrote at the house, as I usually did, I paced the floor between the door and the windows and approaching the windows always thought, I could jump out and end this agony. But on the way to the door I would reflect that when the words rattled out with no real work, an article sounded too glib. The anguish was the same that always goes with acquiring a discipline. To anyone who is thus suffering I give this promise: that the pain diminishes fairly fast. And it is the effort itself that finally unblocks the dam. In the writing profession the unfashionable advice still is good: feel it hot, write it cool. But it's the torment of striving for the cool technique that makes the high windows tempting.

Miss Minnie and Mr. Thompson did not seem surprised when, on the first of the month after I was installed as editor, no checks were distributed. I waited a week and then asked Miss Minnie when we were paid. She said, "Ask Mr. Edwards." I did and he said on the fifteenth. But the fifteenth passed and still no checks. In the year I stayed I never received any proper pay check nor was I ever able to find out what my salary was. I just got along on what I could wheedle out of Mr. Edwards from time to time. This arrangement was so unsatisfactory that when I was offered a job with a building and loan association I snapped at the chance. There too I would find complications, but at least they would be different.

Besides the practical experience there had been bonuses in the Edwards year, extras that belong to the process of becoming a writer. However important it is to learn how to put the right words in the right places, one also has to start turning into that strange being, one who believes that what he has to offer the world is creativity. I made a slight beginning when, in addition to editing the *Investor,* I did some mood pieces about San Francisco for Mr. Thompson's *Coast Banker.*

Scenes, people, talk began to be valued less for what they meant to me personally than for what makes them interesting to anyone. This very steep hill: necessary to climb it slowly but see the effectiveness of all those buildings stacked one above the other and set back in tiers so that they form a pyramid. They all look clean, scoured perhaps by the salty winds, but then San Francisco has few if any factories and no sooty air. Except on the foggy days it is a city of light, light shining on all the pyramid walls, white and pale walls from which the sun is reflected back into the sparkling air.

And San Francisco faces seem bright, both in expression and health, with the clear, rosy skin of others who live by a westward sea — the Irish. Not many trees in the city, though. San Francisco was built upon sand dunes and remained mostly barren till John McLaren got hold of it and planted enough parks, with trees, so that every resident could walk to one. He made his masterpiece, Golden Gate Park, and remained in control of all the parks until he died, when he was ninety-six. I interviewed him for an article when he was over ninety and still sturdy as an oak. So the bundles of waving green fronds dispersed here and there on the sides of the crowded pyramids were the gift of that good man . . . and overhead all those fast-blowing small clouds threw a cover of broken and racing shadows across the sunny facades.

Charles Nicolet was no longer there, having gone to a better job in New York, and the Casa Beguine had moved, to become a mangy little nightclub at the Sutter end of the Stockton tunnel; but I was starting to find the easy-going neighborhood at the foot of Telegraph Hill, a neighborhood that has attracted many Bohemians who have enjoyed it and have given their character to it. I would know it much better a few years later. But already I was eating my lunch in Portsmouth Square, only a block away, beside the Robert Louis Stevenson memorial, that bronze ship on its plinth, and under the same tree where he sat among the old Chinese men and their tiny grandchildren and wrote in a notebook on his knee while waiting until his Tiger-Lily would be free to marry him.

Hollywood never had captivated me, as it does so many, but from the first San Francisco seemed to be the city towards which all my steps had been turning. I loved even the wind-blown fogs rushing around the corners of buildings with coattails flying.

o

In the new job at the building and loan association I was to be the advertising manager, responsible to the vice president in charge of promotion, a Mr. F. He was a tall, spare Scot, ginger-haired and ginger-tempered, who gave me entire responsibility for creating the selling copy, contracting for space in the newspapers and preparing promotional booklets. The first big effort was to be a brochure, 48 pages, printed in two colors, with original artwork. Mr. F. said that I should use the same artist and artisans he had previously relied on. I merrily started the new and challenging project.

The brochure was to be sent to all depositors, urging them to invest in the parent company whose stock would entitle them to shares in the overall profits. As depositors they received only the interest stipulated by law; as investors "they would have a chance for much larger returns." In my copy I put all the emphasis on the nature of stock in a building and loan association, "secure because its prosperity is based on the very foundation of family life, on man's eternal yearning to shelter his family in a home of his own." And there was more on that strain of idealized home life, colored perhaps by my own yearnings. The illustrations showed various aspects of happy living in and around an attractive dwelling. For the cover of the brochure a picture of the headquarters office, a modest two-story building, was redrawn to make it look so imposing that the people going in and out of the mammoth doors could not have been more than two feet tall. This dishonesty quite escaped me. The brochure was sent to all the association's depositors and apparently did suggest to them a quicker way to have the homes for which they had been ploddingly saving. For the booklet became, briefly, a locally famous little effort because it was so successful. I did not know what the average return would be from such a promotion but Mr. F. said proudly that the response to our brochure was considered phenomenal. I was greatly pleased and began to wonder how soon I could ask for a a raise in salary.

It seemed fortunate that the piece had done its job well, for the bills when they began coming in were fairly staggering. At Mr. F.'s suggestion I had spared no expense but I had qualms when I added up the cost of the artwork, cuts, paper, printing, binding, the envelopes and, as I guiltily knew, the overweight postage. One thing puzzled me: at the end of each itemized bill was a surcharge of 50 per cent. Was this customary? I never had bought any printing before and with the statements in hand I went into Mr. F.'s office and asked what the 50 per cent was for. His eyes and smile were noticeably hard as he said. "Never mind about that. Just O.K. the bills as they are." When I went back to my desk it happened that the salesman for the paper company was waiting to see me. I asked him about the surcharge. He laughed and winked with a slight jerk of his head towards Mr. F.'s office. He made no explanation but by then I didn't need any.

I couldn't work under circumstances like those. Employed by the association and paid by them, I would not collaborate in what I felt would be robbing them. The question would not have been quite so clear-cut if Mr. F., and in fact the treasurer, had not required that I validate the bills as correct. In so signing my name I would have been an accomplice, and therefore I told Mr. F. that I was resigning. He made no comment except to say that my employment was terminated as of that day. I took the bills to the treasurer and explained that a personal emergency made it necessary for me to leave before I had had time to look at them. The next month Mr. F. was dismissed from the firm and two months later it went into bankruptcy.

No doubt all the executives had known it was on the edge when they ordered the brochure and hoped by that means to transfer savings deposits into unsecured capital. Many of the depositors were people of small means. Now they had little chance of recovering their money. I realized that my brochure had been to blame and I lost some sleep over that.

2

Even before the firm collapsed I was remembering how impressed I had been, long ago, by Schubert's Quintet, *Die Forellen,* based on the folksong about a trout which lived safely and happily as long as he stayed in clear water but was caught when he swam into a muddied part of the stream. Though quite young, perhaps ten or twelve, I had believed that I was one who was like the trout. Others might not be, but if one were born with a talent, as I had been told I had — a talent in music — then one must stay in the clear water of doing one's best with it. It would be muddy water to play sloppily or compose for trivial, cheap efforts. Actually this was no great moral awakening. The trout symbol was little more than a way to picture my wish to take music seriously.

But the symbol stayed in my mind and it had more meaning when I changed from an ambition in music to one in writing. For there are more ways to prostitute a talent with words than with music: at least it seems so, since words can be used to deceive and they can be used to influence people in wrong directions. No committed writer can thus use his talent without a strong sense of guilt. There is an obligation, hard to analyze, which seems actually to be inborn. If given this ability to create, to pull in ideas from one knows not where, then the gift must never be used irresponsibly.

At that time I had no clear principles about advertising *per se;* until the building and loan association went bankrupt the work I had done on the brochure seemed about on a par with the *Coast Investor* articles, but I could not respect either because I had not really known enough about finance to be giving advice. I had just gone ahead gaily, decorating cold facts with bright phrasing, more interested in making the writing readable than in the value of what was said. And so I had said things that must be regretted. Muddy water. Well, what should I write?

Something of course that would be my own truth. "One's own truth" was a Wellesley definition of writing so distinctly of oneself that no one else could possibly have produced it. That was not to say it was the only valuable kind of writing; facts patiently gathered and honestly presented, or the pointing out of neglected issues, or a clear explanation of what is obscure: there are numerous worthwhile subjects an author can choose, but I was not equipped by temperament to discuss most of them. Besides these however, as I had been taught, there is writing which only incidentally depends on the public world. It is one's personal statement, influenced by experience but largely inborn. For a long time I had felt vaguely — but now sharply — that "my own truth" was what I must offer. The authors that I had particularly enjoyed, like Robert Louis Stevenson, had spoken with their own voices, and it was with them that I had felt most in touch with another human being. They were the ones who could best banish loneliness. But could I ever become a humble member of such a company? At least I could try.

I had been assuming that absolutely individual writing would be drawn from one's subconscious. The mind's conscious level can have been — will have been — influenced by fashions in ideas, by books, journalism, one's associates, friends and relatives; only what is below that level approaches uniqueness. So now I would be discovering what was in my subconscious. I thought I could reach it because I had once found the way to it in producing the musical compositions and poems of childhood years, and to an extent in the themes written at Wellesley. With the present favorable situation, pleasant living quarters and enough money to provide writing time for a little while, I would set out — or rather, *down* — seeking my unknown self. I had no intuition that a descent to the dungeons of the mind could be hazardous.

It seemed logical to start with short stories. Even the characters and the plots would come from those depths, and would evolve into what — in the ambitious terms I thought of it — I had been put in the world to say. I had $261, saved from my salary at the building and loan association, and if I were going to become a creative writer on that, there was no time to waste. Early one morning then I shooed all the bees out of the room and sat down at a window facing the view of the Golden Gate. Ships were making their even way in and out of the channel, the sun shone on the hills beyond, brown that late-summer day, but these pleasant sights were not distracting. I waited with hands on the typewriter keys for my fingers to start to tap out a plot.

Tommy, eight, was almost beside himself with excitement, this being the day his adored older brother was due to come home from the War. Always idolized he was now even more a hero, for he had been decorated for bravery. Tommy boasted about his brother to the big boys hanging around the drug store. A bully took him on: "Your brother ain't been to the war. He's been in prison." The other boys: "Yeah, your brother's a jailbird. Wait till you see his haircut. All prisoners have their hair short like that." Numb with shock Tommy wandered along a brook where he sometimes fished. He would not go home. He never wanted to see his brother again. Worn out with weeping he fell asleep under some bushes. In the morning the police found him there. Tommy locked himself in his bedroom but his brother pleaded, "Let me in. I have something I would be proud to show you." Tommy opened the door, they talked, and he saw the medal of honor and heard his brother explain the GI haircut. Then the story of the big bully came out. The soldier, furious, took Tommy to the store to identify him. The bully denied having called him a jailbird but the other boys' laughter revealed that he was lying. The soldier downed the youth with his first blow. The bully lay very still with his head bleeding where it lay on the curb. The police came, and an ambulance. The ambulance men pronounced the youth dead. And so the police took the soldier away — to prison.

I spent a month expanding that little story. It had seemed to come from the unknown depths in myself and the plot had surprised and disappointed me. I thought the story was rather well written, might even have sold, but I would not submit it anywhere, for sensitive readers would surely have been depressed by it. I didn't believe

that the story was my kind of truth. Why had it come out that way?
I would write another.

This one would be about an elderly actor I'd known in Hollywood. He was cast as a king by Metropolitan whenever they had
such a role, for he had a more regal bearing than many real kings. I
had wondered what he would be like at home. With an ability to
transmute sketchy facts into fiction, as I hoped, now I would find
out.

He and his wife (I assumed) lived with their married daughter.
They shared household expenses and the parents were in arrears
now but soon would make up the balance because he had been
promised a part in a Metropolitan picture. The daughter's husband
did not like this domestic arrangement; that had been understood
but the old couple were terrified at the thought of moving. They
had no savings and unemployed actors had actually starved, as they
knew. One night at dinner the son-in-law announced that he had
sold the house. All knew he had done it to get rid of the elderly
pair. This was a test for the king. Ordinarily he had kept up his
regal manner at home but after a sleepless night he felt unsure of
himself. Yet he pulled himself together for he was due at the studio where he must unmistakably seem a king. As he waited there
for his costume fitting his confidence ebbed and flowed. The costume they brought looked almost like that for a monk. He questioned it: "I have the king's part." "But this time you're a deposed
king," said the assistant. A deposed king: a bad omen and the
actor felt shaken as he walked to the canteen for lunch. On the
way he met the director of the new picture. The director knew
him, called him Bernard, but today there was something not reassuring about the way he stopped him, looked at him sharply, asked
him several pointed questions. As he finished lunch a messenger
brought the king a message: to see the casting director. He was a
young man rather callous, as he had to be in that job, who said
without preliminaries, "Pop, I know I more or less promised you

the role of king in the new picture, but the director has decided he wants somebody else." The king risked asking it: "Why? Because I've played kings so many times?" "Well, no. Pop, you know you are getting old. You're getting round-shouldered. You're starting to crumple. Real kings crumple but not the kings in Metropolitan pictures." The king went out. He would save streetcar fare, he would walk home. An old man, stooped, he shuffled a little as he made his way along Hollywood's street of dreams, Sunset Boulevard.

There it was, the plan for my second story, a tale of cruelty, the son-in-law's, inducing the collapse of the old man's morale and, if a reader's imagination carried far enough, his starvation. Persecution, failure, death: was this a pattern, were seeds like these lying hidden in my subconscious, was I destined to follow just such a development? Had I already, like the king, lost my nerve? I would not be a writer if it would mean spreading a crippled attitude. But I would try once more.

Mike Stroud was seventeen. He lived with his mother, a widow, and sister Natalie who was a teacher. His father had been a very rough character, had beaten up his wife frequently and had died in a barroom brawl when she was pregnant with Mike. She nagged Mike incessantly, telling him he was just like his father and would end the same way if he didn't reform. He was planning to run away and on this night he had reached the end of endurance. He hated his mother and he hated his sister, with her plain face and limp, stringy hair. Mike had gorgeous hair, golden and curly when he washed it, as he did now. He didn't know when he would have another chance, for he was going away in the morning. Before he went to bed he packed a few belongings in a shopping bag, ready to pick up when he would leave right after breakfast, leave for good.

He went to sleep. And late in the night he had a vivid dream,

still very clear when he woke. He dreamed that he had been walking along on an endless desert, yellow and very hot under a blind-
ing sun. His mother and sister were with him. His sister looked
even more bedraggled than usual, and his mother's voice went on
and on, as always praising his sister and in the familiar way whin-
ing that he had been given all the good looks and that wasn't fair.
He was between them, and surprisingly his mother on one side
and his sister on the other were holding his hands. Suddenly, with
an abrupt motion, his mother jerked up her arm and Mike's hand
came off in hers. She threw his hand away. His sister did the same
thing and he lost his other hand. While he was stumbling on, bewildered, his mother tripped him and he fell down. She pulled off
one of his feet and his sister pulled off the other. Now he was
helpless and his mother cackled, "We've got him where we want
him and I can give you his hair." She pulled at his hair and his
scalp came off easily. She put it on Natalie's head where it fitted as
if it were growing there and now Natalie looked much prettier.

In his dream Mike knew that he was dreading the loss of something more precious than hands or feet or hair. It was going to
happen. As he lay on the sand, helpless, his mother began to
loosen his trousers. He struck at her with his stumps of arms and
legs but his mother had what she wanted — his "manhood," as I
wrote it — and now she was trampling it into the sand. He could
see it, it was a bloody nothing. His mother and Natalie walked
away laughing while the scorching sun beat down on Mike where
he lay on the sand, unable to move.

With his last effort before he woke he bellowed with rage — in
his sleep he actually bellowed, and his mother, hearing him, burst
into his room without knocking. "Get *out,*" he yelled and she did
go but left the door open. For a moment he felt that he could not
push it shut, for he had no hands. But then he saw his hand on the
quilt. It had all been a bad dream. For several minutes he lay
there, reassuring himself that he had everything he had had the
night before. Sweat, not from the sun but from his fear, continued
to pour from him.

He got up and dressed but was still very much shaken. The only peace came when he remembered that he was going away this morning — going for good. Tomorrow morning, wherever he would be, no mother would dare to intrude in his room. He would not have to see her again, he would not have to see Natalie. Already he had seen Natalie for the last time, since she would have left early to go to her school. He went downstairs and into the kitchen for breakfast. His mother's talk was as irritating as usual. Why had he yelled, what was he dreaming about? Had he dreamed about where he had gone last night? Where *did* he go? He had come in later than usual. Explain where he went. A mother had every right to know. He must have had a date with a girl, since he had washed his hair. Or was the date tonight? He didn't wash his hair often enough. He didn't know how lucky he was to have such beautiful hair. Natalie should have had his hair. She would have taken care of it. And then his mother said, "If I could I would take your scalp right off your head and give it to Natalie."

Anger exploded in Mike with such violence, it was a fit of madness. His mother was sitting on one of the kitchen chairs, which she had turned aslant from the table. In a leap Mike had reached her and snatching an apron was tying her arms together behind the chair with the apron strings. She could not rise from the chair and cried, "Let me go! *Let me go!* What are you doing?" What Mike was doing was sharpening one of the kitchen knives. His mother was terrified. He kept on sharpening the knife, looking down at her. He enjoyed seeing her helpless and panic-stricken. Now she was quivering and white with fear. "Don't kill me, don't kill me!" she pleaded. He was afraid she would faint. That would spoil what he planned to do. "I am not going to kill you," he told her harshly. He ripped open her dress till her chest was exposed. His first impulse had been to cut his initials into her breasts. But when they were bare he found that they were collapsed and wrinkled. They were collapsed because she had nursed him, but he did not know that. Very well, he would cut his initials above her breasts.

She was still screaming and struggling and he put one hand over her mouth. He was steely calm. "I am not going to kill you," he said, "but I am going away forever and I'm going to leave you something so you will never forget you once had a son. You've never treated me like a son."

He made an incision about two inches long above her right breast. "You've treated me like an intruder that had no right to be in your life — yours and Natalie's." Another incision, not very deep but deep enough to leave a scar. Now he had finished an M. Blood was running out of the wound. But he did not hesitate. On the other side, above her left breast, he cut a crude S. Strange how tough her skin was. His mother continued to scream. He was glad the windows were closed.

He untied her arms. "Get yourself something and mop up the blood," he said. But his mother had fallen. She lay on the floor. She looked as if she were in a faint, but she wasn't because her eyes followed him. He threw a towel down to her. "Mop up the blood, I told you." Those were the last words he spoke to her. He stepped across her and walked out through the hall, picking up his shopping bag and went out the door. Her screams were still in his ears but he drowned them by saying again and again to himself, She will remember me. She will remember me.

If I had had to face the meaning of that story as soon as I finished it, I don't know what immediate revelation it might have brought. I had so deeply identified with Mike as I wrote it that I had not wondered about the plot's significance to myself; I had simply wanted to get Mike out of that house, forever away from his mother's hatred and jealousy. And as soon as the last words were down, I had had to postpone any effort to understand them, for I had to turn quickly to the problem of where to live.

My landlord and his wife had made a trip to Southern California and when they came back said that they had bought a house down there, in an orchard on a highway. They were going to raise bees and the wife, sitting out at the side of the road, would sell honey. She spoke regretfully of this change but said it had become necessary for her husband to leave his teaching post. For some reason they didn't understand, the rest of the faculty at his high school had taken a concerted dislike to him. Their animosity made his life intolerable and so he had resigned and wishing to get completely away from San Francisco, they had sold this Steiner Street house.

With the decision irrevocable the gentle scientist was dumbfounded to find that he was well liked by his colleagues. They gave him a farewell dinner at which speech after speech told of the high esteem in which he was held, how much they would miss his considerate nature among them, and what a loss his going would be to the school. They gave him a handsome clock. His wife told me all this with tears running down her cheeks, for she had not wanted to leave San Francisco. She could not explain how the misunderstanding had arisen, but her husband had always underestimated himself. He had so much goodwill — I could testify to that, for it shone out with his every glance — that he automatically expected the same response from others. When they did not express it so freely, he assumed that their goodwill was lacking: that was as close as his wife could come to an intimation of what had happened. It seemed likely that she was right.

There, I thought, was a legitimate story: sadness but nothing sinister. I would have liked to attempt it if I had not had to seek a new place to live at once, while I still had enough money to pay the first month's rent. I was down to my last $28.

I found a room on the third floor of a rooming house. It cost $15 a month and so after I'd paid a drayman $2.50 to move my trunk I had $10.50 left. This was an emergency I had not anticipated, because the Steiner Street couple were known to be very lenient about delayed rent. Now that cushion was gone, and at the lowest depths

of the 1930's depression. I was not very much worried. I would
look for a job as a typist.

That intention had vanished within a week, for there seemed to
be thousands of girls out of jobs. They filled the crowded employment offices and stood in long queues beside the walls of the corri-
dors. When I finally would reach the desk for an interview, I found
that what I had hoped were my good qualifications were in fact otherwise. It didn't matter that I said I could type very rapidly; when I
explained the other jobs I had held, the interviewer usually said,
"You will never be satisfied in a typing job." In one or two agencies
where I intimated that I had run out of money, "So have a lot of
these girls," said the interviewers with glances lingering on my
well-tailored suit. I had only the smart Hollywood clothes I had
brought to San Francisco, and they were obviously a handicap. I felt
self-conscious, apologetic, in them. Besides the agencies, I applied in
department stores and companies that might employ large numbers
of girls. There the answers were "No vacancies," or "We only employ local people."

President Roosevelt had been installed but the work programs
which would give help to millions of unemployed were not yet set
up. And appeals to my family were out of the question, for my father's factory had failed and my young brother was just getting a
start; I would not be a drag on him. As hunger became an increasing problem, absolutely the only solution I could think of was the
Salvation Army. But my family were the kind of people who *gave*
to the Salvation Army, we didn't ask them for help.

And so, what to do? The answer was obvious: forget about food.
I bought two pounds of coffee and a pound of grapes and that left
$1.10 for more grapes. Fate would just have to come to my aid if it
would.

It was a terrible little room that I'd rented, very small and furnished with only an iron cot, a straight chair, a bureau and a wash-stand with a gas plate on top. In the bottom part of the washstand, where a chamber pot had once been kept, were a cup and saucer, a plate, a coffeepot and a frying pan. One could survive with that equipment, I supposed, if one had the money for fried eggs and an occasional chop. Crumbs in a drawer suggested that a previous tenant had had bread. I put the plate on top and the grapes on it. I would not eat a whole meal of grapes, just keep them to have three or four if hunger became unbearable.

I will explain about hunger. The first effect is restlessness. It probably is akin to the feeling that makes an animal leave its nest or burrow and search for food. The restlessness does feel like a search and it should be possible to turn the lack into a search for ideas and spar-kling words but in real hunger the restlessness is a physical sensa-tion and if it cannot be satisfied it becomes very demanding. Although there is nothing to look for, no food in the cupboard, one moves about the room thoughtlessly, opens and closes drawers, picks up a pillow and puts it down, adjusts the curtain, obsessively straightens the rug. The rug was a runner that had a wrinkle across the center and I had a continuous battle with it to try to make it lie flat. Pushing out on both ends I could smooth it down, but let me go out of the room or lie on the cot, within a few minutes the wrin-kle was there again. The rug was like an animal, dog or cat, that in-sists on sleeping in only a certain position.

Outside there was nothing to see except the backs of some shabby apartment houses. A dirty curtain kept blowing across the sill of a window, constantly flapping. I felt like that curtain, moving around to no purpose, and decided that I would go outdoors for a while.

On that day I found a small park, only a square block or two but one of John McLaren's green places to which "any resident of San Francisco can walk." A few benches were there: lovely. Now I had some place to come and sit in the sunshine. The restlessness was transferred to my head. In circumstances like these what did one think about?

Think first about the two earlier stories, the boy whose bragging had put his brother in prison, and the old couple who had been turned out of their daughter's house. Cruelty was the theme of both, and the boy's pain seemed the more depressing. He would have to know he had been responsible for his brother's arrest because he had bragged to the bully. To the raw ingredients of sorrow would have to be added his guilt — so much sorrow for such a small wrong. The cruelty seemed to be fate's, vindictively punishing.

Fate seemed to be involved too in the actor's impending starvation. After the studios had begun giving him kingly roles, arrogance must have grown in him. He would still be a king in his son-in-law's house, and the son-in-law would not endure that.

Here it was then, the same disillusion that had been present in my themes written at college.

The story about Mike and his mother was naked horror. I could recognize the application to my own life. It would have been more logical to make it a story of daughter and mother, but a daughter could not have been castrated, not at least physically, as in Mike's dream. But what was the meaning of it? That mothers hate their children, of course. That they may want to kill them. And one's other relatives kill. *"It is likely that many people who seem to die natural deaths have in fact been poisoned by their families"* — not just kill in a sudden fit of anger, but plan long enough in advance to get poison. Why be surprised that my story had brought this gruesome fact into the light? Hadn't the knowledge lain in my mind, not very far under the surface, ever since my mother first warned me about those poisonings?

And if it was so common for relatives to kill, then one had to accept that others do. People, the ordinary people one met every day, would commit murder and no doubt many had. People I knew? Paul Powell, who had seemed so gentle? He had said, "If any man ever tells you what it is all about, I will come and kill him." He certainly was exaggerating but, see, he had had the *thought* of murder. I ran through a list of people I'd known, both emotional and mild-tempered ones, and the single exception to those who would consider murdering and therefore might do it, was, I thought, my father. My father had no malice in his nature at all, he was one of those who are born innocent-hearted — not innocent in the sense of not recognizing evil but in the sense of having none of it in himself. I could think of nobody else of whom I believed that was true.

No wonder then that, under an appearance of calm, one moved about with a kind of terrified caution. I did. I had an unfortunate manner that I had realized must seem ingratiating. Anyone might assume that I was seeking favors of one kind or another but now I understood that actually I was trying to disarm possible killers. I was trying to avoid giving people the slightest provocation. If many others were not thus appealing to be allowed to live, it was only that they had not sensed the danger. But I had, and I would have to go on through the rest of my life knowing it.

There were a few of us who went to the little park every day. Two old men, one with a cane, never sat near each other. They looked utterly lonely, and could they not share the sadness of being old? They did not even glance at each other; one could guess that they avoided seeing another man who was decrepit, worn out, because each of them knew so well that that was what he had become.

But there were two women, not long-time friends apparently, who always drifted to the same bench and talked to each other. It seemed rather mindless talk, what I heard of it, variations of, "So I said to my daughter . . ." At least they were holding at bay their own loneliness and perhaps each had the illusion that she looked the younger.

Which way was better? For me, it seemed, the choice would have to be disillusionment. But sometimes the cold truth was intolerable.

The sunny weather had held, till a day came that felt chilly. A few clouds were in the sky. I would go back to my room.

I shouldn't have turned this way, for now I shall have to go past the grocery store and my money's all gone, and also my grapes. See the apples and pears and bananas outside on the trays — chewable, nourishing bananas — how easy to slip one into a pocket. But no, I have not been reduced to stealing. The children are all in school. I should like to see children, running and shouting, well-fed children full of ongoing life. But what I keep seeing is ill-clad men and women, many old, some of them, too, looking hungry. There is nothing exceptional about being hungry these days, but things should work out. I don't know how.

Lean against this wall. I could just be waiting for someone. The dizziness will soon pass. It doesn't. Suppose I should faint, fall down on the sidewalk? Might I come to in a police station and perhaps be given a meal? A disgrace. Keep thinking. Concentrate on this fence. It's only four houses farther. I can make it. Move slowly, carefully. Concentrate.

Back in my room after the slow climb up the stairs I lie on the cot. The washstand and bureau and chair are swimming around the bed but they soon settle down in their places. This is better. Better not to go out any more. If I lie still I can think more clearly.

In spite of the vast unemployment, if only I could have *food* I could surely devise some unique way to make money. What might I do? Maybe I could take old people or children out for the day. There must be prosperous relatives who would pay for such help.

The visions become concrete and sharp, only not sensible. I, laughing, skipping, am leading a bunch of very elderly people, also laughing and skipping, through Chinatown. How foolish. I am not thinking straight.

It is Sunday and I have taken some children out to a park. We are all laughing. I toss them up into the trees where they pump themselves up and down on the branches. One has flown away, just flew off with some birds. A pretty notion. One might put it into a children's story.

Exhausted from hunger I drift in and out of sleep. I am taking a bank manager through a printing plant where I shall be making a booklet for him. He is impressed by how much I know. But sickeningly the factory turns out to be making automobiles. Myself at work in a library but someone has left the door open and a cyclone comes and sucks all the books out and away. As a cyclone had once sucked the breath out of my lungs.

Wake up! Think what to do. I couldn't get any sort of job in this state. I have come to an impasse.

A small new thought began to intrude. It seemed lucid enough but at first it hardly was recognized. It was like a tiny leak from a pinhole-opening in a gas pipe — in the beginning not even a whiff and for some time afterwards only a vague sense of something different. But then finally *there,* a thought that no longer could be avoided.

The thought was, why live?

Now it could not be ignored, this possibility of no longer living. Suppose I did live and the hunger problem was solved in some way. Nevertheless, wherever I went I would still be among people one couldn't trust. And there seemed to be something provocative in my nature. If a mother had found that she couldn't endure my existence, probably others couldn't. One could never feel safe enough to relax. No. I did not wish to go on.

It seemed rather sad that my life, which had been so promising during those years at Wellesley, had come to this sordid end. To die of
starvation here in this terrible little room would be the ultimate failure, but to die before I had reached that limit, to die with purpose,
would still be strong. (How many who contemplate suicide have
had that deceptive thought?)

Finding the means was easy. I had an unopened bottle of sleeping pills, given to me by that hiking doctor during my first weeks in
San Francisco. Those should be enough. The time was about 1
A.M. A soft gentle rain was falling. I stood at the open window,
breathing in air that seemed deliciously fresh. Pouring out half the
pills, all I thought would go down at one gulp, I swallowed them.
The rest were then in my hand, now to follow the others . . . when
a dog barked. I was startled, for it seemed the bark of the little white
dog I had betrayed long ago. He kept on barking and I thought of
the way he had tried to keep up with my bicycle going down the
hill, of my last glimpse of his flying feet and the wind flinging back
his ears. Was it indeed the same dog, sending a message across the
years, a needed hallucination — or an actual dog in San Francisco
that night? If an actual living dog, how did I know he was white?
Perhaps fate was touching me with the only voice to which I could
respond. For how could I leave a world where there were small
trusting dogs?

I threw the rest of the pills out into the rainy dark, fell onto the
bed and at once felt myself drifting away from life, drifting up and
out into swirls of gray mist.

o

The next morning the landlady came to my room to learn why she
had not seen me lately. When I couldn't be roused she found the
empty medicine bottle, which had the doctor's name on it. She
called him and he came and did what was necessary — I am not

clear about what that was. And he persuaded her to bring me food until I was straightened out.

He guessed that I had run out of money and the next day we talked about solving that problem. When I told him about my brother, who had a good job in Chicago, he insisted that I should ask him if he could help with a loan. That would not be an imposition, the doctor said; these were dreadful times and many would starve if their families did not come to the rescue. It was even a good thing, he said, that the depression was drawing families closer together. They were recognizing their dependence on one another. I doubted that any of my family wanted that, but I did write to my brother, who responded at once with a generous check. And while I waited the landlady was giving me meals, food that the doctor had recommended.

I was not glad to have been brought back to life. Starving would probably now be avoided, but starving had never been the chief difficulty. That was the disillusionment, the prospect of going on with the old familiar fears, the lack of trust in anybody, except my father perhaps and he was out of reach. It would need more strength than I ever would have to take up the burden of always being on guard and desperate.

As I lay in bed convalescing however, I remembered something that had happened in Hollywood. When I was at Metropolitan Paul Powell, who liked my face (it was no longer smashed in), had persuaded Mr. Sistrom and Al Christie that they should put me in movies. Paul had visualized a series built around one character, who would be myself. No one explained the plan to me until it was complete, and then Paul had said, "You will be a kind of waif, always in dreadful trouble but things will turn out right in the end." Curiously I was not thrilled, in fact hardly interested. Perhaps I knew intuitively that nothing would come of it. But we went through with the screen test. The makeup man smoothed up my features and Paul directed as I acted in one little scene after another. He thought they were good until we saw the film in the projection room. The results were rather astonishing, for the camera had caught what the men apparently had not seen in my living face — a look that went far beyond the dismay they had planned for the story line, dismay in tolerable proportions they thought audiences would find moving. What the pictured face showed was a battlefield of more violent emotions — terror, desperation, guilt, bitterness. The film was scrapped and no more was said about my dawning picture career.

But I had been shocked by the revelation of so much turmoil. If all that was going on at a lower level of my mind, it had better be brought to the surface and straightened out by some process like psychoanalysis: so I had thought at the time. The resolve had been formed that some day I would be analyzed, but that intention was pushed out of sight among other distressing elements, and I went on being distracted by the melodramatic studio events, the move to San Francisco and the two financial jobs. Then writing the stories had taken me down into the realm of horror again. Now for the second time I clearly knew what should be done.

The next time the doctor came I told him the suicide had not been due to hunger but to "some disturbing ideas" I had, that I had tried to resolve them myself but couldn't, and so I believed I needed the help of a psychoanalyst. Would he recommend one? He said, "I am a psychoanalyst, and if you like we can start right away to get you straightened out."

That doctor a psychoanalyst! The very thought set up an emotional clamor. For he seemed so neurotic himself that one couldn't imagine his giving wise guidance. He was painfully tense and self-conscious, and with such a busy personal manner that I had already thought, There is something in himself that he can't face, otherwise he wouldn't keep jumping around that way. How could anyone pour out excruciating memories to a man who would never sit still but must always be crossing and uncrossing his knees, pushing up his glasses, running a hand over his head, pulling his chin up out of his collar, shifting his weight in his chair? He could not even listen with normal restraint to what any average patient was saying, but must keep darting in with premature comments. Probe one's inconceivable depths with this man? Impossible. But he was already consulting his datebook. "I will see you at three next Monday."

The first talk did not go well. I was defensive — and angry because the uncongenial doctor, intruding aggressively, had sabotaged my great effort to find a way to live. When I left he told me to come back on Thursday. Three days to decide what to do. Only one thing seemed possible — ignore the man, try not to look at him, don't hear when he keeps breaking in with uncomprehending remarks. Just talk and talk and talk and try to believe that some help can come out of finding words for what is unspeakable. Try once more.

For fifteen or twenty minutes I did that, let flow a stream of shattering memories. Then I chanced to look at him. His face was pale, his mouth inert, his eyes unfocussed, for he had lost nervous control. Perhaps what I was saying had shocked him. More likely he was realizing that this was a case for which he was not equipped. Whatever the reason, his morale had collapsed, he was paralyzed with self-consciousness.

This was indeed a final horror: to make oneself utterly vulnerable, to expose one's deepest need to another and have him fail. For a hideous moment my sanity swayed. But a sweeping fury took hold of me. *One* of us had to be crisp:

"Tell me," I said very sharply, "what was your analytical training."

The doctor struggled to pull himself together. "I have done a lot of reading —— "

"Under *whom* did you study?"

"No one. It wasn't necessary. I've done a lot —— "

"You have no qualifications at all."

"Oh, yes, I have a very good understanding of the analytical techniques."

"Have you been analyzed yourself?"

"No, I —— "

"An analysis is the first requirement of anyone planning to practice. Even I know that."

"In my case it wasn't necessary. Because I have such a good understanding of —— "

"How many other patients have you tried to treat?"

A pause; then, "One."

"Man or woman?"

"A woman."

"How long has her analysis been going on?"

"We were interrupted. She had to go into hospital."

"A mental hospital?"

A murmured, "Yes."

I walked out of his office, went down in the elevator and to the nearest telephone booth were I dialled the University of California in Berkeley and asked for the Psychology Department. Could they tell me the name of the best psychoanalyst west of Chicago? A short wait and then someone else came on the line—my lifeline — and said, "The two best analysts anywhere in the West are right here in San Francisco." He gave me the names and I dialled one of them. A strong, slightly foreign voice answered. I asked if he could give me an appointment and he said yes, the next day at two o'clock.

I was terribly shaken by the experience with that unscrupulous doctor, for I didn't have strength enough on that day to hold onto hope. Back on my bed in the rooming house I fell into despair. Why go further? Why see the analyst tomorrow? He too would fail to help me, in some different way. Nothing had ever come right and so nothing would. Dignity, integrity, required that I kill myself and this time do a final job of it.

But the next day I went as far as the lobby of the Flood Building, where the analyst had his office, and found his name on the directory: Dr. Carl Renz, on the eighth floor. There was a light well in the center of the stairs. I would see him and if all was not promising, I would come down the light well. But I had twenty minutes to wait and walked across Market Street and into the Emporium, San Francisco's largest department store. It was fairly crowded, and in the confusion of all those people I lost my composure again. It would be useless to see Dr. Renz. I should take my life *now*. Beneath the dome I turned back towards the door, fully intending to throw myself under the wheels of the first heavy truck that approached.

Ahead of me was a little girl, about six years old, with her mother. The child was walking backward as the two went towards the door, and she was smiling up into my face in the most friendly and beautiful way. It was a smile of determined encouragement, and she held her eyes on mine as if waiting for some reassurance. I was impressed, for it seemed an omen, but I still wondered how she had happened to be walking backward, why had she turned around if she had not first seen my distraught face, and how could she have seen it if she had been walking ahead of me in the normal way?

It has never occurred to me till this moment, as I am writing these words, that the little girl may have been imaginary. She seemed so real that once, years later when I was very happy, I thought of putting a "Personal" advertisement in the *San Francisco Chronicle* thanking the child, if she remembered, because her smile had saved my life. Now I believe that the child may have been myself as I was at the age of six, and that the hallucination was a sign from the subconscious monitor urging that one last time I should try to live. (But of course the child could in truth have existed.)

With a surge of hope I went up the Flood Building elevator and into the door with Dr. Renz's name on it. He came forward, a large man, tall, with a kind but authoritative manner, one who would take hold of problems and *solve* them, one in whom a troubled patient could have absolute trust. My tears burst out suddenly and so copiously that I couldn't even give him my name and I continued to weep uncontrollably through the entire time I was there. I sat at the side of his desk and as he faced me he was quiet, only now and then moving a small brass lion. Sometimes he spoke a few words soothingly, as one would to a child but a child who has had a real fright. Otherwise he smiled and his tone was lighter. I was wearing bangs, a word he may not have known, being foreign, but perhaps he was just being whimsical when he asked, "Why do you have those hairs hanging down?" And he asked more questions but not insistently. Most of what he said, in one way or another, was the promise that he would help and together we would find the way out of my dark distress.

At the end of the hour he stood up and I was able to check the tears, since I would have to go. He said, "I live across the Bay and usually I don't come over on Saturday. But I think you might like to see me tomorrow and so I will come. At two o'clock again?" And then gently, "In the meantime you won't do anything foolish, will you." I shook my head with some sort of smile. "Tomorrow you will be able to talk. And I will be listening."

To this desperate near-end I had come by the determination to write my own truth, to explore what would be found in obscure depths. As I had suspected, creativity may reveal an unknown self. That the discoveries can be unbearable was intimated in A. Alvarez's recent book describing the suicides of a surprising number of twentieth century writers, as different as Sylvia Plath and Ernest Hemingway, who risked making those soundings.

I am still awed by the kindness of fate which allowed my own dive to take me into such healing, beneficent hands.

viii

LA VITA NUOVA

There were giants . . . in those days. Genesis 6:4

CARL RENZ — not Doctor then — was born in Alsace-Lorraine of a German mother and an Italian father (the family name was Rienzi). From his German side he had inherited a respect for scholarship and from the Italian, warm human sympathy and quickness of understanding: exceptionally good equipment for a psychoanalyst.

His childhood was spent in Germany, France, Italy, and Russia, longest in Russia where he absorbed the rich, dark mythology of those talented people. He went to Tübingen University (founded in 1477) where he took a medical degree and was planning to practice in Europe, but on a voyage to America he fell in love with a beautiful girl from California, and when they were married he agreed to settle in San Francisco.

After ten years of working with patients he became convinced that psychological factors play a large part in physical health and decided to make his specialty the treating of patients' minds. Wanting as always to give his work the soundest possible background, he returned several times to Europe and studied separately with the three masters of psychoanalysis, Freud, Adler, and Jung. He found Jung's approach the most congenial but adopted some of the theories and techniques of the others, out of them all developing his own analytical method.

He spoke eight languages fluently and his cultural background was a wide sweep over Europe. Details like these would not be known at once to a patient, but Dr. Renz's intelligent and assured manner immediately inspired confidence. One of the first things I learned was that he had had musical training and was a pianist — his brother was then editor of Germany's best-known musical magazine; and so music provided an untroubled subject for our first conversations.

But could he really be trusted? Since I believed that no one except my father could be, the progress of the analysis, my very life at first, depended on what Dr. Renz was as a person even more than as scientist. In our second talk Dr. Renz said that he never took more than six patients, so much time and energy being demanded in an analysis, but he said one of his patients had finished that very week, "and so, fortunately I can put you into that vacant place." I already knew that patients in psychoanalysis are supposed to pay well for their treatment, and I told him at once that I had no job and no money. He brushed that information aside. For the present, he said, he would continue to come across the Bay on all Saturdays and holidays, and on Sundays I should write him a letter — we would never be out of touch. Such compassionate help, and from a stranger who didn't yet know the desperate need (or did he?) was enough to persuade me to hold in abeyance the inclination to leave the perfidious world by suicide.

Dr. Renz sensed the chaos that existed in my subconscious, and his way of exploring it was the standard practice of dream analysis. He explained that this was his method and asked me not to read anything about dreams for the present, so that the spontaneity of my own might not be distorted. Dreams would be bringing the traumas up from my subconscious into full light of day, where my rational mind would defuse them. Both drugs and hypnosis were (and are)

used by some analysts to set in motion this dream mechanism, but
Dr. Renz said he felt that a patient's improvement was likely to be
more permanent if he did most of the work of releasing the memories himself. It would be a bold thing, he warned, to come face to
face with suppressed anxieties, but it could be done here with perfect
safety because he would give all the support I could possibly need.
There was nothing whatever to fear but one must go forward with
courage. There was a stout-hearted spirit in the very way he pronounced courage — "couratch" — his chin going up a bit. He said
there were drugs that gave one the sense of courage, but if one tried
to achieve it oneself, one's glands responded with the real thing. I
would find that was true. There had been, were even then, disasters
in his own life, I later learned. One would not have suspected it.

There were not as many surprises dredged up as perhaps Dr.
Renz expected. I had always been aware, consciously, of all but one
of the more decisive events in my childhood. That one came out
through a dream but not until after several months. Other dreams
did bring out details of the incidents I was telling about, and what
the dreams revealed, shocking to me, was what had been my subconscious reaction to the cruelty of my mother. I had always
thought that I had been very cool, taking care with a calculated patience not to disturb her. I had been rather proud of my efforts to be
"a nice child." But what the dreams showed was that all through
those years I had been filled with explosive anger. I had been out-
raged by all the evidence that I was hated and by the many times I
had been falsely accused of weakness, of instability, of deceit. Now
the pent-up indignation came spilling out. My very face in the mirror changed. It looked like the face in the Hollywood screen tests,
distraught and unpleasant. Those days must have been a trial for
Dr. Renz.

He did nothing to check my new attitude. Indeed he listened

with what appeared to be sympathy and some signs of shock (probably simulated) to my unmotherly treatment. After weeks of such
talk my anger was finally dispersed; and then came a new
development — I began to wonder if I had provoked some of the
hatred. The dreams disclosed ways I had shut my mother out of my
life. And one reminded me of a snapshot I had once seen, of myself
sitting on my father's lap with my head back against his shoulder
and a look on the small face that said clearly, "This daddy is *mine*."

I asked Dr. Renz why I hid all my anger when I was growing up.
"Try to discover why," was all he would say. Many times, I
thought, I could have protested, for example about being deprived of
food, and I didn't. After the cyclone in Cleveland, when my mother
showed plainly that she was sorry I hadn't been killed, I could have
said, "All the other mothers came to school with dry clothes for
their children." And when she tried to persuade me to commit suicide, I could at least have said, "That's a pretty strange thing to hear
from a mother." I didn't really believe at this late time that I would
have been endangered if I had made such remarks — and why
hadn't I?

The answer had to come out in a dream, a dream of the only
memory I had not been able to describe fully. It was an incident
when I was six. I had remembered it long enough, four years, to be
able to talk to John Craig about it, but then I had lost it. In a general way I knew consciously that something unpleasant had happened. I could describe the Sunday morning: the rain, Elizabeth's
boredom, how much my mother had hoped from her being with us,
the goat's escape and my father's fall in the mud and my defending
him from my mother's ridicule. The rest of the day was blank. Had
I even been slapped, perhaps lightly shaken?

The aftermath too was remembered vividly: the sudden illness,
the tic, the neurologist, my many new and enormous fears. Why
such extreme reactions to whatever had happened?

I had been dreaming profusely, those dreams of anger and guilt, and when I described them Dr. Renz always said, "What does that remind you of?" He had taught me to answer without trying to reason out any significance, since the subconscious speaks in symbolic language and with minor details it will sometimes reveal important meanings. A quick response to "What does that remind you of" would often produce the kernel of truth we were looking for.

One day I took him a dream about windows — most unpromising.

"What kind of windows?"

"Casement windows. Rather high. They were oblongs of light but they darkened ——— "

"What does that remind you of?"

Now suddenly I was hysterical, was screaming I think, because I knew that the windows were those in the upstairs room at the Brownells' house, and the windows went dark because I was being strangled. Again I could feel my mother's hand closing my throat. In the dream it was my life that was losing light.

I am not really sure what happened during the few moments after the dream made the memory clear. Then finally I knew that Dr. Renz was holding my hands and saying, "It is all right. It's all right, you are strong enough to face this. It happened but you lived through it and it can't hurt you now." He continued to talk, putting all his authority into the reassuring words, and the storm gradually eased away.

I had weathered it only because of the wise support I had had in the crisis. Dr. Renz himself had been ready for it. He told me afterwards that he had known for six weeks what the revelation would be.

And if it had been a different analyst? One less skilled?

At the time of that climax Dr. Renz had moved his office to the new 450 Sutter Building, and when I left that day and walked up prosaic Sutter Street in midafternoon, I had a fantasy that I walked through a field of wildflowers blowing in sunlight.

A new world had been born for me and a new life had begun on that day.

o

Instead of flowers the vision could just as well have been the faces of people passing on Sutter Street on that memorable afternoon — faces now friendly, harmless for the first time since I was six. That was the way faces looked from then on, but I might have been thinking of flowers because they are symbols of innocence: flowers so guiltless, so incorruptible, were the face of the world on the day my great fear was cast off.

One might expect that it would have seemed amazing and wonderful to be able to think of people, now, as no longer potential murderers. Instead it seemed perfectly natural. It is normal to expect a certain amount of good will in casual passersby and immediately that seemed normal also to me. A certain habit of caution hung over, but no longer panic. The panic was gone forever.

As soon as the invisible memory of the violent Sunday burst up into consciousness, Dr. Renz and I talked about it. Or rather he listened; I did most of the talking while he, with a questioning look or a smile of agreement, guided my thoughts to the right conclusions. At last I knew why I had been so timid during the childhood years: subconsciously I had known that a mother like mine might attack. When she said, "It is likely that many people who seem to die natural deaths have in fact been poisoned by their families," that suggestion had stayed only a short way below the surface and was apt to come up into daylight at any time, when I might be happy or troubled, and I had supposed that my fear of other people was due to her intimating that anybody might murder. Now however I believed, and Dr. Renz agreed, that my deep distrust was due to the experience of having my breath nearly stopped. I had long under-stood that my mother wished I were dead, but a wish is a pale threat compared with a hand on one's throat. Being finally able to face that experience consciously, I knew that normal mothers do not want to harm their children, not hour after hour and day after day. Most parents feel antagonism occasionally, but in this case a mother had had those strange impulses continuously. Why?

That question had come up several times and at last Dr. Renz was willing to answer it. For more than a year he had been reading the correspondence between my mother and me and from the evi-dence in the letters and our talks he had decided, he said, that "we have to assume that your mother has paranoia." He spoke in a cas-ual tone, probably to avoid making the information too startling. But I didn't realize at that time what true paranoia would mean: that she never had been responsible for her attitude or its expression, that she simply was showing the signs of a mental illness. "Paranoia" — why, that was just a fad word, I thought. "Oh, don't be so paranoiac about it," meaning don't be so touchy or so extrava-gantly angry. I had said things like that myself. And so I didn't fol-low up what Dr. Renz was then ready to tell me. I remember the moment and how I changed the subject. To Dr. Renz the sugges-tion of paranoia would have been significant and he may have thought that I was refusing to accept unwelcome knowledge. It is possible of course that he would have been right.

When that information became clear in the later talks with Dr. Isaacs my mother ceased being an ogre who had presided over my childhood and could be seen as the gracious person that she essen-tially was. But perhaps it was just as well that I failed to under-stand Dr. Renz and that my disillusionment continued for a little while longer. Before many more months a great compensation would come out of it.

My analysis had started in April and Dr. Renz saw me every day except Sunday until mid-September. After that he felt that four times a week would be safe, later three times and then two. The analysis came to a natural end after nearly two years. He was pleased with the way it had gone. Shortly before Dr. Alfred Adler died he was in San Francisco and Dr. Renz included me in a dinner they had together. With his usual light touch he said that he wanted to show me off as one of his successes.

Nevertheless he thought I should recognize the limitations of my emotional recovery. When, remembering the tormented mother on the Hollywood streetcar, I told him that I never wanted to marry, he did not disapprove. He said, "Wherever you are, you may always have to be able to go away." But he didn't think I should therefore be deprived of love. A relaxed but discriminating attitude towards sex was one of the benefits he attempted to give — not to give it with any ponderous pronouncements, more often with small debonaire asides in the course of our talks. For example, regarding the current fad of wearing no stockings: "It is all right with me if women want to go out on the street with naked legs but they are wrong if they think they are being alluring. The irresistible women were those I knew when I was a student. They wore skirts to the ground and eight petticoats. I know — I used to count 'em."

The jolly remarks were not all of it. He tried, like a wise parent in fact, to put in my mind a vision of love that is guided by sensitivity and finesse. On a piece of paper he said he hoped I would keep he wrote: *Love is a delicate plant. It will wither if treated roughly.*

I am not sure he was even aware of something else he had given: a view of life that was sane, tolerant, and very civilized in the sense of encompassing many cultures. All this was not proffered in any one talk, rather expressed in his characteristic comments on incidents I would describe. Being himself, he would always hold up a picture of sanity against which one could measure exceptions. Sanity is what any analyst tries to present, of course, but with Dr. Renz it seemed effortless and spontaneous, typical of him later too, when I knew him after the analysis was over.

As it neared its end, the transference had to be weakened and finally broken. At an early point he had explained the meaning of the analytical transference — that a patient transfers to the analyst deep emotions previously felt, probably towards a parent. In this process the patient gains an enhanced confidence in the analyst which facilitates the emerging of the sometimes-frightening memories. In my case what was transferred, temporarily, was my devotion to my father, to whom I could have told anything if we had been closer in understanding and if he had not usually been away. Dr. Renz played his part with a convincing impression of fatherly tenderness and concern. But the time comes when the patient has to be set free from that bond — a rather unhappy experience for all patients in analysis, I imagine, but even during that period I could admire the subtle way Dr. Renz loosened the tie, with a little coldness on one day, indifference on another.

When my analysis was all finished it was permissible for me to know more personally Dr. Renz and the perceptive young woman he had recently married (his first wife having died), and sometimes I spent weekends at their house, filled with foreign treasures, on a high hill in Marin County. Besides the satisfaction of having such good friends, I was very interested then to see in what ways Dr. Renz at home was different from the analyst in his office. He was still interested in my welfare; what was lacking was the protectiveness; and what was gained was the knowledge of his rich and now more varied personality.

But the concern never had been all technique, all acting. I was very fortunate to have fallen into the hands of one who believed, with Dr. Jung, that psychotherapy rests on a genuine relationship between two human beings and that the relationship is "the significant thing to which all theories and methods should be secondary." Dr. Jung insisted that "any suffering should be shared" — and I had the reassurance all along that Dr. Renz was sharing mine. I don't underrate his skill and intelligence, but the thing I had needed most he had been ready to give generously: his response as a human being.

A compassionate giant.

o

To be free of panic was the greatest benefit I gained from the analysis. Now, I thought, my mother and I can have the same kind of pleasant relationship that she has with her circle of friends. I believed that when she found I at last had become adult, no longer afraid of her, she would respect me and welcome a new kind of bond.

That prospect seemed nearer when my brother married and he and his gentle, understanding wife came to live in Berkeley, across the Bay from San Francisco. Two children were born, and to be near them my parents moved to Berkeley, my father having retired. Here we were, all our family together again and, it was hoped, under much happier circumstances.

It didn't work out that way, not for my father nor me. He was pleased with the boy and girl; "They are good children," he said in a way which meant "the family strain is sound." But something had happened to him. Most of the inner radiance was gone. He himself felt its lack. As he said towards the end of his life, "Something that was there isn't there any more." One thing that never was gone was his spirit of helpfulness. My parents had invested in a plot with two houses on it, planning to leave it to my brother and me, but my father decided that I would do better with a place of my own and after he was seventy years old went back in business in order to buy me a three-apartment building on the edge of the campus. Later, when he was suffering with a terminal cancer he was still painting furniture for us; and when he was in the hospital in a two-patient room he had to be moved to a single room because, in his delirium, he was trying to take care of the other patient — when he could do nothing else he kept moving his bed so that he would have a view out of the window. My dying father didn't even need to be rational to wish to brighten the situation for someone else.

I continued to live in San Francisco, only eight miles from Berkeley, but I did not often see my parents. For my dream of a friendship with my mother had proved a chimera. Her dislike of me was as ferocious as ever — of course, as I now know, because the psychosis was still there and would always be there. And yet she was proud of my achievements, such as they were, and said so generously in letters. Her aversion was almost entirely a physical, neurological thing, which she could not justify psychologically because I was not turning out badly, I had not disgraced the family, her early predictions had not been realized. It was an ill-fated relationship, doomed by those hours of my dreadful birth, and I wish my mother could have known the reason for her extreme antipathy, for I am sure it caused her distress. Up to the last infrequent times that I saw her she continued to refer to Stevenson's Dr. Jekyll and Mr. Hyde with always the comment, "There are people like that"; and even her claim, her belief, that relatives often poison members of the families may have been a delusion to make it easier for her to come to terms with some of her memories. When she died, at the age of ninety-two, I had to know that I, her first-born and only daughter, had brought her nothing but suffering through most of a long life.

I saw her less than a dozen times during her last twenty years —
and that was her wish. When I left Alaska, after being there for
nine years, I was homesick for friends in the San Francisco Bay area;
if I had any roots they were there, and I longed to go back. But first
I would test out the emotional atmosphere: had it improved, as il-
logically I always hoped that it would? I wrote to my mother pro-
posing that I should return and live in Berkeley, but she, in a desperate letter, outlined many reasons why I should go somewhere
else. None of the reasons was sensible and the one that would have
been was omitted: that she literally could not have endured having
me there.

I had contracted that lingering ailment, undulant fever, from un-
pasteurized milk in Alaska, and in that debilitated condition could
not decide what to do. My doctor in Nome (physicians have often
been my most helpful friends) said just the right thing: "You may
not have a loving family, but you have the world." Yes, the world
— large enough so that one could always move on, and being a
writer I could live anywhere. (An echo of Dr. Renz's warning:
"Wherever you are you may always have to be able to go away," although he had meant that the pressure would come from within myself.)

While I was growing up there was never a day when I was not
made to feel that as soon as possible I must be gone — not just to
support myself but to leave, to take myself to some distant place. I
didn't mind then; it was not just that I was being turned out, but
that I would escape, escape from a trap. It is more normal, however,
to want to belong somewhere, to feel secure enough to believe in
lasting friends, in oneself, in life's welcome; to have Erik Erikson's
"basic trust," which most psychologists believe must be acquired in
one's early years, or it never can be. And I have not achieved that;
however, recognizing the reason, I do consciously trust my friends,

even trust their affection though I don't often dare put it to any test. Thanks to the analysts I have lost my fear of people and also the sting from childhood memories, but the impulse to leave, even to be the first to leave an evening party, is absolutely compulsive, and I only feel any real confidence in a friendship if I have made it clear that I will not put any weight on it. And so, although I admired my mother for her intelligence, her beauty and charm, and most of all for her gallant spirit, I cannot feel warmth of love for her memory. There is too unavoidable a sense that I must go through life always saying goodby.

She was seventy when my father died and the more than twenty years she continued to live could be described as a triumph. Her mind seemed to sharpen right up to the end, when she was reading two or three books a week, which she got from the library herself. When she was eighty-eight her banker said to her, "I wish you were younger. I would put you in charge of my insurance department." Her end was sudden and merciful, a heart attack while she was entertaining two friends at the apartment hotel where she lived. She had not dreaded death. In her animated way she had said she was very curious about what the next world would be like.

One of her younger friends, Mrs. Geraldine Morgan, wrote to me after her death, "In spite of her years she walked with the carriage of a queen, was tall, erect, lovely, gracious, interested in people and always talked about things of the present." After my father died she may have discovered that she had loved him more than she had supposed, for she spoke of him with increasing appreciation. For whatever reason, as I was told, she seemed to become more relaxed, more contented and gentle — and did even I contribute, by staying away? I hope so. I know she was comforted by her church and religion. After her death her prayer book was found. It was much worn.

Dr. Isaacs, who could put in its proper and minor place the one scar in my mother's mind, said, "She must have been a fascinating woman." Most of her friends would say the same thing, and so do I.

For that she was: fascinating.

2

In the 1930's when companies the world over, from corner groceries to financial empires, were toppling, one kind of business was not only thriving — it was coming into a flood tide of prosperity: advertising. That was the decade when modern advertising techniques were perfected and were so immediately successful that they seemed an Aladdin's lamp. Firms on the edge of bankruptcy were diverting funds to the new wonder craft and immediately beginning to flourish themselves. Before that time advertising had either been of the medicine man, preposterous kind lampooned as "This will restore hair, improve your love life and put a shine on your shoes"; or else the claims were polite and modest: "This is a good product whose value is guaranteed by the 50-year reputation of its manufacturers." There had been only the simple attempt to sell goods, not to change the personality of the buyer in order to make him more susceptible to the sales appeal. But psychology had caught on. Advertising men, better than most of us, had learned about fears and frustrations and with Yankee shrewdness were adapting that knowledge to profit-making.

They were bringing into the advertising profession many psychologists of high academic qualifications who worked with the methods familiar in laboratories, *i.e.*, with extensive experimentation, tests of different kinds of appeals, analyses of buyers' weaknesses and sensibilities, with surveys of buying habits. The psychologists did not stop with these background results; they helped to find ways to exploit the public's reactions, and this groundwork in advertising ap-

peals was done so well then in the thirties that the same techniques
are used today, almost without change.

There was some sense of foreboding that scientists, those respected if "bloodless" men, were selling their skills to dupe the public. But more widely there was a willing acceptance of what was almost a new kind of entertainment. Advertising was widely talked
about, less with wariness than with interested approval. It was like
a game: public buying habits swung one way and another as rival
companies such as coffee manufacturers launched their different
campaigns. To those who believed that advertising disarmed and
manipulated people the conjurors defended themselves by saying
that advertising can induce and assure prosperity. Today there is
still an effort to soothe critics of advertising with the same argument.

Advertising rescued me from my own financial depression, for I
got into this burgeoning field very soon after my hunger had been
dispelled and I could think clearly again. Radio was the medium. I
had a small set and in listening to the dramas and talks, it seemed
obvious that this was something I was equipped to do. All that time
spent in Mr. Dudley's office studying dialogue, and then the three
years at the Metropolitan Studio, hearing more than 150 pictures
analyzed for dramatic effectiveness, must surely have been as good a
training as most of the radio writers had. Ideas crowded into my
head and the first one I presented anywhere, at H. Liebes & Company, a store selling high-class apparel for women, was accepted.

It was a serial — a "strip show," as they were then called — built
around a young pair in love who were exploring San Francisco together. To build the incidents I had the pleasure of exploring San
Francisco myself and the commercials caused me no anguish; I simply
described what the girl wore each day and said that it came from H.
Liebes.

This was exactly what had been missing in Kansas City: the color and stir of a crossroads of cultures. The radio characters visited Chinese homes, had dinner at a Japanese hotel where they ate in a private dining room, sitting on the floor, first having refused the bath that was offered all guests. They went to the Sutro spa where there were seven pools with water in temperatures to please every swimmer; to the Cliff House, a spectacular restaurant hanging over the sea; to Telegraph Hill, where observers of long ago signalled the names of approaching ships to those who were waiting below at a dock on the Bay. The characters (I first) went out for a day on an Italian's fishing boat and had dinner on the boat later when it was anchored at North Beach. They (I) spent an evening at the restaurant — speakeasy — of Izzy Gomez, the half-caste Brazilian whose almost hypnotic personality had made him famous with newspapermen throughout the world.

One of the places visited was Gump's, renowned importers of Oriental art. Gump's had become established during the Gold Rush when they were furnishers of the city's elegant bordellos; later when many of the girls were married to men who had made mining fortunes, Gump's furnished their homes. But gradually they had specialized in Oriental imports. On my visit I was shown the Jade Room where there were jade statues worth hundreds of thousands of dollars; and other exhibits, for example of Chinese porcelain — one set of dinner plates priced at $500 each plate.

Most stunning of all were the examples of Cambodian sculpture. The deep forests which had overgrown the ancient capital of Angkor Thom and the nearby temple of Angkor Wat had only recently begun to give up their treasures. Discoveries in surrounding groves, and imported by Gump's, included human hands of incredible refinement and, most notable, heads so subtly carved that they had an expression of youthful eagerness when viewed in the sun of the early

morning, of practical realism when the sun was overhead, and at
sunset of deep disillusionment. Mr. Abe Gump, head of the firm,
had provided a special room where the heads, one at a time, could
be viewed. With floor, walls and ceiling of sky-blue velvet, the room
had a lighting system which simulated the sun's passage, whereby
this astounding achievement of Cambodian sculptures (probably
A.D. 1000 to 1250) became real. When I was shown the heads, by
Mr. Robert Gump, one of the founder's sons, I exclaimed, "Oh,
please let me write the publicity for them!" Rather amused because
I had been so swept away with admiration, he said, "All right, if you
think you can do it." It was one of the most satisfying assignments I
ever was given.

My radio characters listened to tales of the earlier San Francisco,
of people like Emperor Norton, a beloved old man who, in his senil-
ity, thought that he was an ex-emperor and how all San Francisco
collaborated in sustaining his belief by giving an elaborate annual
banquet for him. Ah, San Francisco! I was completely enchanted.

I wrote, cast and directed the Liebes program and it ran for several months, until the rainy season arrived and the canny sponsors
thought it was unrealistic for the loving pair to be prowling about
during storms. But the program had attracted attention and the
week after it ended I was approached by an advertising agency who
wanted someone to create a network show for a milling company. I
wrote a sample script for them and got the job. The new program
too was a quick success, gratifying because I could go on fulfilling
my obligations to Dr. Renz and my brother, and the work helped to
restore my self-confidence. It fitted in well with the analysis, since
my time was my own except for the period when we were broadcast-
ing. Luck, I felt, had stopped playing hide-and-seek with me as it
had done for so long.

In the advertising agency I was introduced at once to the most sophisticated and cynical advertising techniques then being practiced, and for a while it was fascinating, in a rather horrible way, to observe how well they worked — indeed to be working them myself. The sponsor, a western milling company, had recently been absorbed by a larger eastern flour-milling organization which exercised some supervision over the advertising. We had a western advertising agency and were allowed to create our own format for the program, that is, the entertainment feature, supposedly western in tone, but the main advertising appeal was dictated by the eastern flour mills, who had an agency in Chicago and relayed to us the tried and proven appeals worked out for their eastern advertising. The executive who ran the western agency had been sent out from the East. He had little to offer except an emotional intuition of what would break down sales resistence, but he was a good one to handle a flour campaign because he personally was obsessed by food and believed it could solve every problem. When my assistant was sad for a while because of a broken engagement he told her that she would get over it in a week if she ate a huge meal every night and went right to bed in a hot room. Each day he asked what she had had for dinner and was angry that she was not following his advice but the poor girl had lost her appetite. He was a very tense, very apprehensive man and kept a cocked revolver in each drawer of his desk and his table — not a man easy to work with but I was grateful that he allowed me some freedom in planning our entertainment features. I was supposed to change the format every six months, a requirement finally abandoned though the need for the frequent switch kept us on our toes. Eventually the company decreed that we should switch to a soap opera. To avoid the sentimentality already typical of those shows I devised a family with an unsympathetic father and two teen-age sisters who fought with each other, giving a chance for some sharp, funny dialogue. The serial caught on and was still running when I bowed out of the program.

Radio was a medium I could have liked very much if it had not been so appalling to write the commercials. In the shows themselves it was something new to be painting in backgrounds through dialogue and sound effects; to study voices, to assemble a cast with voices sufficiently different in pitch never to be confused; to learn to recognize the particular timbre that will pick up well on a microphone and that has an arresting quality. Some people could, as often said, read the telephone book and hold attention while others could have the most compelling lines and immediately lose their listeners. Some voices come down to the same tone at the end of each sentence, a fault that still is not always avoided.

I listened to voices everywhere, on the street, in cable cars, at parties. And another thing I learned is that voice quality has only a moderate relation to age. One of our freshest voices belonged to a woman with several grandchildren whereas some young actors' voices sounded already bored. I heard in a hotel dining room in Victoria a voice for which I would have created a whole radio serial, it was so poignant. The young Keats would have sounded like that, I thought, and turned around to see who was speaking: an Englishman, a retired British Army captain, eighty-four years old I was later told. For the family serial I wanted a very cold, heartless voice to impersonate the father of the family, a banker, and I was having great difficulty in casting that part because the one thing that cannot, must not, be found in a radio actor's voice is chill. I heard the very voice I was looking for, this time too in a hotel, at Lake Tahoe, and I asked the hotel hostess to take him my card. On it I wrote, "Would you be interested in working on a radio program? The job would be fairly permanent." The man sent his own card back and I read, "Certainly not. What an extraordinary idea." I turned the card over. The man was president of one of San Francisco's oldest and largest banks.

In the sponsored programs and a few that I did on the side for the

San Francisco Community Chest, I was trying particularly to get a new degree of conviction into the dialogues. Too many broadcasters then had come to radio from the stage and they had the same dramatic mannerisms that had proved hard to overcome in the movies. They were obsessed with what they had been told was the need to "project themselves" and they kept violently throwing themselves at the audience. For our broadcasts I made up the slogan, "Project from quietness." Only a few actors could do that but we built up a cast of those who could. Pauses were, I felt, my best discovery. In real life one seldom comes back in a split second to anybody's remark, and I tried to make the cast really "think out" their answers before they spoke. What I was seeking was naturalness — the quality that is so well realized in many radio and television programs today: just truth, really. It was something rather new at that time. The casts found this attempt stimulating and developed their own contributions to it, especially our star, Jean Scott, an actress who had been working in London and brought exceptional intelligence to the problem of radio realism.

And then, after trying so hard, all of us, to present what was creative truth, three times in each program we had to swing into commercials that, to me, were as false as the waxed mustache on a stage villain — but rising sales of our flour proved that the audience believed the sales messages too. What the dramas and interviews did was to produce an atmosphere of credulity; listeners believed in the radio performers and so they believed the commercials. That was the first deceit.

The theme of the commercials was dictated from the East though we were expected to carry it out with a western slant. For the first two years the theme didn't change. It was "Your family will praise you" — if you bake enough cakes, pies, dumplings, bread, muffins, rolls, waffles, pancakes, whatever is made of flour. On each program we gave a recipe but more time was spent in describing the baked miracles that invariably would win praise, the most glowing extravagant praise, for the housewife. The whole assumption was that the women in the twenty-eight western cities where our programs were broadcast were crawling around almost incapacitated by inferiority complexes. To win a few words of approval they would spend extra hours every day in the kitchen — baking, with our flour of course. Cakes baked with *ordinary* flour would win only disgusted glances. (The word ordinary, but now exhausted of meaning, was just coming into advertising use. Our manager wanted it brought into every commercial.)

Sometimes the commercials were dramatized; Jean read others as narratives. They all described family upsets, leading quickly into a recipe, a mouth-watering description of the result, expressions of love all around and a final torrent of praise for mother.

Finally that theme, "Your family will praise you," was abandoned and I would remember it almost fondly when the next theme got under way. For it was this: "Your neighbors will envy you" — for the things you bake, of course. We never could say, "Your friends will envy you," because, the manager explained, "many people don't have friends and so it is snobbish to mention them, but everybody has neighbors." I wondered whether it is true that many people don't have friends, particularly the cozy kind of women who like to spend hours baking cakes; but if they don't have friends maybe it is because their idea of a desirable relationship is one based on envy. The manager assured me that the new theme was proving wildly successful in the eastern advertising of the parent company. I was skeptical about its going over in the friendlier atmosphere of the West, but I was wrong. The campaign surpassed the highest expectations. Western cooks, too, were promised the warm satisfaction of being envied, not envied for skill but for having the wit to choose

our brand of flour, and ours because it produced a very special quality that we were instructed to emphasize every day: "a tender
crumb." The kitchen witch who knew the means of baking a tender
crumb could apparently dress in her sloppiest clothes, neglect her
children, hang out the dirtiest wash but still be the object of envious
glances.

And so I was beginning to think in these terms of manipulating
our listeners, of coercing them, really, by psychological means. Many
hints were available through the agency and through studying other
radio programs. I had become well aware of the way to use suggestion in order to sell a product like flour.

"Avoid logical argument. Stay with promises." Since a woman's
neighbors were never her friends how could they, logically, know
whether her cakes had a tender crumb or a rubbery crumb like those
made with ordinary flour? When did they ever taste them? No
matter. Just promise their envy.

"The voice presenting the sales message should speak with authority." Jean Scott, who read our commercials so "sincerely," had
been brought up in hotels and never had cooked so much as a soft-
boiled egg. Her own ambition was not to excel in a kitchen but to
play Shakespeare with John Gielgud in England. But being an actress she *sounded* authoritative.

"Talk in simple words and simple, uncomplicated sentences, no
sentence ever longer than two typewritten lines." That is, talk as to
a child. Feeling childlike herself, then, the listening housewife will
become more suggestible, as children are.

"Appeal to the most basic, primitive needs" — like a mouthful of
collapsing crumbs baked by a housewife whose ego was starving.

I had a recurrent nightmare: of sinking in flour helplessly as one does in quicksand. It was becoming impossible to go on.

Try writing radio programs for other products? I had been asked to submit program ideas for a brand of gasoline, a line of cookstoves, and a hobby shop. All the interviews had revealed that what was wanted was a knack for exaggerating the products' value. In the case of the gasoline and the stoves I had been talking to advertising agencies and was learning still more about the ethos of advertising. Bright young men, hot with self-importance, tried with all their ingenuity to inflate the worth of the items their clients were selling. In the magazine advertising they showed me for other products a five-ton truck was illustrated with a girl in red tights stretched out on the hood, a cigarette with a view of a mountain stream, a brandy with a girl whose resistance was close to collapse. These subliminal promises were supposed to enhance the actual value. *Enhance* was a word constantly used in the agencies.

But does any purchaser of a five-ton truck believe that he gets a girl with it, does any smoker expect that a particular cigarette tastes like the water of mountain springs, does any male really think that one brandy is more aphrodisiac than another? Yes, many do. For most advertising is planned to appeal to instincts that function below the level of rational thought, instincts that are quite ready to believe the most absurd suggestions if they promise satisfactions for sex or hunger or thirst, or praise for a damaged ego. No reputable advertiser would make false measurable claims for their products. They would not state that a five-ton truck would carry eight tons, or that their cigarettes contained anti-cancer drugs, or that the fifths of their brandy really were quarts. They didn't, at least not often, misrepresent actual facts — but they didn't present many facts. They based their promises on the enhancements, the fantasy extras.

I wrote some sample advertisements for the flour company that put the emphasis on the products' legitimate values: *honesty of emphasis* was a slogan I had idealistically composed for myself. For I believed that well-thought-out arguments, with the emphasis where it belonged, would have an appeal because of their obvious truthfulness. These commercials were not gravely sober; the descriptions were colorful but pointed out, I thought, advantages that might not have occured to a listener. In every case they were tossed back across the desk with the criticism: "This is not selling copy."

Enhancement was what was wanted and I had been able to give it, I had had the knack, but I would not have it very much longer. The words for that kind of compelling persuasion just would not come; a psychological or emotional reluctance interfered. When I told the agency manager that I wanted to change to commercials in which there was "honesty of emphasis," he was flamboyantly offended. Didn't I realize that every one of my scripts was read by the firm's attorneys and if there had been any dishonesty that could have brought on a lawsuit, they would have found it? The only dishonesty he could recognize was the kind for which he or the company could be sued. He was not honest, himself. His whole mind had gone over to the advertising psychology.

I was reminded of him last year in England when the BBC, which does not broadcast commercial programs of course, put on a panel of advertising agency men to defend their selling arguments. They seemed incapable of answering questions logically. The problem came up of commercials that advertise products which are dangerous to health or life. They all said that the public "has the right to buy lethal products if they want to." No one admitted that the advertisers create that want and then use clever psychological techniques to coerce the public into buying the dangerous products. None of the challenging questioners was able to make those advertising men give genuinely reasonable replies. And I was convinced

again — what I had never doubted — that I had been right long
ago in San Francisco when I decided that commercial radio was not
for me.

As my analysis neared its end I talked to Dr. Renz about my career, still a career-to-be since radio never would be a fulfillment. He
suggested that I should write a short story in my free time; see what
would come out, now that analysis had removed the panic. The
story wrote itself, for I was still able to open a line to the deeper,
creative levels where, Dr. Renz and I assumed, my subconscious
would speak with a new voice. The story did not involve deaths or
poisonings, no real horror, but its message was disillusionment. It
concerned "Kate," a hospital nurse, thirty, very efficient but lacking
romantic promise until she met a young man from the Hawaiian Islands while on vacation and he proposed. A more experienced girl
would hardly have taken him seriously but Kate prepared for the
wedding, to take place in Honolulu. She cut all her ties at home
and set forth with a large trousseau and assured expectations — to
find her fiancé already engaged to someone else. At the end Kate
was left, her hopes abandoned, in a strange city, without friends, and
with too much pride to return home.

Dr. Renz had wanted to read the story, a slight, simple tale. He
was disappointed in it, for he had believed that I would have gained
a brighter outlook from the analysis. Try more stories? Each of the
dozen turned out, in brief form, the same way — still, as before, in
defeat. When I told Dr. Renz that all my ideas seemed to emerge
on that theme, he asked if I thought the public would want to read
fiction like that, could I build a career on the creation of depressing
material? I thought that perhaps I could if I wrote strongly, effectively enough.

But now something else had come out: an unfamiliarity with
real-life situations. The nurse was conventional, she was in fact

based on a young woman who was another tenant on Steiner Street, but most of the characters I could imagine were somehow grotesque; they were outcasts, or half mad, there was something monstrous about them, they were like Mr. Dudley or other people in Hollywood, or Mr. Edwards, or the dishonest man in the building and loan association, or the manager of the advertising agency with his several guns.

Or if the characters were not monstrous themselves, they were abandoned children or old people turned out on the street. They had impossible hopes and ambitions and the way that fate treated them was outrageous. All disturbing; and if these convulsed elements were reflecting my childhood and the bizarre events since I was grown, at least I knew they were not life as it is in most cases. What I longed to portray were scenes of more normal living. There would surely be drama, human and moving, in the fortunes of average people — but when I tried to construct some plots with that sort of drama, I felt ill-equipped. I didn't know many average people, or at least know them well enough to have a clear sense of their destiny.

No doubt a time comes to every aspiring writer when he takes stock of the subjects his life so far has given him — the places he's seen, the kinds of people he's known, the situations he has experienced. He will add to these with his imagination, perhaps will add a great deal, as the Brontës did, and Jane Austen and George Eliot, but unless he will be writing adventure stories, fantasies, it seems to be an advantage to have a background of fairly normal events upon which to do the embroidery. It was that which I was beginning to doubt in my own equipment.

All the way, from the proxy parents to Dr. Renz, everywhere there had been someone giving me help, more than my share of help, certainly more than I ever returned. It had come often in rather desperate times, but it had come. I had survived. Why then did life, not just for me but for everyone, seem a dubious benefit?

The kind of stories that so far emerged from my depths had become distasteful. I doubted whether such subjects would really inspire the hard work I knew writing would be. For what sense of fulfillment could a writer expect in presenting the lives of eccentric people coming to sad ends, to betrayals, to loss of hope, to the death of trust? Would there be any self-respect in adding to the world's gloom?

I knew of course that a mood of disenchantment was increasingly found in the work of artists in many fields. That didn't mean that I had to be one of those who lead *down*. If society was disintegrating, should one give it another push? Not necessarily. There was another choice: silence. One could be a bystander, observer of falling developments without, oneself, adding with even one's minor talents to the momentum. I would have nothing to say. I would not be a writer.

This decision was reached in rooms planned as a workshop for giving expression to my own truth — my truth concerning the lives of others. I should have questioned earlier what was the truth about my fitness to do that, my own horizons.

3

It seems surprising that most writing schools don't discuss the best atmosphere for creative work. There are some interiors where I at least could not write a word, one being a modern room with four square plaster walls, a blank window or two, adequate heat and light and all with no trace of character. On the other hand I once rented a flat in London that had in its drawing room five tables heavy with ormolu that served no purpose but to hold bric-a-brac — numerous porcelain trays, boxes, figurines, vases, a candelabrum, a tree made of minute shells, and seven motionless clocks. Other *objets d'art* crowded the mantel and the Victorian desk. Walking around I instinctively kept my elbows pressed to my ribs. The owner said that another author had produced a book there; I knew his work and found it too full of whimsies, and for me the profusion of ornaments, many distractingly beautiful, made any clear, organized writing difficult.

Perhaps the best atmosphere for creating will always be simple, although with a few possessions that feed the spirit, books, a picture or two, objects with personal meaning. It is good if there is a feeling of times past, even shabbiness that will give a sense of life's continuity. These conditions are what Bohemians seek intuitively and are what I found as soon as the radio program gave some security.

After closing the door on the squalid small room where I nearly starved, I moved in with a woman I didn't know who said that she was a dress designer. It turned out that her flat was a very strange place. She was a mistress of a formidable Red Indian and had other friends who belonged to some occult group, perhaps the forerunners of hippies for none of them seemed to work and they streamed in and out all day. I told Sylvia, the designer, that I couldn't concentrate with so much going on and would have to leave.

Heart-of-gold Sylvia took on herself the task of finding me an apartment and all the furnishings for it. The apartment, which seemed just right, was in a small, ancient building on the slope of Nob Hill, on Joice Street at the top of the steps that lead down to Pine. There were two rooms, neither large but with such a wide doorway between that they seemed to be one. A trundle bed rolled away under the bathroom, up two steps; and there was a tiny kitchen. The woodwork was dark but the walls were covered with

clean light paper — all acceptable, but what gave the whole atmosphere quality was a bank of windows looking out into the branches
of eucalyptus trees. At all but one of the windows were flower boxes
in which were planted geraniums, flame-colored and white. In the
years I lived there they never ceased blooming. The fourth window
had been equipped with a bird-feeding tray.

One could see immediately that the windows should be the apartment's main feature. We replaced the stained shades with bamboo
blinds and to frame the windows Sylvia gave me percale draperies
with a pleasing small geometric design in brown, yellow and white.
We put Japanese tatami mats on the floors; and in the MacAlister
Street second-hand furniture market found a substantial youth's desk
and some walnut chairs, all very nice when refinished. Sylvia sold
me for almost nothing a provincial oak table, an upholstered chair
in a rosy-rust shade and a carved Spanish daybed which proved to
have bedbugs in it. As terrified as if they'd been carnivores, which
of course they were, I called exterminators who lighted fumes that
also got rid of the cockroaches against which I was carrying on an
uneven battle.

I had two pleasing things of my own, gifts of the Steiner Street
bee people: a hand-woven bedspread in gray and blue which I hung
on a wall, and a carved walnut powder table and mirror. I bought a
set of Mexican pottery dishes and Sylvia gave me some cooking
utensils.

So there it was, my own household, not a home as I thought of it,
rather a practical place to work. There were written all but the
earliest of the radio scripts, and there was nurtured the dream that
some day I would produce writing in which I would speak with my
personal voice. In the beginning I had not been afraid of what my
own truth would be. Living at last with no sense of panic, with instead something I dared to call happiness, I believed that here in the

exhilarating city of San Francisco I could start to spread my own clear colors about, in books if not on walls as my father did.

But two years passed and the light of that hope went out.

o

Few places are more depressing than a workshop when there is no prospect of work to be done in it. That the apartment became when I gave up the thought that I ever would write again. The desk, the typewriter with the pile of clean paper beside it, always there for encouragement and I still hadn't been able to put it away, the simplicity of the rooms with their cleared-for-action atmosphere were a reproach, as if I had already let them go derelict. But this hiatus didn't last long. It had happened again (a monotonous pattern): the vision of an enticing career, training for it, a taste of success in it and then the abandoning of the whole enterprise and a quick descent into illness. This time as always the illness was unexpected. At night I was well, the next morning the only way I could cross the rooms was by lurching from chair to chair — no aches or pains, just this ridiculous dizziness. The doctor, a different one now, said, "Your blood pressure is only half normal strength and you'll have to stay in bed until it comes up a bit." For how long? He wouldn't predict.

I phoned the assistant to take over the radio program and then I lay on the Spanish bed thinking. The problem was plain: to dredge up a new incentive for living, a new argument to persuade the knot of nerves in the heart to resume its exceptional push. This time suicide wasn't tempting. There were many things one could do, surely, besides writing. But anything I would *want* to do? I began to compose a sonnet: "Farewell to Words." Words, which I loved as many women love jewels, words no longer would be my bright beautiful playthings. From the first line the sonnet became an elegy. I sank deeper into the mattress.

Outside in the eucalyptus trees a flock of small birds, linnets, hopped and fluttered, splashing in and out of the clusters of leaves. They seemed eager, as if they had just discovered these trees and must find out all about them; but they had come to the garden each winter, they must already know every gracefully swinging twig and secluded hideaway. How could they be so endlessly active, they so small and fragile while I, immense thing, could hardly raise myself off the edge of the bed? Was there some wonderful rightness in them that let all their vitality flow unimpeded into their living?

They were birds of sparrow size, the males being mostly a rosy scarlet, the females warm brown and off-white. The daybed, extending along one of the living-room windows, brought the birds into my natural line of sight, and it was pleasing to watch the males flitting about the crimson blooms on the branches. For the eucalyptus trees were blossoming then in late February. Their flowers develop in gray-green cups with lids that fall off at the right time, releasing big pompons of silky threads, brilliant red. When a bird left a bough one could imagine that a flower had taken wing.

This, the rainy season, was not yet time for mating linnets to announce boundary lines but anyway they were singing, garlands of notes that always ended with the sweetest of codas: *chwee, whurr,* three tones apart, from the dominant down to the mediant. Most of the time there were several of the songs pouring out, and behind and around them was a musical chatter, all sounding pleased.

For a long time I had been putting crumbs on the tray outside one of the study windows. Now I phoned for ten pounds of birdseed and kept a supply scattered among the geraniums. One of the flower boxes was less than an arm's length from my head, and since all the windows were always wide open, the linnets were fearful about coming that close. Yet curiously they did want to, although there were plenty of seeds farther away. It seemed a challenge to be so near the big human face with its disturbing inquisitive eyes, and those strange appendages, hands, lying on top of the blanket. Not safe! But compelling. A dilemma. The simple solution would have been to forget this particular window but the linnets would hover above the geraniums, skim off, soon to come back. Before long then they would alight and pick up a seed, while their pretty red crests stood straight up with excitement. There were seeds as well on the interior windowsills but of course that was too far to venture.

One day one of the females came to the window box in a pitiful state. She had lost a leg, perhaps caught by a cat, and probably some days ago because she had become so thin that she was a little skeleton with a skin of feathers stretched over it. Her feathers had lost all their lustre, the polish which helps to repel moisture, and she appeared to be drenched whereas the healthy birds never became quite so wet. The eyes of the female were dull and her cheeks were sunken. The look of death was upon her. I felt that if I could take her in my warm hand some of my strength might flow into her . . . but instead she must totter about on her one weak leg as she tried to feed among the geraniums, pelted by rain.

But suddenly she had fluttered in out of the rain and was eating the seeds on the indoor sill. And several of the other linnets, made bold by her daring, were with her. It seemed hardly possible that she would live, though perhaps being able to dry off might give her a chance. Soon all the seeds on the sill were gone and the wounded one flew away with the rest of the birds. By the time they came back a feast was there and a chopping bowl full of seeds stood on a nearby table. The Brave Lass, as I had begun to think of her, again took the audacious step and flew to the table. Not long after her some of the others came in. On the next day the linnets were fluttering from sill to table and once the Lass came for a moment to perch on the peak in the bed covers made by my foot.

At first the linnets were tense, always quick to explode away through the windows, but gradually they became more relaxed. It was progress when they began to chirp while they were inside, that sweet liquid chatter seeming so much like talk. I thought that here too they were sounding pleased.

The Lass appeared to be gaining weight. She could stand without wavering quite so much, although when she hopped the leg sometimes gave way and she used her wings to move even an inch or two. Now and then she would lose her balance when she leaned forward to pick up a seed. She was a sick little bird even now and I hardly dared hope for her, but I was growing fond of her and could she sense that I was? And would such an impression have given her confidence?

In two or three days the birds were flying about the rooms. And not only flying; they were finding favorite perches and staying inside for hours. Some of them stood on the tops of picture frames, one or two on the edges of vases, one on a framed photograph on the powder table and one on the typewriter. But most of them sat on the picture rail in the living room and the plate rail in the study. They spaced themselves out the way swallows do on a telephone line: rows of alert, bright-eyed little beings filling the rooms with cheerful and vibrant life. Not every bird in the flock was there, though on one day I counted forty-three linnets inside.

I was learning important things about reassuring any wild creatures that pay us the compliment of their trust. When the birds first began to come in I lay perfectly motionless, tensely so which was tiring. Then gradually it became clear that the birds felt more safe when I relaxed, changed position, even rose to sit on the edge of the bed. Finally I could go into the kitchen without alarming them if the motions were still relaxed. Someone, a cat for example as well as a human being, is more ready to spring when muscles are taut. The intention behind relaxed muscles is not to attack. I did move quietly but that simply seemed natural. It was not necessary to think about it, it was the obvious reaction to such sensitive little companions.

The linnets dashed out if the phone or doorbell rang and were gone one day when a caller arrived. I was in bed and so after a while, being helpful, she said, "Shall I clean off your table? It's just covered with seeds."

"Thank you, don't bother. The birds will soon have them scattered again."

"The birds! Do birds fly in here?"

"Those linnets out there. That's not remarkable. Why shouldn't they be inside when the rooms are warm and dry and there's always food in here?"

"But aren't they afraid?"

"No. I don't know why but they aren't."

I didn't know why but suspected that there was some connection between the birds' confidence and my feeling that it was perfectly natural for them to be in here. We have an affinity that is almost personal with inanimate things, cars, furniture: why not a closer association between human beings and those who are wild? We share the earth, all of us are alive here for only a little while, and we have essentially the same needs, food and shelter and the companionship of our kinds. The superiority is not all on the human side either; we have brains which have developed further but most of the birds and animals are more fleet and graceful and they have keener senses than we do. Many observers have found that they are drawn to us if we do not repel them. And when there is no question of one hurting the other, as between the linnets and me, why shouldn't we be at ease together and even have some communal feeling in being here in the same environment?

There was another thing: communication. I had communicated my harmlessness and perhaps my concern to the birds and they had communicated many things to me, especially their spirited interest. Our eyes often met now, and something would pass between. I should not, however, withdraw too far into my human pattern of analyzing, defining. "The paralysis of analysis": it could imprison one's natural spontaneity.

When my thinking had got that far I remembered the lion in Hollywood and how my sympathy reached him across all that movie gear and, bounding down through the people, he came to where I was sitting. I really never had wondered why he had done that; but certainly I had been feeling something like kinship and would have felt it towards any creature who was suffering such harassment. He was right and the strident trainer was wrong. It didn't seem to have needed a special kind of awareness to have recognized what was happening and have taken the lion's side. That's all that was needed — a sense of fellowship.

I had stayed in a hotel once where another guest, an explorer, kept a wild ocelot on the roof while he tried to find a zoo that would buy it. I used to go up on the roof for some sunshine and it seemed as normal to make friends with the ocelot as if it had been a domestic cat. The ocelot made the overtures in fact and liked to lie with its fifty-inch length stretched across my lap. The explorer came up one day when the ocelot was draped over my shoulders. From behind he said tensely, "You are in danger but if you keep perfectly quiet I think I can get the ocelot away from you." I took the ocelot in my arms and handed it to the man and laughed and said, "We understand each other. I have not been in danger."

The feeling that we and the animals should share a communal

good will is not very rare. One thinks of Joy Adamson, Jane Good-all, Lois Crisler, and Adolph Murie and many others less well known — and especially of children. When my nephew was six I took him up into the mountains. From the beginning all the birds, squirrels, chipmunks and deer came to him. An envious little girl tried also to win the wild creatures and sat for an entire day holding out nuts but without any result. John told her, "It isn't enough just to hold out your hand. You have to feel a certain way inside." I had not prompted him, and I was reminded of how at home, where he had an aquarium, he would speak of "my friend the snail." It was in his temperament to have that easy fraternal impulse and probably most children have it. A few years ago Araby Colton, president of the Canadian and American Wolf Defenders, brought some purebred wolves to Carmel Valley and invited the local children to come and play with them. For both children and wolves it was a great celebration. They tumbled together and the children scrambled all over the wolves and no one could say which had enjoyed the occasion more.

o

The linnets flew back and forth through the windows, even the window nearest my head, and there was one tragedy for which my thoughtlessness was to blame. All four windows were always open, with the bamboo blinds down to the bottom of the glass-covered space so the birds would not make the mistake of trying to fly out through it. But one day when the birds were inside and suddenly I felt chilly, I pulled down the window nearest me. Within the next minute or two one of the females, taking off from the other side of the room, flew at speed into the glass and broke her neck. She fell on the bed and I picked her up, still almost breathing, and held her

against my cheek. And made the surprising discovery that she had
an exquisite fragrance, very flowerlike, sweet with a hint of light spici-
ness. The seeds she had been eating did not have that scent; it was
something that had been added by her own little body. And was
that scent common to all the linnets and did they perceive it in one
another? It was too delicate for my crude nose to catch at the usual
distance, but the linnets were often close together and birds do have
the olfactory nerves that allow them to perceive fragrances.

There were happier events. I was now putting seeds on the sill of
the window beside which I lay, seeds that were not more than
twelve inches away from my face. One of the linnets, always the
same one, came there to feed. He came most often at dusk, when he
was a little sleepy. After he'd picked up a seed he would husk it in
his mouth very slowly and afterwards he would stand for a dreamy
moment or two before he picked up another. Our eyes met, by his
choice. We had a little relationship.

Something that happened one night seemed very interesting. The
sun had set but its rosy light was still on the many small clouds that
were blowing across the garden. They moved rapidly, a pink dap-
pled cover that kept coming up over us. When my eyes turned from
watching the clouds to glance at the linnet I found that he too was
watching them. His eyes would focus on one or more of the pink
fluffs, follow it past the tops of the trees, come back and follow others, again and again. He had eyes that saw colors and were the
clouds giving him pleasure? Otherwise why did he stay so long,
until the colors were gone?

As we know birds and animals better we learn that most of them
are more observant than we are, and the more materialistic of us assume that they are just looking for prey or enemies or other factors
in their practical lives. But later I was to find that many scientific
experiments have proved that some birds and animals have what is

called a pre-aesthetic sense. The ability to distinguish between circles, triangles, and squares has been proved for wasps, turtles, fishes and many of the more highly developed animals. Some, from crows to monkeys, have shown a preference for abstract designs which have balance or symmetry, or are smooth or parallel; and when we come to original work, the choice of colors and designs in the structures of bowerbirds are fine enough to make us proud of our evolutionary origins. There are other examples of aesthetic sensitivity in animals but no detail ever thrilled me more than the sight of that small linnet absorbed in the sight of the tinted clouds blowing by. Why not suspect that he was enjoying them for much the same reason that I was? *

There were many surprises and the Lass furnished more than her share. One was the way she reacted to storms. As she gained weight and the state of her feathers improved, her leg had been growing stronger. She did not lose her balance now and could hop nearly as well as the others. Early in March, then, some early spring gales struck San Francisco. Some of the birds spent more time indoors but as many retreated into the vines that covered the building. The Lass — only she — continued to perch in the eucalyptus boughs, now swinging widely. As they whipped about she would lose her grip and I wished that she would take refuge in some safer place, it seemed so probable that she would be hurled against the building or down on the ground. But she fluttered back every time to the branch, actually near the end where the motion was the most wild. Hour after hour, day after day, she carried on this fight, she so ill-equipped to hold onto an insecure perch and so often flung off by the wind, just as every loose leaf and flower capsule was being flung.

Why did she do it? What was the motive that put so much spirit

* Editor's Note: A résumé of what is known about animals' pre-aesthetic sense is given in the last chapter of Sally Carrighar's *Wild Heritage* (Houghton Mifflin, 1965).

into this tiny life? The routine was a good way of course for her one leg to develop more than the usual muscular strength, but would instinct function in such an abnormal situation? Or mysteriously did she just have an urge to do the hard thing? Some birds and animals do have that impulse. The three Chinese geese that brighten my life at present have been provided with an adequate masonry house. They frequently spend the night in it if the weather is pleasant, but when it is cold, with a gale-force wind and rain slashing down, they stay outside. Possibly that is nature's way of helping to keep them strong.

The linnets poured out their songs now when they were inside, usually when they would be standing on one of the windowsills, facing out. Spring was coming along and perhaps they were beginning to have territorial urges. There was evidence that they were starting to mate. I knew from previous years that most of the courtships would take place here, and then when the pairs had formed they would fly away, to nest in orchards, my bird book said, where there was plenty of food for their young.

I had a new worry about the Lass, for one hardly could hope that a cripple would have that experience. Some species of birds and animals are cruel to an injured companion. Although the linnet flock had not threatened the Lass, instead had depended on her to take the initiative — mating: that would be different. Could she even support the weight of one of the cocks?

The males and females were divided about evenly and they had been a sociable group, with no differentiation due to sex in their treatment of one another — until March when the males began to have a new boldness and the females a growing shyness. Soon there were little encounters, advances on the males' part and retreats on the females'. A male would stay near his chosen one, telling her by his very posture what he wanted. His head and tail would be up, held high, showing that he was a very fine fellow, while at the same time his wings dropped in what seemed supplication. But what of the Lass? Would she be left out of nature's creative festival, now beginning?

I was not doing her justice. For a change came over her. Handicapped she might be, but now she developed an exceptional feminine grace, the most intriguing ways among all the female linnets, I thought — so humbly, so wistfully, she would turn her head and chirp in a voice that became ever softer, more pliant. The most splendid male, the largest and brightest in color, was aware of the cripple's appealing manner. More and more often he sought her out, and when he was perched beside her she would sink lower and lower, quivering her wings, and when the beautiful male started to sing to her, as courting male linnets do, she responded with a delicate song of her own.

The day soon came when her happy future was sure. As she perched alone on the rim of the flower box, this most eligible of all the cocks came swooping in from a tree. He had brought a large insect which he transferred from his mouth to hers. It was the act that would seal their bond. In a day or two more they were gone.

All through the late winter she had shown spirit and energy, and one does not have to be human to achieve more abundant life with those qualities. Watching her I remembered how Dr. Renz had said that morale can be created, and so I set about trying to have an effect on my sluggish heart by something akin to determination. But it still was true that I had to think of something, some work, I really wanted to do. My life had fallen apart so completely, there was nothing ongoing about it. I was willing to try to pick up the threads, as they say — but what threads? The answer would not be postponed very much longer.

As the linnets began to leave another visitor had moved in, a visitor who would influence all the rest of my life. Most unexpected; I still marvel at the way and the time that it happened.

As soon as my radio program had started to prosper I had bought a new console set, a Philco on which music came through especially well. The radio stood in the study opposite the wide doorway between the rooms, and since I lay and slept on the Spanish bed facing that doorway, the programs were piped directly to me, and I had a remote control by which I could turn the programs on and off from the bed. A fine program of classical music was broadcast each night at ten and I ended the evenings listening to it. The birds had gone to their perches outside but the memory of their songs and chirpings stayed in my mind, to blend with the human music coming out of the radio.

At least that was the explanation that seemed logical in the beginning, when birdlike or flutelike notes accompanied all the solos and symphonies. But I began to doubt that the sweet obbligato was only in my imagination for the melodies also carried on through the announcer's talk; and then the new songs were continuing after I'd turned off the radio for the night. Lying there in the dark I would listen gratefully and with growing wonder to the small song, which would trill out of the radio for at least ten or fifteen minutes after the other music was silent.

Had one of the linnets stayed inside, although it didn't sound quite like a linnet's voice? Not likely either because the birds did not sing at night. It must be some freak way in which my radio was relaying sounds from one somewhere else. That sort of thing did happen sometimes.

Still, it was a little unnerving. I wondered if I was quite rational. The thing had to be explained and one night I got out of bed, turned on the light and swung the radio away from the wall. As I did, a mouse ran out of the back of it and along the edge of the wall, disappearing into the kitchen. Whether he was the singer or not, he had a neat little nest snugly tucked in among the warm radio tubes. A mouse! Did mice ever sing?

The next morning I phoned the Zoology Department at the University of California and said I would like to know whether a mouse could sing. I was connected with the eminent Dr. Joseph Grinnell who said that yes, very occasionally there were singing mice. They were found in all mice species, just the unusual odd one that had an impulse to sing. No explanation had ever been found.

Had I frightened away this new, musical visitor by discovering his nest? Please heaven, no! I had carefully moved the radio back in place and waited for the next night — since usually he sang only at night, now understandably since mice are nocturnal and probably sleep in the daytime. I needn't have worried. When the radio music came on in the evening my mouse joined in. A play had been broadcast earlier; the mouse did not sing with that but he did with the concert starting at ten. Human music amazingly had enough meaning for him that it touched off his impulse to raise his own little voice.

I tried to find words for it. It was like a bird's song but with more improvisation. It didn't repeat the same phrases over and over but warbled up and down, here and there very much as a human song does. It didn't, of course, actually sound human. It had the wild quality that is in all animals' voices, even those of wolves which are nearly on pitch. In fact the mouse's song too was nearly on pitch. Though so delicate it sounded, I thought, more as if it came from a flesh and blood throat than the song of a bird ever does.

I was still attempting to find better words for it when I had to get out of bed and walk up and down because of a thought so startling and so exciting: *this* is what I should write about! Birds and animals! I could after all be a writer, a nature writer. Of course! Take

back the words I had thought that I must abandon! Take back the
stifled hope that I might devote my life to some kind of significant
writing. There could be no finer subject than woods and fields,
streams, lakes, and mountainsides and the creatures who live in that
world. It would be a subject of inexhaustible interest, a supreme joy
to be learning to tell it all straight and truthfully.

My whole future life burst open that night like some great and
beautiful flower, blossoming in the span of a thought.

ix

HOME

EVERYTHING had to be different now.

No more Mr. Dudleys, Edwardses, financial crooks, employers with desks full of guns.

No more households depending for happy loving on tender crumbs.

No more actresses marrying lovers' undertakers, or Indians coming scowling out of landladies' bedrooms; no more contraltos singing Indian love calls from hilltops at night; nothing from now on like the fantasy life of Hollywood.

No more gardens abuzz with diseased bees or man-made lakes with mud beaches and dead trees in the shallows.

No more years of reeling from one weird event to another among grotesque personalities.

From this day forward a purposeful avoiding of the half-world of the half-mad: this was the resolution immediately following the night of the mouse's song. For I saw that bizarre worlds could be *rejected*. Why had they not always been? For one reason because my personal world had always included some part-mad elements; it had been only a part-world but it was familiar when I was a child and so it seemed familiar when I was grown and I fell into the way of being at home in it. But another reason I did was that I had a pe-

culiar tendency to drift. I had called the habit "going along with
life," "accepting what comes," "letting fate dictate my choices." Mr.
Nicolet's study of fate, making fate seem inevitable, had been an influence, but I probably was impressed by the study because it seemed
to confirm my own impulse to take events passively. "Roll with the
punch": I had collected slogans that would seem to justify what was
my own approach to life.

These sudden conversions are always a little suspect — was it
hysterical, would it be permanent? Whatever the motive of mine, it
was a switch into sanity and it has lasted for several decades, with
undiminished enthusiasm which probably now will not fail. My decision the night of the mouse's song made everything fall into place.
At one stroke my scattered and fragmented life had a purpose. *I
was born for this:* the new change was not less than that revelation.

And clearer thinking, coming just when it was needed, was made
possible because suddenly there was a full supply of oxygen-laden
blood going into my head. Now that I had an incentive to be up
and well, the heart was no longer sluggish. Its good strong beat had
me out of bed within days and normally active in less than two
weeks. It did not then falter for many years, for I had tapped Tho-
reau's "tonic of wildness."

The vision of the new future showed up the fallacy of the past:
that I wasn't one who made plans. Now I *was* planning and naively
was finding it thrilling, like the development of a skill. Two things
to decide: what kind of wildlife writing to do, and how to finance it.
There would be years of research and of wilderness observation,
preparations that could not be self-supporting. Perhaps even the
eventual writing itself would not be. No matter; it still would be
my life work.

There were various ways one could write about animals. My first
thought, of a weekly report to some newspaper of the events in a

mountain wilderness, soon seemed too superficial. It would be more worthwhile, also more interesting, to write narratives showing in some detail how various animals live, especially how their lives are part of a network. That network is now a familiar subject, ecology, related to conservation because we know how serious it can be when the elimination of one or more species breaks down the whole pattern. By the present time eloquent books have been written on this situation. But my emphasis would be slightly different: to portray the pattern but devote most attention to individual creatures in it. I wanted to tell how these animals were related to one another but to show chiefly what was interesting to the creatures themselves. They did not see themselves as strands in a net. They were concerned with surviving, finding mates, rearing young, and getting through every day with as little stress and as much satisfaction as possible. How did they do it, each one with his numerous neighbors? There was no book I knew of when I was outlining that project and no book I found later that described minutely the activities, hour by hour, day and night, of a particular limited group of animals. That was what I would write.

The biology courses at Wellesley had not stirred any wish to become a nature writer because the courses dealt with the least interesting of biological subjects: anatomy and taxonomy (the classification of animals). It was, of course, not really boring to learn the various forms that stomachs can take, or the fact that seals' flippers, paws, the wings of birds and our hands are all structured out of the same type of bones, but such things were taught from dead animals' bodies and had little to do with the drama of lives. Yet those dull subjects had been an essential groundwork for what I now hoped to accomplish. (In such impressive ways do the threads of one's own life weave together). The college classes had also given a knowledge of research methods and most important, the conviction that accuracy is essential. All this came back and inspired the resolve that whatever I wrote about animals must be right. The facts must be accurate and one must not make any statements about what the animals feel beyond what can be safely assumed from the way that they act. A new writing technique: truthful as nothing I ever had written had been. At the start I made this test for myself: would what I am saying about this animal seem true to *him*? Many pages were discarded because I recognized that they wouldn't. So there was much to learn, not only the scientific material but the way to present it. Seven years would pass before my first wildlife book was published. The time did not seem too long.

Where to start? Logically one should have enrolled at Stanford University or the University of California and today — but not then — almost anyone planning my kind of project could secure a grant or scholarship. Although I did eventually receive two Guggenheim Fellowships, that was only after I had proved myself by years of observation and two published books; but in the beginning I didn't have money enough for tuition. The scheme I devised was to take temporary jobs and by living frugally to get somewhat ahead with finances. Then I would stop that work and dive into research till the money ran out. It proved to be a very practical plan. For the chance to carry it out I am indebted to a kind woman who ran her own employment agency; I explained my ambition and asked her if she could guarantee that work would be available from time to time as I would need it. She soon found that I was a fast and accurate typist and that employers were satisfied, and so for five years, until I was given an advance on the opening chapters of my first book, that was the program. It was so satisfactory that I recommend it to all aspiring writers.

But I did make some extra money from free-lance writing: some advertisements in *The Saturday Evening Post* promoting the en-

chantments of San Francisco, two conservation booklets, and occasionally some editing. A rich young man was trying to start a magazine, *The San Franciscan,* imitating *The New Yorker,* and I did a
few pieces for that. Finally I could finance a long-term stay in the
wilderness.

Many people who knew what I hoped to do were approving and
made some effort to help. The ones who didn't know were my family. Until I had done all the research and enough of the wildlife
writing to be given a contract for the first book I didn't reveal my
new life to my relatives; for couldn't my mother somehow obstruct
it? She remembered that the Wellesley professors had predicted
that I would become a writer, and she never had lost an opportunity
to deride that chancy profession. She wanted me to become an insurance agent, even though I had such a resistance to figures that I
couldn't make out a tax return without being sick. I don't know
what they thought I was doing, disappearing for months at a time.
They didn't ask; they just accepted that I had distanced myself from
them.

But my great benefactors were the scientists, on whose mercy I
threw myself. In that I was helped by being a woman, for a woman
is not embarrassed to ask for advice or to admit how much she does
not know. I went first to Dr. Grinnell who had told me about singing mice. He turned out to be the Director of the Museum of Verte-
brate Zoology at the University of California, and he not only outlined a program for me but gave me introductions to other scientists
I would need to know. First I met his colleagues in the Museum
there (not a museum in the sense of providing exhibits for public
viewing but of collecting and preserving for study thousands of skins
and skeletons and other types of biological specimens). As well as
arranging that his associates would help me when needed, he made
the specimens available and also gave me an entrée to the Universi-

ty's biology library. In effect I had all the facilities of the University without being enrolled.

And then Dr. Grinnell sent me to Dr. Robert C. Miller, head of the California Academy of Sciences in San Francisco's Golden Gate Park. The Academy is an extraordinary institution. Founded at the height of the Gold Rush by a few men who visualized San Francisco as becoming quite other than a mining camp, it has been a favourite enterprise of several great philanthropists who have left fortunes to endow it, sometimes with the proviso that the city must contribute support — as it does. It was one of the first museums to set up wild-life groups in dioramas of their natural settings, and to establish a world-famous aquarium. A natural history library and a staff of biologists making collections of specimens and producing publications on field observations: these were an unseen activity always considered as important as the public exhibits. Dr. Miller introduced me to his scientists and they, particularly Dr. Robert T. Orr, gave such generous help that I almost could feel I was one of them.

Dr. Orr once said, "She comes in here and asks questions I have not thought of before, and we begin taking down books and discover that no one else has thought of them; so then she goes up in the mountains and tries to find the answers herself." Another who was very patient with my questions was Dr. E. Raymond Hall at the museum in Berkeley. I inquired of him once whether the prey animals like mice are warned by the scent of their predators. Looking slightly startled he said, "Let's find out." He arranged to have several deermice caged, and when they were relaxed and at ease he put in some spoor of a weasel, one of the most deadly mouse enemies. The deermice were obviously terrified. So then when I described a deermouse running over the forest floor I knew it was accurate to show her as dodging away from such scents.

I found my way also to Forestry Professor Woodbridge Metcalf and librarian Edith Francis of the U.S. Forest Service, both extremely helpful; and to Mr. Joseph S. Dixon who probably had more personal knowledge of the California wildlife than anyone else at that time. When he was sure that my interest was reliable, he sponsored my membership in three scientific societies through which I received their valuable periodicals; later I occasionally wrote for them. At last I was finding my feet in my new profession. It was Mr. Dixon who recommended the wilderness area that became the setting for my first book: Beetle Rock in Sequoia National Park. He was a National Park Service naturalist, and when I came under the shield of that organization, their Lowell Sumner and other naturalists took an interest.

The explanation for all that outpouring of help is that biologists who are concerned with the behavior of living animals seem to be that kind of people. They are a type of men I had never met before, so natural and well-balanced I wondered sometimes whether association with animals had given them those characteristics or whether they chose the study of living animals because they were born with a wise, serene temperament. For they all had energy and initiative but no aggressiveness, none whatever, and they showed no signs of a tense ambition. They had no prospect of riches or popular fame and they were not even working in a branch of their science that would have wide publicity, like molecular biology. They didn't expect to change anything or apparently wish to. They just had a great interest in animals' lives and when they learned something new about them, that and their colleagues' respect were their form of fulfillment.

Those biologists who are studying living animals in their own environments are now, of course, called ethologists, but the word had not yet been suggested in the late 1930's when I first knew their predecessors. They often made field trips, the "field" possibly being the ocean, a forest, a desert, or perhaps an Antarctic ice pack, and the men had to be skilled campers and explorers because those were rough expeditions. Later they enjoyed assembling their specimens and notes, analyzing them and writing up their findings, usually to be printed in one of the scientific journals, but the field men didn't seem to be under any driving demand that they publish. Most of them had adopted some specialty that appealed to them personally, a category of creatures such as waterfowl, seals, amphibians, or some large subject like migration or population densities. In addition to those broad concerns most of them seemed to take a particular interest in some individual species, perhaps a very familiar one like deermice or robins, and by patiently gathering observations over the years they would prove that the species had previously hardly been known at all. Not only in California but later in Wyoming, then Alaska, then New England and more recently in England at Oxford and Cambridge I have met, and been helped by, other ethologists. They have all been generous and comfortable men. Of almost every one it has been true that they have had peace in their eyes.

2

By June of the second year I was ready to go up to Beetle Rock. If it would not do as the place where I would finally stay long enough to know all the birds and animals and give them a different life in a book; if it would not be the place, I must find another but I didn't expect to be disappointed. I already had done enough research to know what birds and animals should be there, for Beetle Rock is in the Transition Zone, and the Transition Zone has a characteristic wild population. I was already living there in imagination. But to *see* it! To see my new world, the one that would replace the human world, which had often proved unsatisfactory! A large personal

event, this, significant, and what would it really be like? The technical sources gave the facts but not the experience. Now I would
go.

Sequoia National Park is about half way between San Francisco
and Los Angeles and it would be wonderfully uncrowded, Mr.
Dixon said, because residents of the northern city preferred to go to
Lake Tahoe and Yosemite for vacations, and those in the south went
to the nearer San Bernadino Mountains or out onto surrounding des-
erts. Sequoia was a refuge not only for wildlife but for naturalists.
(By now tourists have found it.)

The train ride was my first sight of the great fertile valley that
stretches for more than four hundred miles down the center of California, vast stretches of vineyards, orchards and cotton fields between
the coastal mountains and the snow-capped Sierra Nevada heights.
At Visalia half a dozen of us were picked up by the Park coach and
started an incredibly steep winding climb, nearly 7000 feet, up the
mountain slope to the east. We started down in the lowlands,
where trees were only brush-high but came rather abruptly to firs
and ponderosa pines of which we could see only the tall straight
trunks, for their crowns were out of sight above the roof of the
coach. The trunks grew thicker; now some, those of the sequoias,
were more than ten feet in diameter — to what heights would such
trunks be lifting the tops of the trees? Finally the coach stopped
and we stepped out, those of us who were first-time visitors unprepared by anything we had heard or read for the scene around us.

These were trees of course but utterly unlike any trees we had
known before. To a height of about a hundred feet many were simply immensely thick pillars, straight and clean-sided, with no twig
or branch to break the upward sweep. When their boughs did
break out, they rose in most cases more than a hundred feet higher
— some nearly two hundred feet more — of green tangles that

seemed to have caught the white cloud puffs motionless in the sky. The crowns of the trees were more lofty than the ceilings of some of the largest cathedrals (Nôtre Dame in Paris is 115 feet high), but were not oppressive for they were so far above ground that always, except at noon, the sun slanted under them, to fall in shafts through the trees and onto the earth, red-brown and easy beneath the feet, being carpeted with evergreen needles that had fallen for many centuries from the canopy of the branches.

No doubt most of us knew that these were among the oldest trees, the oldest living things in the world; but we would not have had to be told. Their vast age was obvious from their size. Many were giants when Pericles, Plato and Socrates were advancing the Greek civilization, being then trees more than a thousand years old. They had stood here on this mountain slope through all of mankind's recorded history and to sense that, in walking below them, was like a personal experience of eternity. We here today would be alive for only a few of the countless years, a sobering thought but one that was curiously enlarging. Small though we were, we were part of a greatness. In our brief moment we were part of timeless events — of ongoing life.

Not far from where the coach stopped was the General Sherman tree, with a diameter at its base of 36 feet and a height of 278 feet. Its lowest branch is 150 feet from the ground and is six and a half feet in diameter and more than 150 feet long — this branch alone being larger than the largest American elm. The tree, as proved by a core drilled into its heartwood, is 3800 years old. When it sprouted, human beings were just starting to make written letters and to fashion tools out of copper.*

* With a pleasing suitability the name of these ancient *Sequoia gigantea* was derived from that of an Indian chief, Sequoyah, who gave his people their first written alphabet.

Why have the sequoias been here so long and grown so tall? For one thing their cells have a little-understood power to renew themselves. The bark, as much as two feet thick, is resistant to all infections and even, somewhat, to fire from lightning; and the inner wood is curiously immune to decay. It has been estimated that these sequoias will be here, living *and still growing* after a hundred more human generations. The external conditions too have been beneficial. Abundant moisture from the deep snows of the mountain winters, mineral nutrients from the granite soil and, above all perhaps, the light here, so rich in ultraviolet rays and so remarkably clear and resilient, have produced stupendous growth also in other cone-bearing trees, some companions of the sequoias being white firs rising to 200 feet, ponderosa pines to 230 feet and sugar pines to 245 feet, all soaring to great heights before branching, and living for many centuries.

Some visitors are said to resent it a little when anyone speaks during their first few hours at the Park. I didn't, but I noticed many times that voices seemed quiet here. There was a hush in the tones; even the children did not scream and shout. I was glad to have some human beings about, but glad also however that Mr. Dixon had suggested my asking for the last cabin out in the forest.

The cabin, of unpainted weathered wood, was a single small room with two windows, cots, two small benches and a table with wash basin and pitcher. No covering on the floor, plain green curtains that pulled across the windows on wires for privacy; no screens. The mealtime arrangements were sensibly outside under a canvas awning off one end of the cabin: a little wood stove, a table, and a cupboard that locked with a padlock. It held cooking utensils and had a typed card tacked onto it? "IF FOOD — ESPECIALLY BACON, MELONS AND JAM — ARE LEFT IN THIS CUPBOARD BEARS WILL RIP IT OPEN." There were a bucket and dipper for water, available at a standpipe half way down a slope. I took the bucket indoors at night for fear that bears would drink out of it. Outside too, for relaxed enjoyment of the view, were a canvas chair and a double seat. Before my Beetle Rock book was finished I would have sat there for many months.

Those were the living arrangements, absolutely ideal for a stay in a wilderness. Rough, and no plumbing, but at such times, I discovered, one curiously shifts into a different gear. Civilized comforts are no longer important. Simplicity is, and simplicity is a boon in itself, it is a deep kind of emotional satisfaction and I had that at Sequoia partly because of the minimum physical satisfactions. Below that level there can be misery, as in living in tents during long spells of rain, or in having to get one's water by melting ice, as I did for a year in Alaska where the indoor temperature might be ten below zero F. in the morning and the ink and the hand lotion frozen. One's body aches for warmth in that situation, a handicap if one is trying to work. But Sequoia was perfect. I could have lived there indefinitely.

o

When daylight could just show the windows distinct from the walls I woke. What had called me from sleep was not the minimal light but something heard. crystal sounds seeming so joyous they could have been my own thoughts. What they were of course was the famous Dawn Chorus of birds.

Soon, when there was enough light to fly, the males left the nests to sing at their territorial boundaries. But first there were chirps and cheeps, bright murmurings clear as raindrops, and subsongs, as the ornithologists call them, which are gentle improvisations on the fine full-throated challenges that the males would sing on their borders.

The subsongs just seemed to be the birds expressing the way they were feeling this morning — slightly sleepy but glad to wake up, I concluded lying listening to them. Birds, most often mother birds, also have "whisper songs," but if they were part of the Dawn Chorus they would have been too soft to be heard by me.

Now the cock birds could see to make their flights from the nests, out through the boughs of their trees to the edges of territories. There they proclaimed that their homesites extended to *here,* and as those splendid anouncements — the typical songs of each species — began ringing out, I thought how pleasant it was that this property sign-posting should be in most cases beautiful. Men call it challenging because men like challenges, but to me the songs seemed to express pride too, and satisfaction, and one can guess that a song which is lovely would be just as effective in holding off trespassers as if it said, "Don't you dare to come over here," which might operate as a taunt. Some of the subsongs went on as a background to the territorial songs. Nice if mammals too, including ourselves, had a Dawn Chorus to welcome the day.

I had asked the man who carried my bags to the cabin where Beetle Rock was. "Right over there to the left," he said, and I could see a gleam of white through the trees. Not liking to crowd impressions however, and the trees being enough astonishment for one day, I had waited till morning to go to the Rock.

My source books had called it an outcropping, a word new to me which was defined as "a sheet of exposed rock" — hardly suggesting this field of gray and creamy white stone on which one would seem to walk right out into the sunny sky. It was about two acres in size, nearly square, clasped on the north and east sides by the forest but with the other sides forming a sharp curving rim over a canyon. From this rim the Rock fell away in a cliff to a stream below, tumbling and gurgling when I arrived in June but nearly dry late in the summer. It was enjoyed by most of the Beetle Rock residents while it flowed, water to drink and play in.

The upper field of the Rock might be a sheet but cracks and clefts broke it up much as a beetle's back is divided — not the reason however why it was called Beetle Rock. An early-day entomologist had found a rare beetle on it, after which it became "beetle rock" to him and gradually was so called by others. I had tried, unsuccessfully, to find out what his beetle was so I could see if it still was there, but wildlife would not be scarce; that was plain from the first sweeping glance and hearing chirps and songs from the forest border.

As well as the clefts there were small knobs and stone terraces, and earth and dust had blown among these, forming toeholds for grass, flowers, brush such as manzanita and chinquapin, and even a few young trees. Any animal seeing the Rock for the first time would recognize its advantages immediately, especially the warmth. The sun beating down on the granite made it even too hot at times, but there were all those shady spots under the brush where one could cool off and rest also hide, which was important. By mid-morning the warmth had created a rising column of air on which two red-tailed hawks and a golden eagle were soaring, around and around, the benefits of the Rock extending even into the sky. The birds' circular gliding defined its shape, for they seemed motionless on the pillar of warmth until they drifted out over its edge, when a few wingbeats would bring them back into it.

Anyone on the Rock also could feel that he was high up in space, for he could look off to the ocean a hundred miles away. The stream at the base of the cliff flowed along between ridges, which spread apart as they fell away on the lowlands below where, beyond the wide valley floor, was the coastal range and beyond that a shimmer. One could imagine that it was sunlight on waves but perhaps it was only the sky's brightness above the water. (Smog now obscures that view.)

Walking around the rim of the Rock I discovered that there was a ledge part way down the face of the cliff. Where I started, at the Rock's northwest corner, the ledge was narrow; two creatures would have to be friendly to pass on it. But it widened until at the opposite, southeast corner, it held a little spring-watered meadow and there, digging up what were probably lily bulbs, was a bear. He could not have been very hungry because his motions were indolent. This probably was the end of his morning meal for he has left the meadow and is coming back on the ledge to a nook where the grass is flattened, perhaps his resting place — yes, for now he lies down. First he lies on his back and rolls from side to side slowly, voluptuously. A strange creature to be in a wilderness, seeming so slack. Even I in my ignorance knew that a wild society holds together because most of its members are so alert. But the bear has no enemies, except man and not even man here; and although he enjoys a good meal of meat, if he is too lazy to get it the bear can just reach out and eat any green leaves. This bear has now turned onto his belly, with forepaws outstretched and his wobbling head gradually going down for a sleep. I had been prepared to like all the animals here but I didn't believe I liked bears. And with that thought — a premonition? — a cold little fear trickled into my mind.

Back on the top of the Rock two handsome lizards were having a confrontation. I had noticed one of them earlier, his chameleon stripes, green on his back and yellow on his sides, were growing bright as the sun warmed him through. Now he was up on his toes facing another lizard and both of them had compressed their sides to throw out ther iridescent blue belly- and throat-spots — a display intended to be intimidating. Next they were chasing each other, off the Rock to a pine tree, up on the trunk, circling it, dropping off to speed over the ground again, swift and graceful; their six-inch bodies made silken and fluent lines with their longer tails. Was this a game of tag or a boundary dispute? When I knew lizards better I learned that it could have been either. After the skirmish had ended the original lizard returned to his place on the stone. As it grew warmer still his colors became very light to reflect the sun's heat, but there was too much of it finally and he slipped down a crack out of sight. Since he was always the temperature of his surroundings he had to take care not to become too hot.

Bird songs were filling the air. Persistent were the small sweet horn of a red-breasted nuthatch and the querying of an olive-sided flycatcher, perched high on a dead branch and repeatedly flying out to catch insects. His call seemed a complaint, perhaps meaning, "Where *are* all the flies?" In contrast a junco nearby in a seedling pine was singing his festive song, like a tinkling of little gold bells. On an upbeat too was a chickadee's *dee, dee, dee,* as well as a more melodious robin's song. And then suddenly, startling really, a sooty grouse cock began to drum: *broo, broop, broop, burro broo broo,* a crescendo and then a trailing away and sounding remarkably like a tympanist beating a kettledrum that was tuned so low I couldn't determine its pitch. I later learned that it is about one octave lower than a horned owl's hoots. It seemed an amazing sound to come from vocal cords and it didn't. It is made by the large air sacs, one on each side of the cock's throat, expanded until the skin over them is stretched tight — not in fact very different from the parchment head of a kettledrum, except that the air sacs are pumped rather than beaten.

The sacs are bright yellow and when inflated are rimmed with black and white feathers. Meanwhile two orange crests rise above the cock's eyes and his tail is spread out in a black and white fan — a spectacle meant to impress the hen grouse and perhaps to throw her off guard. It might do it too. One day, in another summer I turned around in front of my cabin to find a grouse cock displaying to me. I never had seen a cock do that before and I was so surprised — all that gaudy color and the big bird advancing with dragging wings — that I dropped the book I was holding. On that first day on the Rock I tried to decide where the drumming was coming from but couldn't, not surprisingly since it is known to be ventriloquial. Meanwhile a bird's rounded shadow passed over the Rock, the hen grouse sailing down to the riverbank. He probably had been drumming to her and she may have been going to him. Or she might have been leaving him, since I couldn't tell where he was.

Nothing I saw that day stayed in my memory more sharply than one of the small golden-mantled squirrels. Up on his hind feet moving along the grass growing out of a crack, he was pulling the seed-heads down with his forepaws to eat them, using the paws almost as adroitly as delicate little hands. Those squirrels are attractive anyway, with the black and white stripes down their backs and their bright copper-colored heads — like red-headed chipmunks, though larger — but it's the gentle way they move that is so endearing. They have a quality Paul Powell in Hollywood used to talk about, a quality that crosses not only national lines but racial and species barriers. Paul gave a few actresses credit for it and said that ducks have it and wire-haired terriers — an appeal that melts opposition. Another species that have it are golden-mantled squirrels.

After the one had finished the grassheads he went to a tiny pool in the granite were it seemed there was room for only one creature to drink. And here dashing down the trunk of a ponderosa pine came a chickaree, a tree squirrel. Vivacious in all his ways, he bounded over the ground to the pool, perhaps, one could imagine, because he had seen the golden-mantled approach it. The chickaree was larger and heavier than the other, he seemed to have all the advantage, but the golden-mantled quietly appropriated the pool even though the chickaree sputtered his protests and danced around a bit. Inner force won the day. In a wilderness one sees this happening fairly often. It is a quality as mysterious as innate leadership and may be related to it.

Late in the morning one of the red-tailed hawks left his high soaring and came to the Rock. The hawks were a pair. They lived on the other side of the canyon but frequently, it developed, one of them would come over to see what he could get of the prey so numerous at the Rock. That day he alighted in one of the firs on the border, as it happened a fir where a jay was perching. Instantly there was a shrieked alarm: *Tchah,* repeated with every breath, summoning three other jays who came streaming in, helping with their alarm calls. The four jays darted around the hawk at close range, like wasps, with a clamor as sharp as would have been jabs by their beaks. The hawk, turning his head from side to side angrily, flew to the higher boughs of the nearby sequoia. The swarm of jays went right along with him, and by then he might just as well have left, for every creature around the Rock had gone into hiding. The fear was almost as tangible as a scent. I could feel it, could almost share it. And the hawk must have known by now that his search was hopeless; yet he stayed, leading the tormenting jays into three more trees. Then he gave up and when all the jays knew he was routed, the deputies left for their own home grounds and the jay at the Rock flashed his wings a few times and tossed his crest as though pleased with himself.

And well he might be. The policing by jays is one of the most interesting aspects of wild societies. Of course when he has young to feed the jay may take nestlings and eggs from his neighbors, and he is not above imitating the voice of a hawk to watch everyone flee.

But overwhelmingly he and supporting jays benefit other animals. And besides, jays are beautiful.

The Sequoia jays are the Steller species, named for Georg Wilhelm Steller who accompanied the Russian Vitus Bering on his discovery of Alaska. Steller was the first naturalist to see and describe many of our western birds and animals, and none must have pleased him more than these stunning jays with black crested heads and breasts and vivid blue wings and tails. Sailing down from a tree they look like electric blue beams of light.

They were the handsomest flyers at Beetle Rock and on the first day and later I always watched one of them when he was on the wing. By then I had made a rather full study of what was known about flying techniques, including film showing slow motion, and I took with me notes made from more than a dozen sources. Even that summer, so near the beginning, I was able to write several paragraphs about the jay's flight that went into the Beetle Rock book. The details still seem worth knowing:

> On the swift rise the wings almost relaxed, letting the wind fling them high, with quills opened like slats. At the top of the stroke came a splendid flip of the end-feathers, then the Jay felt his breast muscles grasp the wings and pull them into the slower down-beat, quills now locked in a solid sheet . . . His wings had moved gracefully, only three beats to a second, like the great buzzards', while the sparrows flapped thirteen times in the same interval, and the humming birds two hundred times . . .
>
> Since birds seldom ascend at angles of more than forty degrees, the Jay mounted the cliff in a spiral. He left the branch with a strong forward push into the canyon wind, swung around and placed his wings well to the front, a position which made him tail-heavy and gave his body an upward tilt. He flapped vigorously and also curved down the wings' trailing edges so that each had a deepened arch in which the wind caught and helped to lift him . . .

The Jay set his wings, drawn back to make him head-heavy, and launched himself from the branch. Down forty times the height of a human being he fell, then levelled out by advancing the wings and spreading and lowering his tail. The change in the shape of his body stalled him at the precise point to alight on a pine bough . . .

The wind was irregular, as disturbed as a river. The Jay rode its uneven stream without flapping, with only small, sinuous changes in his body's form. The shoulders, elbows, and wrists of his wings were ever slightly turning, bending, rotating, adjusting themselves to the air's pressure, pliant all over their surfaces. He steered with the wings even more than he did with his tail, though his tail too was supple and helped the bird keep a steady course through a wind that would have tumbled him wildly if he had not made himself its responsive partner.*

When the jay had composed himself after driving away the hawk, he came down for a meal of ants in a rotting log near where I sat leaning against the ponderosa pine. Alighting with a strong forward speed, he bounced gracefully to a stop, such a splendid performance that I said "Bravo!" and continued to watch him with admiration; and I rather suspected that he was aware of it. Steller jays are congenital showoffs and he kept turning his glance my way, of course also with caution, as he pecked up ants.

I was on my feet starting back to the cabin when a mule deer buck walked up an animal path from the stream. He was not alarmed and perhaps smelled the raisins in the two pockets of my smock, for he came towards me. I held out a handful of raisins which he took, his teeth avoiding my fingers, only the downy-soft skin of his muzzle touching the skin. I gave him all that I had in one pocket and then turned away saying, "That's all this time. We'll save the rest for —— "

* Sally Carrighar, *One Day on Beetle Rock* (New York: Alfred A. Knopf, 1944).

The deer had struck! His forefoot raked down the back of my leg, painfully though it didn't break the skin, only caused a long streak of bruise. I quickly turned back and said, "You may have the rest," and held out the raisins from the other pocket, for I sensed that he smelled them. When every raisin was gone it was the buck who left: a lesson for the visitor — that animals can understand and accept the fact of there being no more food but not of food's being there and someone depriving them of it. To say no in that situation is an attempt at human dominance and the wild ones don't acquiesce in that kind of relationship. I think that is the most important thing a human being must learn in a wilderness, and possibly the most difficult thing — that we are not at the top of the hierarchy in a society that includes both humans and animals. They make the most graceful adjustments to one another (I would soon see examples of this) and we have to learn some humility. For we are not as swift as a deer, or as poised as a grouse, or as agile as a chickaree, or as aware as a fox or coyote, or as powerful as a bear. There are human advantages but we have to discover how these can be fitted into a wild society — if we want to belong to it. To belong even temporarily, perhaps for two weeks in the year, is a boon, helping us to shed some of the less attractive, indeed self-destructive human traits.

When I went back to San Francisco I told one of the naturalists about that encounter with the buck. He seemed startled and said that only the previous week two men he knew had been on a fishing trip on Mt. Shasta and had been feeding a deer their leftover pancakes each morning. One day the deer — it was a doe — came before they had finished breakfast and one of the men turned from the campfire holding his plate of pancakes away from the deer, perhaps saying as I had, "Not for you." The doe struck with her forefoot and with the extremely sharp point of her hoof ripped open the man's belly to a depth of two inches or more. He died instantly.

The naturalist finished: "Deer are not killers. But they do have quick tempers and sometimes they strike in anger just as a man may do with no intention to murder." One learns about those traits and how not to arouse the anger.

By the time I went back to San Francisco I knew what I would be writing: a book to be called *One Day on Beetle Rock.* It would have ten or a dozen chapters about the creatures that proved most interesting and the other birds and animals with whom they were most involved. They would be narratives, stories, but with the animals not doing anything they don't do in real life. The hardest thing, as I was beginning to recognize, would be to create suspense, for the dramatic events in a wilderness happen suddenly and are over quickly. Only in rare circumstances do they build to a climax. Those were problems that I would have to work out, along with a great amount of studying yet to be done.

In the two months my finances allowed me to stay that first year I had watched sixty species and had a start in knowing their habits. Now the research could take a more definite line. For the next three years I went back and forth, the third stay in the mountains being the longest — from the snows of spring to the snows of the following winter. By then I had written two of the stories and outlined the rest and Knopf's had given me a contract for the book and *The Saturday Evening Post* had bought both the stories.

Before the book could be published my father died. My grief was greater than I had anticipated. However independent one has become, and however worn and ill the father, as long as he lives he is the protector against the indifferent world, the ultimate refuge, and when he is gone one's vulnerability is a shock. There is no choice: one must be grown-up now. But my father did live long enough to know where I had been during the previous years and he had read the two stories and knew that a book had been sold. Best from my

standpoint, he knew me at last as I really was, not as I had been described for most of my life. We had a brief time of understanding
and love, a time not long enough but at least we did have it.

3

That my interest in wildlife was real is proved by the fact that I
often spent months in the mountains even though every absence interrupted a shimmering relationship with a San Franciscan. It is impossible to say much about that alliance because words were barred
from it from the beginning. I had always been suspicious of words
in that situation. In an informal chat I had said to one of the
Wellesley professors that I never could love a man who talked too
much, meaning talked about himself and me, and she said, "You
had better tell him that in the beginning." But of course it would
not be a good relationship if one had to tell him. I didn't have to
tell "Douglas." He too sensed that what we felt for each other could
be damaged by being discussed, worst of all analyzed, or even by
being stated other than very obliquely. Any bald direct reference to
it would have diminished it. We lived it, we didn't talk about it.

I wanted the relationship to be like a work of art, objective, the
conversations and also the closer contacts — all of it in a way like
that beautiful tango the dancer created in Hollywood. I wanted it to
have style and grace and to an extent I think that it did. That does
not mean that warm feeling was lacking, as it was in the dance, but
only that Douglas and I wished to have style and grace in the expression of it.

The very sight of him was an aesthetic pleasure: he was trimly
built, moved in smooth economical ways and had fine brown eyes
and lightly tanned skin, like silk. He was only medium tall and was

sensitive about that. He once said that whenever a group of men are together, every one is conscious of his own height in relation to each of the others'. I wondered if actually that would be true of them all. When we first met I thought Douglas had less self-confidence than he should have, given his pleasing personality and intelligence. But if that was a lack our relationship helped to repair it. At the end he seemed fully sure of himself.

When we first met he was an advertising executive, though with a detached attitude towards his work, enough so that he could say he loathed the word "enhance." With that admission he became, I thought, a bona fide human being. Without much comment he endured my distress during the late stages of the flour program and then witnessed my rebirth into a more self-respecting life. I became a changed person and he apparently thought an improved one. I never tried to persuade him to make the same move but my conversion to noncommercial writing probably was an influence. He resigned from his advertising agency and got an editing job, and became something of a celebrity before long, asked to lecture all through the West. Although disillusion with advertising was not too rare, much later, admitting how pleased he was with his new life, he said, "I give you all the credit." All is too much but naturally we did have an effect on each other's development.

The parallel courses in our careers were the source of congenial talk. Douglas read all my first wildlife narratives and was an excellent critic. Strangely for one who had been in advertising, he was brilliant at sensing anything false. The style could and should be colorful, he said, but not for any purpose except to make the subject more real. In his own work or mine he hated any word put in just to flag attention — gimmickry he called it. Since very few people start with a pure style, it takes a while to get those flaws out of it and he helped.

We both had an almost irrational horror of clichés, in writing and especially the clichés of love. I still do have; I can hardly stay in a theatre when a film or play descends to that kind of talk:

"I adore you!"

"And I adore *you!*"

There was nothing whatever of that between Douglas and me. The praise I liked best was the jokey kind. Said with a laugh, gently: "You cry quite well." I laughed too. But once when he was away on a trip he telephoned from a distant city to say, "I just want to be sure that you do know I love you." He never said it when we were together. But a few times he said it in indirect ways. Once, amusingly naive for a man so sophisticated: "I doubt if there are ten other couples in the world who are as happy as we are." Another time he said, "We were talking at lunch today about close relationships between a man and a woman. I said they can be entirely sweet. The others disagreed. They thought that was impossible. I was sorry for them. They don't know what they have missed."

It all ended sadly, after eight years. The first six were best. Then my Beetle Rock book came out and a nature-hungry public was giving it a fine welcome. I had a contract from Knopf's for the next book, about animals in a Wyoming marsh, and was selling everything I wrote to the national magazines, *The Saturday Evening Post, Harper's Magazine, The Atlantic* and (what bothered Douglas most, I think), *Esquire.* He was a very good editor but his own style was rather inhibited, and perhaps a little jealousy had crept in. Or he may have looked ahead to a time when I would be too absorbed in the work I was doing. In any case he began to be very critical. He often said, "I don't know what there is about your writing, but it just misses." Others did not seem to think it just missed but I could see my self-confidence slipping a little. If this went too far it could destroy what I hoped to do with the rest of my life. I still was determined not to have any children because of the risk of later years with unfriendly offspring; and not wanting children I did not want a husband, for I knew that after Beetle Rock I would expect to go on and on into a farther and farther wilderness. My fondness for Douglas was not strong enough to keep me in one place forever. And besides, I had begun to feel trapped. Dr. Renz had said, "Wherever you are you may always have to be able to go away." That had now happened.

I wanted to end our relationship while it was still good and I said so to Douglas. "But why?" I had never told him the significant details about my childhood because I didn't want to introduce any soggy sympathy into his feeling for me. Now I didn't think that on any ordinary evening I could suddenly say, "When I was a child my life was threatened from time to time. At that age I couldn't escape and so I got a panicky feeling about being trapped. I still feel it when I am in a closed-up situation." You don't make statements like that abruptly after eight years. So I didn't give any reason except that I wanted out, without realizing until afterwards that I was being unfair. Douglas was shocked. Surprised? I don't know. But he had no intention of giving me up. There was a rather terrifying scene. The doctor who came to cope with the aftereffects said that he didn't think I really had been in danger. Alcohol may have been a factor and, "He probably was just trying to frighten you." I chose to believe that; but my tolerance for threats is low, and that memory has made me wary about getting involved so deeply again.

If Dr. Renz had been right, that love is a tender plant, we never at any time in the first six years had handled it roughly. I do know that there is a different kind of love, requiring more of both selves, a greater sharing, even a fusion of two personalities. In such a relationship I might have felt trapped even earlier — unless the man were one I could join on my spiritual landscape, like John Craig whom I had met when I was ten and had never forgotten. But no one else like him had ever come into my life.

o

And so Douglas and I separated; first however there was the pleasurable finishing of the Beetle Rock book. During the long stay at Sequoia, from snow to snow, the plan was to both watch and write, and therefore I needed to have the birds and animals at my cabin instead of around the Rock. They were the same species at both places; it was only preferable to get a group of them to assemble here.

I had advice from my tutors. A range lick, a large cake of salt used in pastures for cattle, is one of the best attractions they said, and it proved to be true. The mammals all licked it and as it became smaller the deer tried to eat it. And water: I sank a dishpan in the ground with a rock placed to slope into it; when the deer lowered the water level small mammals and birds could still reach it to drink. About food, the best, I heard, is a surplus supply of what the creatures gather themselves. Take a shopping bag as you walk through the woods and gather berries, acorns, pine cones and staghorn lichen that wind has blown off the trees, and also the seedheads of flowers and grasses. These might have been enough to convince the wild ones that they would find friendliness at this cabin, but some other natural foods were considered permissible: raisins, carrots, peanuts and sunflower seeds. I took up 100 pounds of those and sent for more. All processed foods, including cake, candy and chocolate cookies are indigestible in wild stomachs. I was told not to throw out table scraps nor especially uncooked rice, which swells in a small stomach and causes the death of the bird or animal. Their instinct is not a good guide. They will eat foods that will harm them.

The biologists had another stern warning: never give what would be more than one meal a day. Otherwise the animals will get out of the habit of hunting for food themselves and the young ones may never learn and will starve when one is gone. If one wants them as friends it is important to *be* a good friend.

I put out the food in the morning but then I wanted my wild guests to stay all day. How to persuade them? First of course one must be reassuring. When I was on their own level they seemed to feel safer. They apparently sensed that a human being who sits on the ground, leaning in a relaxed way against a tree, is in no position to suddenly leap and attack. And what does one do while sitting there? I have a conviction that birds and animals often are bored, or at least they enjoy anything that is harmless but new and stimulating. They seemed to be fascinated by a paper pinwheel on a stick stuck in the ground; as they watched it whirling they came in closer and closer. They appeared to be interested in any continuous small motion that wasn't threatening. John Muir used to twirl his cap on a stick; I crocheted. They had confidence in that monotonous side-to-side weaving of fingers whereas knitting seemed slightly alarming — the finger which kept darting forward (as I did it) was too much like a strike. For a while I carved little figures in Ivory soap, of the birds and animals themselves, shellacked later, and they watched that — not that they recognized the subjects, at least I don't think that was the reason although birds and animals both react to their image in mirrors. (Perhaps I should have taken a mirror into the wilderness. In an aviary I now have a green cardinal from Argentina who spends a long time every day with the other bird in a mirror, his actions having some elements of a courtship. He doesn't know it is himself for he often walks around behind the mirror, trying to find the other bird.) I learned not to sit still at the cabin, as I'd learned with the linnets, but always to move in smooth

ways. It is amazing how many aggressive motions one finds in oneself by observing their effect on animals: human beings walk, drop
into a chair as we say, get up, reach for things, put things down,
turn our heads, gesture, all more abruptly than necessary and that
makes us startling.

I talked to the birds and animals and I talked sense, in a normal
voice not the high-pitched baby talk that is one's impulse. I would
say to a chipmunk, "You whirl so fast you are just a brown blur."
Or to a very shy grouse, "Have you thought of taking a dustbath?
Look here where the earth is so fine and dry." I knew they did not
understand the words, but to such sensitive creatures a tone may
convey more than we realize. I am sure that I would have made a
poorer impression with a deliberate stream of talk, planned and purposeful, for they would recognize such artificiality. It all had to
come out naturally, from whatever I felt at the moment. For in
making friends with the wild ones, I found, it is necessary to be absolutely sincere. I had to act in a friendly way for no other reason
but that I cared about these companions; to seem like a friend because I wanted them to come near so I could watch them and write
a book about them would never have been enough. It seemed that
they had to feel a true sense of warmth, not sentimentality but concern. On the days when my thoughts were absorbed in some writing problem they went away.

Often I sang. Nothing as rousing as *The Star-Spangled Banner,*
be assured; I sang the lullabies I used to sing to my dolls and, better, hummed little random songs, thinking of them as subsongs.
These seemed to provide the right atmosphere and helped to keep
me in the right mood, for a consistently gentle mood is important if
the big human animal is to inspire confidence. Consistent moods are
not always typical of human beings. Letters don't come or they
come with distressing news, or one has had a disturbing dream, or is

catching a cold, or may have eaten too many onions last night — or just feels out of phase. Let that happen too many times and the birds and animals no longer trust us.

They did come to my cabin and finally stayed most of the time. When I opened the door in the morning there they were waiting, about thirty of them, a lovely sight. The tails of the squirrels and chipmunks would twitch, the birds flash their wings, and the ears of the deer turn my way with subtle flickering motions as I began to talk. Before thinking of breakfast I fed them all, the seeds, nuts and fruits from the tin cracker boxes kept in the cabin and whatever I'd gathered the previous afternoon. Since I didn't put out any food for their meal at the end of the day, most of them disappeared then to get their own supper, and that was the time when I went for walks in the forest, incidentally gathering food for them.

The next morning they would have come for it: four kinds of squirrels — a chickaree and gray, golden-mantled and digger squirrels; two deermice that soon moved into the cabin with me; a magnificent four-point buck (the "torn-eared Buck" of *One Day on Beetle Rock*) and a little spike buck and a pregnant doe until she left to have her fawn in the deer's meadow. To the deer I fed carrots mostly, and the big buck became so tame that he would let me come to him with my offering even when he was lying down. He lay for hours each day under a very large sugar pine near the cabin. Among its roots lived a pair of chipmunks and their young and as soon as they heard the door open they whisked up out of their hole. No lizards came; they stayed on the Rock. Late one afternoon a coyote passed and I was glad that my small friends had disappeared by then. And I was well satisfied that the bears left at dawn. A mother and cubs came every night — to the garbage can, not because I was friendly. I watched them at various times away from the cabin but I didn't feel much affinity for them.

The birds greeting me every day were even more numerous than the mammals but did not stay as continually. In the early part of the summer at least, they had nests to build, eggs to brood and young to feed but fortunately for me most of the nearest trees were bird-size, not the tallest, and there were bushes as well — homesites and perches for almost every bird taste. With us much of the time were a Steller jay and a robin, a very shy female grouse and the male who was hoping to mate with her, a splendid red-shafted flicker, coming down in a power-dive to pick up ants on the ground; and besides the flicker, really a woodpecker, there were two others: the white-headed which was tame and bored away in the closest trees for his insects, and farther out and up, one of the stunning pileated woodpeckers, black, white and red and almost as large as a crow. He was not only big and colorful but his constant loud hammering at the trees kept reminding us that he was there.

Our associates with the prettiest songs were the smaller birds. Every bush and young tree seemed alive with them, fluttering about in their delicate way among the splinters of sunlight along the waxy evergreen needles. Two whose territories adjoined and who there- fore did a great deal of arguing in songs liquid and urgently sweet were male ruby-crowned kinglets. Their songs were amazingly loud for such tiny birds and so musical I wondered whether the rest of our group, as well as I, weren't enjoying them. A junco jingled his cheerful gold trill while the wood pewee, with his two falling notes, seemed to say, "It's not quite as good as all that." But the pewee lightened his song during the times when he watched his mate as she built their nest and he stood by, singing encouragement. The red-breasted nuthatch, working over the sugar pine for his insects, kept blowing his one little trumpet note. Less vocal but interesting was the brown creeper at the same task, skillfully turning his white throat-shine into the cracks. Others among us were a warbling vireo who sang almost all the time, a tame yellow and black western tanager, chickadees, purple finches endearingly like the linnets in color and song — and still more.

The songs were fewer as summer wore on but there were always birds' voices around us, twittering and chirping. Dr. W. H. Thorpe in his fascinating book, *Bird-Song,* lists ten different kinds of calls. Two which are opposite in effect he describes as pleasure calls and distress calls. Neither is always literally a "call," that is, with a "come here" meaning. My own thought is that a pleasure call, which is sometimes like a little song, might be the equivalent of our humming or whistling when we are feeling contented. In birds it is most typical of the young. Distress calls do not always mean that a bird is endangered. They may be heard when a bird is cold or hungry or they may be what Konrad Lorenz has defined charmingly as "the peeping of loneliness" of young ducks, geese, and swans. Dr. Thorpe remarks on how even man can recognize cheerfulness in the bird sounds that rise in pitch, the pleasure calls; and the ones that descend as sad or pathetic.

Among the insect-eaters the only birds that came to the cabin for food were those that liked ants, but all came for the drinking water, and to splash in it and to take dust baths on the ground where human feet had made a powder of fallen evergreen needles. For a long time we didn't have any predators there, no weasels, pine martens, foxes, coyotes, wildcats, cougars (which were sometimes near but secretive), not the rare wolverines, or bears in the daytime. Nor did hawks or owls come at first. I watched most of those hunters at other places, but what I saw intimately at the cabin was not a complete picture of the wildlife in this high wilderness. However, one could visualize the predators by observing the prey's instinctive caution. And in this, only the start of a long association with birds and animals, I had to come to terms in my own mind with nature's hunters-and-hunted system. How to accept it? How could one not be repelled by it?

At least one must recognize that the beauty of the wild creatures, the vitality and alertness that allow them to flee or attack *in an instant,* are due to the hunted-hunter relationships. Potential victims must never forget the dangers, otherwise they won't live, and their enemies must be keenly aware at all times of chances to strike, otherwise they don't eat. A cruel arrangement? Yes, from the human point of view but animals that have virtually no enemies and subsist on food as easy to get as green leaves are apt to become sluggish and even ill-tempered. And of various kinds of squirrels, the ground squirrels, which have the easiest, if somewhat vulnerable life, are the dullest and least attractive (except for the golden-mantled). It is something for human beings to think about. We have succeeded in making our lives almost safe. Will our own vitality and alertness survive the lack of physical challenges?

Animals obviously have to have nourishment. Would the kind-hearted prefer that all should be vegetarians? I once wrote in *Wild Heritage,* "As far as we know plants have no sentient life, but there is an impulse in all protoplasm to bring itself to completion, and a buttercup eaten by a rabbit has been denied its maturity just as truly as the rabbit has when it is eaten by a hawk. Perhaps there should also be justice for plants." But justice aside, is an animal always more valuable? Suppose a mouse had eaten the seed of the towering sequoia that grew between the cabin and Beetle Rock. One for one I would consider the tree as worth more than a mouse.

I made two other points in *Wild Heritage.* First, that a bird or animal killing for food does not kill with malice. We may believe it is vicious but when seen at close range the killing appears like a businesslike taking of food for a hungry stomach — not much more emotional than our buying of steaks at a market. And it often is done so fast that the victim never would know what happened. Though not stated till later, those considerations came to me while I was staying at Beetle Rock.

But impersonal and fast though most animal hunting may be, no creature is ever a willing victim, and by one means or another nature gives most of the prey a fair opportunity to escape. A mother bird on a nest brooding eggs or young is at risk, and to help keep her inconspicuous most female birds have dark or dull colors. And camouflage is a well-known protection, saving many a spotted fawn and speckled nestling long before it was saving soldiers. Others who might become victims are very swift, faster if they are in good health than their hunters; deer, caribou, and antelope all escape in that way — but they also need to sense keenly the approach of an enemy. Some prey avoid capture by stillness and others by making themselves inaccessible to most predators. All those skills were evident in the animals at the cabin. And I had to learn one defense that may apply only to human beings.

In each stay at Sequoia I had observed the torn-eared buck and had seen how all other deer would give way to him. The particular herd that browsed around Beetle Rock numbered twenty or thirty animals. The leader had probably got the injury to his ear in fighting other deer to assert his right to first choice of the does. In such combats he would have proved his supremacy — but a herd leader is more than the strongest individual. These leaders are sometimes referred to by men as the master bucks, but once they have won their harem they aren't masters in the sense of having power over the rest of the herd. They are leaders in the true meaning of being guides. They make decisions about when the herd should start down to the lowlands for winter, when to come back to the mountains in the spring, when and where to move if there are human hunters the deer need to avoid. They are the sages, the wise men as long as their faculties are still functioning. Whenever I'd seen the torn-eared buck with the others he had been the one most alert and the others watched him for signs that he was aware of danger. Anybody could read his warnings: the sudden tensing of muscles, the stiff movement of legs if he took any steps, the head flung up, the expanded nostrils to reach for a scent, and above all his mobile ears, now pointing in unison to the source of his dread. At these signals all other deer stopped whatever they had been doing and now also tense were ready to bound away.

On my third summer he still was the leader, the others deferred to him as they had before. But I thought I could detect a little falling off of his caution. A slight sway in his back and less majestic carriage of head suggested that he was showing the first indications of age. The very fact that he spent so much time at the cabin seemed like a slackening of his sense of responsibility. But he was still magnificent and I learned how all other creatures, not just the deer, depended on his alertness to warn them.

As he lay under the sugar pine he was like an instrument finely tuned to pick up distant signals. Often swinging his head, he was apparently testing scents, but his ears were his chief antennae, the tear in one not being serious. Large ears, as the species name, mule deer, suggests, they moved independently — unless the buck heard suspicious sounds, when they pointed together. At other times one ear might turn to the stream below while the other attended to sounds from behind the cabin; or one caught a sound from the right and the other one from the left. They never were still. They were scanning the whole horizon continually and flickering with the most delicate nuances of motion, most of the time responding to sounds that did not reach my ears at all. I tried to imagine how it would be to have that apprehension of everything that was happening within the very wide range of the buck's hearing, to know so many things that would be out of one's sight. Was he aware of a chipmunk's cracking a seed in its underground burrow, of the small weird hum of the bear cubs while they were nursing on the ledge of the Rock, of all the whisper songs of bird mothers, of a squirrel's lapping of water below at the stream — and if it had been a louder lapping would the buck have suspected a coyote or cougar? Perhaps that was why he was sometimes up on his feet in an instant, his nostrils quivering as they reached for a scent and his ears focussed together, so exactly that one knew the precise spot from which the sound came.

And did the buck distinguish between the bright sharpness of wind in the oak trees (to a human being sounding like taffeta rustling) and the overhead murmuring of the wind in the firs, pines, cedars and tall sequoias? When the wind eased away the sound seemed to drop in pitch, bringing to human ears the suggestion of sadness that Dr. Thorpe detected in the falling of pitch in bird calls. The wind in evergreen trees is often described as a sighing; so it seems to us and I can believe that it had the same emotional tone for the buck, since these impressions seem to be universal. And did the buck, that summer, have an instinctive sense of his own downgoing? The next year, my fourth and last summer there, the buck remembered that I had previously been occupying that cabin, and he came again to lie under the sugar pine. But one day when I had laid some food on a flat stone and the buck was eating it, another buck came around from behind the cabin, a younger, stronger deer, imperious in his manner. And the torn-eared buck stepped away to give a new leader the food. I wept.

During the longer summer when he still was unquestionably the leader, he had a friend who stayed all the time near him, not the pregnant doe and the spike buck who came and went, but a female grouse. It was one of those curious relationships between members of different species that occur now and then, for example with badgers which are likely to invite a fox or coyote to share their burrows, after which the two animals may become almost inseparable. It could be said that the grouse always rested beside the deer because she was relying on his alertness and undoubtedly that was one of her reasons. But she could have been farther away, among the other birds and animals, and have noted his actions just as the rest of them did. The buck, for his part, often watched her. It seemed obvious that the two were aware of each other.

I don't know how many days she had been there before I discovered her. She stayed on the far side of the buck and was shadow-colored, but she was a large bird, about the size of a pheasant without the long tail, and I think the real reason I didn't see her was that she had a stillness so complete, it was like a disguise. It was an uncanny talent. Few birds except mothers on nests are absolutely quiet for long, but once after a red-tailed hawk had flown over I watched the grouse and for eighteen minutes she did not even wink. Her eyes were remote, as if in consciousness she had removed herself and by that means avoided any intensity of emotion that might attract notice. And when she finally came forward her walk was so smooth and quiet, even then it appeared like stillness. She placed each foot in exactly the center line of her body and being thus always in perfect balance, she could stop at any point in her progress. I tried that and found that a human being can't do it without making adjustments to redistribute his weight.

Insects furnished part of the grouse's food. In taking them off the ground she didn't peck here and there jerkily as a hen does; she waited until the insect was under her throat and she could reach for it with the least possible movement. Poise and calmness spread out from her. It spread to myself. Stillness, I told myself as I watched her, is beautiful.

In the early part of the season she was a little lame, and from the amount of time she spent in the sunshine, lying with one leg extended beyond her wing, I thought that it probably ached. Of all the birds and animals she was the most shy about trusting me. I thought that the lameness, due perhaps to a recent attack by some predator, might have made her more than normally wary, and believing that it would help her to regain confidence if she accepted my friendliness, I made a special effort to get her to eat from my hand. I knew she liked peanuts because she would pick them up off the ground but she wouldn't come nearer than four or five feet. Finally one day, when her friend the buck was not there, she did come and very cautiously took a nut from the offered handful. Just then the buck walked around the side of the cabin. "Oh, don't disturb her now!" I said impulsively. At those words, which of course he didn't understand literally, the buck stopped completely, he even held one front hoof off the ground until the grouse had finished the nuts and moved away. As he walked to the sugar pine then I noticed for the first time that he avoided stepping on flowers. Even his hind feet avoided them. One is in a different world with wild creatures, one of infinitely fine sensibility.

Was the lameness the reason why she was not receptive to the grouse cock that was courting her? He was often there but whenever he came too near she moved on, sometimes even flying away from the neighborhood of the cabin. The first time he went into his full courtship display she had just gone and so, perhaps in desperation, he displayed to me, as described earlier. It was such a sudden and spectacular transformation that even the buck was startled and got to his feet. All summer the female did not give in to the cock. I presented her story in *One Day on Beetle Rock*. *The Saturday Evening Post*, which also published the story, titled it "The Spinster of Beetle Rock," but she was not a spinster permanently because she had a brood of five chicks the next year. She mothered them with firmness, and if she had thought them threatened she undoubtedly would have done as other grouse mothers do, flown right up into the face of the human intruder. The father of her young was not the handsome male who had courted her the previous summer. He had come to a fatal end, unhappily there at the cabin, but not until after she had overcome her timidity. For all her shyness she actually was a forceful bird. Her strength was shown with our little tree squirrel, the chickaree. When nothing else was absorbing his electric energy he would tease her. Darting around her and chirring in a voice that was meant to be taunting but actually was pleasant, he kept trying to get a reaction. She would seem not to be aware of him till he came in too far, when her feathers would rise and her eyes flash with anger. Ordinarily he would retreat. This went on day after day.

Once then when he was not there the grouse had a dust bath. There probably were some mites on her skin, for extending her feathers widely, she threw dust with her feet all through her plumage, onto her back, wings, sides, down to the base of the feathers. Fluffed out widely she waited a bit to let the dust smother the mites. The chickaree had seen her. He raced down his tree and began jumping around her, dashing up to her face and back as if he really intended to nip her. Suddenly when he was close she hissed and gave an immense shake that covered the squirrel with dust. With a shrill protest he ran back up the tree.

He was always in motion. Like other chickarees thereabouts he had a territory, his consisting of seven trees, and he patrolled them constantly to be certain that no one intruded. It was breath-stopping to see him leaping from tree to tree on branches so high in the sky. Sometimes the gap was many times his own length — he would surely fall! He had a chickaree friend that he allowed to come into his territory and the two chased each other in games of tag, taking chances greater than ever — a brilliant performance and actually good practice for their defense against predators. Sensibility was the buck's defense, stillness the grouse's, but the chickaree's was speed. Swiftly he could be off the ground, avoiding coyotes, foxes, snakes and other hunters, and up in his tree he could dash through the foliage so fast that even the hawks and owls were handicapped unless they could catch him asleep. He could be noisy and was, with always a sweet liquid voice; he could be much more conspicuous than most prey, and yet part of his liveliness was no doubt due to temperament as much as to assumed safety. As I wrote of him in the book, "He took the bright chance and its touch fell upon all his ways."

I had a personal reason to remember his bold courage for a long time — a startling experience but I respected his bravery for I could have caught his tail and in anger hurled him against a tree. The cabin was in his territory of seven trees and he felt that he owned the ground space in front of the door. But two other chickarees came for nuts, and to avoid fights I worked out three miniature territories on which to feed them. These were flat rocks, two placed near the corners of the cabin and one in front. Very quickly the three squirrels learned that they would only receive a nut on their own rocks and amusingly all three would come, often at the same time, and sit each on his rock and call if I was inside. I would come out then and toss them their nuts. This had gone on for weeks, I knew the squirrels apart and none had ever gone to any but his particular stone. Our chickaree had the one in front. But one morning one of the other squirrels went to his rock and sat on it and called. Absentmindedly I threw him the peanut to which he was not entitled. At that instant our chickaree arrived.

I have told that much of the story to several biologists and asked what they would have expected to happen. All said that the rightful owner of the rock would attack the trespasser. But he didn't. He attacked me. In his fury he climbed my body as fast as if it had been a tree and ran out on my arm and dug his claws into my wrist so deeply that the scars lasted for many months. This transferring of anger from his intruding neighbor to me seemed to reveal a surprising degree of intelligence and moreover a delicacy of feeling — outrage that I could not be trusted, that I had betrayed an accepted agreement.

This was but one of many proofs that birds and animals have a very strong sense of fairness.

I had offended the wilderness code and again offended it with nearly disastrous consequences. For I stared into a pair of wild eyes, which is not permissible. Wild eyes can put us in touch with our primitive selves, with unsuspected strength. We feel a hint of the energy displayed by the flying, bounding, leaping, climbing, searching creatures who seem so incredibly tireless. So there are the eyes, telling us that we once were as they are. But their eyes do not look directly, inquisitively into others'. They look across yours and glance away, and glance back. But if we look straight at them the birds and animals quickly become restless and then either attack or leave. The bear attacked.

At the time I was writing a story about a black bear mother and her two cubs that I had been watching frequently. Because mother bears are quick to anger I had not gone as close to them as I wished. I had wanted to study their faces, to try to see whether I could get any feeling of what a bear's consciousness was like — dull and lazy or sharp and suspicious, inquisitive, tolerant, or sometimes seeming like the Big Brown Bears of Alaska who don't eat human beings but tear them to pieces savagely? These Sequoia black bears were supposed to be harmless unless provoked but with irritability quick to rise. I was immensely curious.

And then one evening at dusk I was heating two saucepans of water on the cookstove outside the cabin. As I waited I watched two exquisite young deermice who came out of their hole at the base of the sugar pine. These are beautiful little creatures, deer-brown above, white below, with white feet and furry tails — in no way like house mice, though of course I felt tender towards all mice since it was the song of one that really had sent me here.

The two mice under the tree probably wanted to run about looking for seeds but if they ventured so far apart as twelve inches they rushed back together again, clinging like two little maidens. Then I happened to raise my eyes. From around the side of the tree was peering the face of a large male bear — in the cinnamon phase, and those cinnamon bears are supposed to be surly, whether or not because other bears are supposed to shun them, as animals often do avoid one who is an odd color.

My only thought was, here is a bear's face, less than eight feet away, a fine chance to study him. I was staring, of course — with the bold, aggressive looking of human beings. I knew better but I continued to stare.

He was attacking! Half rising to give himself height, he had hurled himself towards me. Grasping the pans of hot water I threw them full in his face and rushed for the door. I fell going up the steps with the bear close behind, enraged now, but I tumbled inside and banged the door shut with only a second or two to spare for he fell against it. The lock had the old-fashioned wrought-iron type of latch and marvelously the bar did fall into its notch. That very small piece of mechanism was now my security.

Or so I thought for the first few minutes. But the bear began ploughing around the outside of the cabin, apparently pitching himself against the walls for it sounded as if some heavy body had struck them. I sat on the edge of the bed, huddled into my fear. One hour, two hours, three hours passed. I was remembering how I had heard that on occasion when visitors went away leaving bears' favorite food, the bears had tipped over the flimsy cabins to get it — not often but it had happened.

The bear kept up his siege of the cabin all night. I could hear his snorts. I didn't sleep of course. And when the early light came it showed the bear standing up with his front paws on one of the windowsills. He was looking in and on his face was a viciousness I had not dreamed existed. My heart simply caved in with fright.

He didn't try to get in through the window and soon, when the park attendants came to bring firewood and collect garbage, he left. I had a respite from fear and stilling a slight hysteria, fell asleep.

When I went out for breakfast the bear was there, perhaps fifty yards away down the slope in front of the cabin. He had been watching the door and then he watched me as I moved around the stove. I cooked no bacon or anything else that would smell delicious and the breakfast I did make I carried inside to eat. I had to get away from that cinnamon-brown face and its look of threatening anger.

The park rangers had been in the habit of coming around every few days, being interested in my group of wild companions and the writing about them. One dropped by that morning. The bear was still there. I described what had happened and the ranger apparently took it rather seriously. Especially he didn't like the bear's staying. He helped me to make some piles of rocks here and there, on each side of the cabin and on the steps. In an emergency I could throw them and perhaps gain a head start. He said that he would return in the evening.

He came and learned that the bear had not left all day. The bear had moved back and forth on the slope a few times but not very far away. He was always in sight and continued to keep his eyes on me and the cabin. The ranger thought I should stay somewhere else for a week or so, but if I did wouldn't my creatures disperse? I said I did not want to leave. The ranger did not think the bear could tip over this cabin, or at least so he assured me.

For three weeks the situation continued. Sometimes the bear would leave for a few hours, probably to get something to eat, but he was there most of the time and always from late afternoon on. The men tried to lure him away but were not successful. Meanwhile he had begun coming in closer. Sometimes he was only thirty or forty feet away.

During those weeks a curious thing happened. I regressed to a very primitive instinct, an imperative need for something solid and strong touching my back. It would be an animal's way of insuring that an enemy could not approach from behind. Ordinarily human beings don't have it, perhaps never have had it, and yet there it was, a sensation as physical as intense thirst but very different. We have no other sensory feelings to which I can compare it, but it was absolutely irresistible. I *had* to sit with my back touching the wall and for as long as the bear stayed I did, though I tried to argue myself into believing that I was no safer there. When I could feel the wall the sensation ceased but if I leaned away even as much as an inch it returned instantly.

I called it the need for "a shelter-touch" and later described it in a deermouse I wrote about.

As the weeks went by the park authorities expressed some alarm. Everyone knew what was happening. Other park visitors came to see the bear, though they stayed pretty well back. I ate my simple non-fragrant meals, got my bucket of water each day, and fed the birds and animals although I was too tense to be an easy companion with them. Then early one evening two of the rangers called. They said it had been decided that there was too much risk in allowing this to go on any longer. The next day they were going to shoot the bear, or else try to trap him and take him away to some distant part of the park.

I have seldom felt more humiliated. I, friend of wildlife, believing myself a naturalist by now, couldn't handle myself in a wilderness. No other visitors had had any trouble with bears that year, although sometimes they did. But I, the expert as I assumed, was going to cost the bear his life, for that, I believed, was the rangers' intention. I felt very sick about it.

The rangers left. As they said goodnight we looked for the bear. He was not in sight. It was only dusk but I began to get ready for bed and had taken off my dress when the voice of a stranger called from behind my cabin, "Your enemy's out in front."

I don't know what happened. Was a cupful of adrenalin released into my blood? The weeks' tension broke and I was simply beset with fury! Flinging open the door I dashed out in my slip and snatching up handfuls of rocks from the step I tore after the bear. I screamed at him, words I hadn't even realized that I knew, and was hurling rocks at his face and hitting him too, for he was less than ten feet away. He reared but not with rage this time, with stunned surprise, quickly let himself down on all fours and ran away fast down the slope. Trembling I pulled myself together and went back into the cabin.

The bear never returned. The rangers did not dispose of him and I settled down to absorb my lessons.

First of course, one must not stare at any wild animal, a stare being invasion of privacy, rudeness they will not tolerate. But second, an overpowering sense of outrage can be a defense in some circumstances. The bear had threatened too long and my fear had turned into its opposite. But one shouldn't depend on outrage to save one's life. I am sure it would have to be genuine, no phony attitude ever works with an animal and the excess adrenalin really would have to be in one's blood, perhaps emitting an odor. There would be some occasions, with a bull moose in the belligerent rutting season, I think, when humility might work better. But best, try to achieve something like the wild ones' alertness and not get into these tight situations. If I had not stared and had gone quietly, unobtrusively into the cabin when I first saw the bear, I feel sure there would not have been any incident. And I still think that the wilderness is a very good society.

o

Many people assume that the true state of nature is anarchy. That was not what I found, at Beetle Rock or in more remote congregations of wildlife. There were dramas, some very sad, and occasionally I was in danger, but what impressed me more were the stability and the sanity. They seemed almost spectacular. After all the giddy and irresponsible people I had known in the human world, here in the wilderness there was a code of behavior so well understood and so well respected that the laws could be depended on not to be broken. There was always the need for alertness, required by the hunted-hunter relationships, but otherwise birds and animals knew just what to expect of each other. They could be sure their associates, whether of their own or different species, would act in dependable ways. If something ought to be done, it was done. What is, in the literal sense, integrity — "reliable adherence to a code of behavior" — was almost infallible.

There were contests for mates but once a pair-bond was established it was accepted as final, both by the couple and by anyone else who might covet either of them. It might last for a lifetime — a pact usually preceded by a rather long courtship as in the case of geese or, elsewhere, wolves. Or it might be the species rule that it only would be for the raising of one brood or litter; but the devotion and loyalty during that time was absolute and so was the sense of responsibility for the young on the part of one or both parents. Most parents wore themselves to a ragged extremity of fatigue by the time the young were grown but they never shirked the task — not even though the fatigue, exposing them to disease and predators, might mean that they would live only a tenth of their possible lifetimes, as is the usual case with wild birds.

Sometimes there were deviations but on the lenient side. A female cougar, having her own territory, would allow another cougar to trespass if she had young to feed. An unmated female bird would sometimes assist a mother; and mothers would often baby-sit for each other. One can envy a wolf mother who not only is sure of her mate's fidelity for a lifetime and knows that his sense of responsibility for the young will not fail; moreover the family group often includes uncles and aunts who also will feel responsibility for the cubs. Not amazing devotion, just one example of wilderness ways.

A bird or animal could lay claim to a homesite simply by moving into it, but he would not do that if it already belonged to another. On the edges of his property there might be disputes over boundary lines, sometimes with a "showing of fists," but there were no deadly fights on that issue. The wild ones are masters of compromise. And as soon as ownership of the site, the plot of ground or the niche in a tree, had been established, the home itself, the burrow or nest, belonged without any question to the one who had dug or built it — unless the owner left or died. In that case a new owner was quick to move in, suggesting that others had been aware of the home's advantages all along.

It seemed remarkable to me that a more powerful bird or animal, or one higher in rank, never tried to take a desirable home or mate just because he was stronger or was superior in a hierarchy. The weaker or humbler one might be expected to give way on a path or at food or drink, but his family and home were inviolable, his without argument.

About food there did not seem to be any intense possessiveness.

The remains of a kill the predator no longer wanted was community property — it could be eaten by anyone. While the hunter was first enjoying his meal there would usually be a circle of lesser creatures standing around waiting to have their chance, and if they darted in for a bite ahead of time, the owner of the catch might growl a little but he would not attack. One day our chickaree cut off eighteen cones from a tall tree in about as many seconds, let them fall to the ground and then raced down the tree to bury them. Meanwhile a digger squirrel, not able to get his own cones by climbing, began pulling some of the chickaree's into his burrow. The chickaree didn't waste time in more than a brief sputtered objection. He got busy and buried the rest of his cones, first giving each one his lick sign which said, "This cone is mine." They would still be there in the ground when he dug them up in the winter.

And water: it often happened that two would meet at a rain pool or the drinking pan at the cabin. If there was a little personal friction between them, as sometimes there was between the robin and jay, they argued a bit about which should drink first but they never injured each other. It was much more typical for thirsty creatures to wait without bluster, because there was a well understood — and observed — custom of taking turns.

Tempers never seemed to be short. Once I was watching a mourning dove and a sparrow, perched a few inches apart on a branch, when the sparrow left the branch and clamping his beak on one of the dove's tail feathers, hung from it and with a reverse wing-beat tried to pull it out. That was the nest-building season and no doubt he wanted it for his lining. The dove, though keeping her balance with difficulty, did not protest, not even when the sparrow tried to get a feather again a few moments later. It wouldn't come out so he flew away and she settled back into a dove's usually peaceful emotions.

And there was no meaningless anger, no psychosis here.

If there was a contest, as between bucks over a doe, the one who was losing would turn away, leave, and that was the end of it; and a wolf, sensing defeat in a fight, exposes his jugular vein to the victor's teeth, the victor in that case being "honor-bound" not to harm him. I think of those animal contests sometimes in watching a tennis match and seeing the winner run up to the net to offer his hand to the loser. The tradition goes back a long way.

The deer and wolf rituals are only two of many inherited forms of behavior which prevent members of the same species from killing each other. Around Beetle Rock, as in other wildlife communities, many and various species could be observed, all with different habits and needs but living in close association. Aside from the prey-predator situations, were there not countless conflicting requirements that would precipitate fights? The issues were there but almost always were solved with tolerance. The powerful did not assert their superiority with any unpleasant display of strength, and the weaker or smaller ones never showed any resentment in yielding.

Among some biologists — not always those who know birds and animals well in the field — there is a habit of downgrading any pleasing animal habit or action as being due "merely to innate directives" — formerly called instincts. They imply that behavior is automatic and no credit therefore is due the animal. Admittedly the same type of scientists often define human actions as mechanistic. But they don't state a reason why wild parents are selfless and human parents sometimes are not; and they don't recognize the many other situations when the wild creatures adhere to wilderness codes although self-interest would seem to suggest otherwise, or the many times when the powerful exercise restraint. (And when the end of life comes I also admire the dignity of the animals in wishing to die alone.)

I am familiar with the biologists' Law of Parsimony, which requires that an animal's behavior be interpreted in the simplest, most primitive possible terms. In most cases that means considering animal actions as automatic, without conscious thought or sensitive grades of feeling. Now however there is much interest in the ability of animals to learn, and since their memory and adaptive skills have surprised many a scientist, the Law of Parsimony is being eased up a bit. There is an interest, moreover, in behavior that is neither inborn nor learned but is rather an expression of the inner state of an individual animal at a given time.

Dr. K. von Frisch, the tireless observer who has described the precise dance-language of bees, has been illuminating also about the bees' temperament. Many of us have assumed that bees are like insect robots, going about their tasks in such rigid routines as to make them seem almost as mechanical as ball bearings. But now it appears that a bee colony includes "eccentrics," (von Frisch's term): "Anyone who has watched these dances . . . will recognize with amazement that these insects, however much innately tied to the fixed traditions of their species, have yet kept a degree of individual freedom." One of the worker caste spent half her time "marching slowly and at ease round the combs, now cursorily inspecting a cell, now making brief contact with a neighbor."

Nothing very mechanical about that; nor about an elderly male chimpanzee observed in the field by Dr. A. Kortlandt of Amsterdam's Zoological Laboratorium. It was the chimpanzee's custom to go to a certain place where he could see the sun go down. He went every evening and he would stay until the sun had set and the color was gone from the sky. Then he would turn away and find his place to sleep (like the male linnet watching the blowing clouds).

These are but two of many examples of birds and animals that have been seen to express a certain degree of freedom from inborn habits. The lyrebirds of Australia experimenting with vocal sounds — they imitate pneumatic drills and car horns as well as the exquisite songs of hummingbirds; and birds and animals showing distinct preferences for certain designs, usually the more smooth or symmetrical; and any of the creatures at play: all these show that they have at least a small chance to make choices. Nevertheless they are, as von Frisch says, innately and closely tied to their species traditions. Otherwise the wilderness code of behavior would begin to break down — and it doesn't, unless man interferes with the wild conditions.

Basically wild behavior is biological. The fixed traditions have been acquired through the long millions of years while the present species have been evolving; and these traditions have become established in animal genes *because they are the ways that work*. This is the kind of behavior that has insured survival, just as physical features like camouflage coloring or long-range eyesight have helped to insure the survival of the species that have them. The sixty species at Beetle Rock, like the species in all other wild communities, are here today because they have been the fittest, the fittest in their behavior.

That behavior conforms to our definition of "moral." The responsible care of young, the fidelity of mates if that is the species custom, the respect for others' property, the fairness in taking turns, the rituals that prevent conflicts from being fatal, the lack of malice, the tolerance, the mildness of tempers: these are some of the principles of the wilderness code that have insured survival. There may have been other species at some time in the past that did not observe the biological commandments (which is to say, those commandments were not in their genes). They may have neglected their young, or violated the bonds between pairs, or pirated others' homesites, or they were too belligerent, or malicious, or made a habit of fighting competitors to the death. Such species do not exist today. In their behavior they would have been the unfit, and they would have been eliminated. Evolution rejected them.

Once the wilderness code was ours. Once we were a species that survived in a wild community, among our animal neighbors, because our species too was one of the morally fittest. And when we became more human, when we emerged into the stage of cerebral thought and language, so that we could find words for our moral standards, we did not have to look further for them than our own biological background, our inherited customs and usages. Even before we had any religious feelings we must have been moral people. Only later would we have attached those standards, those wilderness values, to our dawning religious consciousness.

In different parts of the world the religious impulse took different forms, but almost everywhere the long-known social rules were incorporated. For many centuries these religions have provided a code of behavior very similar to the wilderness code. Now we in the West seem to be losing religion's guidance — and is the biological behavior still in our genes?

Once I asked an Eskimo mother how she taught her children the difference between right and wrong. She said, "We don't teach them, we just remind them. When they are born, they know." No doubt many children of other races are born with an impulse towards the good biological behavior. That may be what we mean by the innocence of small children. But do we keep reminding them of what they know? How can we, when many of us have forgotten what that behavior is?

If we are going to try to find our way back to nature's principles, it would seem helpful to rediscover how the animals live. The commandments recognized in the wilderness could be our lifeline to mental and emotional health — to survival, among the fittest. But we are apparently bent on destroying the wilderness, which could be the most tragic development in the history of the human race. For if the wilderness is reduced much further, we shall have no clues to nature's moral sanity — none except our own now-devastated instinctual guidance. Can we find that again, shall we have enough sensitivity?

"The Ten Commandments are strictly observed by animals, much better than we observe them." That was a comment by Jacques Monod at an international conference called by the Nobel Foundation to discuss mankind's chances of survival. M. Monod, a past Nobel prize winner, is a molecular biologist at the top of his profession in France and renowned throughout the world.

Job said it long ago: "Ask now the beasts, and they shall teach thee; and the fowls of the air, and they shall tell thee: Or speak to the earth, and it shall teach thee; and the fishes of the sea shall declare unto thee."

o

Late in June of the long summer our little company were enjoying a sunny morning, the birds singing, the mammals scampering about, when tragedy struck. The female grouse was there and the cock, who had been booming for her, approached through the surrounding bushes. He was conspicuous in his courtship finery, bright yellow throat sacs, orange crests over his eyes. In less time than it takes to read this sentence then he was up and away through the sky in a goshawk's talons. The goshawk must have concealed himself in a thick clump of foliage and came down from the tree like a shot — a "bullet hawk," he is sometimes called. There was no sound; one moment the cock was there and the next he was gone.

The door of the cabin was open, and in a wave of terror all the rest of the creatures including the birds swept in. Many had been inside at other times and now they found safety here. Any small previous irritations were forgotten, the jay and robin were eating and drinking without competition, the chickaree and the digger squirrel picking up nuts side by side, and the female grouse and the golden-mantled squirrel, who had sometimes shown jealousy when I had fed her, were all harmonious now. Feeling safe under the roof they didn't attempt to hide, they walked and hopped about. I had scattered food on the floor and their fright quieted as they began to eat. Even the torn-eared buck, lonely perhaps, tried to come in although he had not been in danger. He had his forefeet up on the sill when one of the rangers walked by. Amused, he told me that I must keep the deer out for if he did enter he would probably panic and jumping about he might break a leg. We put a bench in the doorway.

I sat there among the refugees, a dozen within an arm's reach and two on my lap. It had not occurred to me that I would create an emergency by assembling this group at the cabin. There would have been no such concentration of prey otherwise and I felt guilty about the loss of the cock, although I did realize that in his erotic mood he might have been careless about displaying in some other place. What worried me more was the future. It seemed hideously possible that the goshawk would keep coming back and one by one would pick off my birds and animals. But that didn't happen because it was their own impulse to spend every day inside. I fed them there and brought in the drinking water and salt lick; later on in the afternoon they would go out to do their own foraging. The goshawk did return and sat in the tree near the door several times but then he apparently realized that there was no longer a gathering of available prey and stopped coming.

It was a sweet experience to have all these birds and animals in the cabin with me. They seemed as much at ease here as anywhere else. When they had finished eating they would relax, some would sleep, the birds perched on the two-by-fours that braced the walls.

One day when I was looking around at them with satisfaction and out through the door to the wider green walls beyond, I thought, suddenly, This is a home I have come to. I know now what home means to most people, not only walls but a shelter-touch for the heart and mind. Here I have found it, home at last — and with all these delightful children.